TH

WICKLOW

WAR DEAD

First published 2009

Nonsuch Publishing,
119 Lower Baggot Street,
Dublin 2
www.nonsuchireland.com

© Tom Burnell and Seamus Burnell, 2009

The right of Tom Burnell and Seamus Burnell to be identified
as the Authors of this work has been asserted in accordance
with the Copyrights, Designs and Patents Act 1988.

British Library Cataloguing in Publication Data.
A catalogue record for this book is available from the British Library.

ISBN 978 1 8458 8949 4

Typesetting and origination by The History Press
Printed and bound in Great Britain by Athenaeum Press Ltd.

Contents

Introduction

There were seven children born to Patrick (Pakie) and Peggy (Margaret) Burnell in Finglas during the 1950s. Margaret, Paddy, Tom, Seamus, Paul, Greg, and Michelle. Four of the lads served in the Irish Defence Forces here at home, on the South Armagh, Monaghan, Cavan, and Louth borders during the troubles and overseas with the United Nations on peace-keeping duties. Their relations had fought in the First and Second World Wars and two of them died during the Irish Civil War. It is no surprise that they would have an interest in all things military.

Like most Dublin families, at least one of their parents come from out-side Dublin so it was not surprising that every one of Pakie's children moved out of Dublin to the countryside for a peaceful and slower pace of life. Some things are taken for granted by people who live in rural areas not least of which is that they are surrounded by history and no one appreciates this more than the 'blow-in'. Tom and his wife Ruth now live in Tipperary and have successfully completed and published *The Tipperary War Dead*. It was only a matter of time before Seamus (who now lives just outside Carnew) and Tom got together and decided that the subject of Wicklow during the First and Second World Wars should be properly addressed.

This had been attempted before and there was little help offered by the populace to complete it. Seamus placed an advertisement in the Wicklow papers asking for photographs of the fallen so they could be used in the final tome. Only one newspaper cutting was given and the Wicklow Historical Society said it had been tried before and 'no one wanted to know'. Well, Tom and Seamus wanted to know and they decided it would be done anyway. The war-dead databases available to them (Tom is an ex-War Museum Curator) were hauled out from their dusty resting places and they dived straight in. Seamus and his daughter Jodie Burnell scoured the graveyards, cemeteries and churchyards for any hint of a war grave. Covering the entire county was no easy task but it had to be done so that all aspects of the subject would be covered adequately. With a rudimentary list from the Commonwealth Wargraves Commission they set forth and after two months of trekking through some of the most remote and overgrown cemeteries in the country, the task was finally completed. They also had to go through the period newspapers in hard copy as no microfiche technology was available. Every available issue of the Wicklow newspapers (First World War newspapers exist only in hard copy, are deteriorating rapidly and may not exist in the very near future) from 1914 to 1919 and from 1939 to 1946 had to be read and any references to war casualties were photographed and logged. These newspaper articles and references are included here in text form. When this was done they put all the data in alphabetical order and the end product you now have in front of you.

This book also contains all casualties of the two World Wars buried in County Wicklow including those who are not native to this soil. The disproportionate number of Wicklow casualties sent to watery graves by German torpedoes (mostly men from Arklow) surprised the authors as did the unfortunate airmen who came to rest here in the garden of Ireland from places far afield. Wicklow men were involved in every action of both wars, on land, sea and air. Some of them died of their wounds in England after receiving a 'blighty' (a wound that made them eligible for a military discharge and a pension). However the majority of them died on the battlefields. A surprising number of these have no known graves and remain just a name on a memorial. Others died of their wounds at home.

History is a collection of facts, not a selected collection of those facts but all of them. Seamus and Tom do not express opinions on the data found, they just place it in front of you.

If no one else remembers these unfortunate men and women they will be remembered here in this book.

The German Military Cemetery in Glencree poses a problem as their records are not in English. Although photographs of the cemetery are included in this book the investigation of these casualties must remain a future project.

Terminology

Killed in action: The soldier was killed during engagement with the enemy.

Died of wounds: The soldier was not killed outright and may have made it back to the Regiments Aid post or Casualty Clearing Station before he eventually died of his wounds.

Died at home: Death by drowning, suicide, accident or illness in Ireland or the UK and not necessarily where he lived.

Died of wounds at home: The soldier was not killed outright and may have made it back to the Regimental Aid post or Casualty Clearing Station before he eventually died of his wounds back in the UK or Ireland.

Died: Death by drowning, suicide, accident or illness.

A

ABBEY, John: Rank: Lance Corporal and Lance Sergeant. Regiment or Service: Irish Guards. Age at death: 24. Unit: 1st Bn. Date of death: 8 August 1915. Service No: 3913. Born in Baltinglass, Co. Wicklow. Enlisted in Carlow. Killed in action.

Supplementary information: Son of Patrick and Mary Abbey, Weaver Square, Baltinglass, Co. Wicklow. Grave or Memorial Reference: I.B.13. Cemetery: Guards Cemetery, Windy Corner, Cuinchy in France.

ACTON, (also listed as BALL-ACTON), Charles Annesley: Rank: Major (T.P). Regiment or Service: Royal Welsh Fusiliers. Unit: D Company, 9th Bn. Age at death: 39. Killed in action. Date of death: 25 September 1915.

Supplementary information: Of Kilmacurragh, Rathdrum. High Sheriff Co. Wicklow. Served in Crete in 1898, and China Expedition in 1900. Older brother of **BALL-ACTON, Reginald Thomas Annesley.** From De Ruvigny's Roll of Honour: Son of the late Col Charles Ball-Acton, C. B., The King's Own (Yorkshire Light Infantry), by his wife, Georgina Cecilia, second daughter of George Annesley (Viscount Valentia Coll); grandson of Lieut-Col William Acton, of West Aston, Co. Wicklow, J.P., D.L., M.P. Born: Peshawar, India, 14 February 1876. Educated in School House, Rugby; Oxford Military College, and the Royal Military College, Sandhurst. Gazetted 2nd Lieut, 2nd Battalion. Royal Welsh Fusiliers, 5 September 1896 and promoted to Lieutenant 16 December 1898, and Captain 31 January 1906. He served in Malta, Crete, Egypt, India, and in the China Campaign (Medal), being Staff Captain at Welhei-Wel from 14 April 1900 to 2 June 1901. He succeeded his uncle in the family estates 25 August 1908, when he discarded the name of Ball. He retired from the Army the same year. On the outbreak of war, having offered his services to the War Office, he was gazetted captain in the Reserve of Officers, and rejoined his old regiment 7 September 1914; promoted temp, Major 19 July 1915 and went to France the same day. He was killed in action near Givenchy the first day of the general

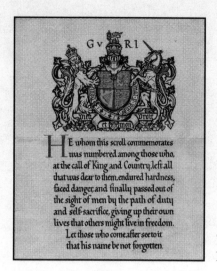

HE whom this scroll commemorates was numbered among those who, at the call of King and Country, left all that was dear to them, endured hardness, faced danger, and finally passed out of the sight of men by the path of duty and self-sacrifice, giving up their own lives that others might live in freedom. Let those who come after see to it that his name be not forgotten.

The scroll that always accompanied the Death Plaque or the 'Widow's Penny'.

advance, 25 September 1915, while helping a wounded soldier. Buried at Festubert. He served as High Sherrif of Co. Wicklow in 1913, and was J.P. for Co. Wicklow. Grave or Memorial Reference: He has no known grave but is listed on Panel 50 to 52 on the Loos Memorial in France.

ADAMS, John Edgar: Rank: Lieutenant. Regiment or Service: Royal Artillery. Unit: 6 H.A.A. Regt. Age at death: 32. Date of death: 1 March 1942. Service No: 151925.

Supplementary information: Son of Frank E. Adams and Sarah Anna May Lee Adams. Husband of Kathleen Ruth De Quincey Adams of Newcastle, Co. Wicklow. Born and lived in Surrey. Grave or Memorial Reference: 6.A.2. Cemetery: Jakarta War Cemetery. Indonesia.

AHEARN, Thomas: Rank: Private. Regiment or Service: Royal Dublin Fusiliers. Unit: 2nd Bn. Date of death: 21 March 1918. Age at death: 25. Service No: 9379. Born in Newbridge, Co. Kildare. Enlisted in Dublin. Killed in action.

Supplementary information: Son of Mrs Mary McDonnell, of Lacken, Blessington, Co. Wicklow. Grave or Memorial Reference: He has no known grave but is listed on panel 79 and 80 on the Pozieres Memorial in France.

AINSWORTH, Charles James: Rank: Major. Regiment or Service: Royal Artillery. Unit: 59 (6th Bn. The Hampshire Regt.) Anti-Tank Regt. Age at death: 39. Date of death: 13 July 1944. Service No: 96418.

Supplementary information: Son of

Percy and Alice Maud Ainsworth. Husband of Daphne Ainsworth of Humphrystown, Co. Wicklow. Born in Bolton and lived in Berkshire. Grave or Memorial Reference: IV.A.12. Cemetery: Brouay War Cemetery, Calvados, France.

ALCOCK, Frank: Rank: Private. Regiment or Service: Royal Dublin Fusiliers. Unit: 2nd Bn. Date of death: 4 July 1916. Service No: 14246. Age at death: 20. Born in Athy, Co. Kildare. Enlisted in Wicklow. Died of wounds.

Supplementary information: Son of Joseph Alcock, of Magherymore, Wicklow. Grave or Memorial Reference: I.D.7. Cemetery: Couin British Cemetery in France.

ALLEN, Francis: Rank: Private. Regiment or Service: South African Infantry. Unit: 'B' Coy. 2nd Regt. Date of death: 18 July 1916. Age at death: 29. Service No: 6143.

Supplementary information: Son of Anthony Allen, Ballymoney, Donard, Co. Wicklow. Grave or Memorial Reference: XI.K.2. Cemetery: Delville Wood Cemetery, Longueval in France.

ANDERSON, John Calder: Rank: Private. Regiment or Service: Canadian Infantry. Unit:

195th Bn. Service No: 907433. Date of death: 3 March 1920. Age at death: 38 also listed as 68. Born: 29 December 1851 in Carrickmacross, Co. Monaghan. Enlisted: 18 March 1916 in Regina, Sask while living in Kerrobert. Occupation on enlistment: store clerk. Height: 5'8½". Complexion: fair. Eyes: blue. Hair: fair. Religion: Presbyterian. Next of kin listed as Ellen Anderson Ballybolan, Ashford, Co. Wicklow.

Supplementary information: Son of Robert and Helen Anderson, of Ballyvolan, Ashford, Co. Wicklow. Grave or Memorial Reference: P.13.B B.G.13. Cemetery: Regina Cemetery, Canada.

ANDERSON, Peter Thomas: Rank: Flying Officer. Regiment or Service: Royal Air Force Volunteer Reserve. Unit: 209 Sqdn. Age at death: 25. Date of death: 22 February 1941. Service No: 84833.

Supplementary information: Son of John Sloane Anderson and Sylvia Perring Anderson. Husband of Mary Eira Anderson (*née* Morris), of Wicklow. B.A, M.R. C.S, L.R.C.P. Grave or Memorial Reference: He has no known grave but is listed on panel 29 on the Runnymede Memorial, UK.

APPLEBY, Francis: also listed as **James Francis**) Rank: Private. Regiment or Service: Irish

Guards. Unit: 1ˢᵗ Bn. Date of death: 14 January 1918. Service No: 8571. Born in Rathdrum, Co. Wicklow. Enlisted in Wicklow. Killed in action. Grave or Memorial Reference: II.B.34. Cemetery; Level Crossing Cemetery, Fampoux in France.

APPLEBY, John Patrick: Rank: Rifleman. Regiment or Service: London Regiment. Unit: 8th Bn and 1ˢᵗ/12ᵗʰ Bn. He was previously with the 12ᵗʰ (County of London) Battalion (Rangers) where his number was 8172. Date of death: 2 December 1917. Age at death: 22. Service No: 485015. Born in Wicklow. Enlisted in Dublin while living in Dublin. Killed in action.

Supplementary information: Son of Joseph and Margaret Appleby, of Rathdaughtergan, Baltinglass, Co. Wicklow. Grave or Memorial Reference: He has no known grave but is listed on Panel 11 on the Cambrai Memorial in Louveral, France.

ASHFORD, John: Rank: Private. Regiment or Service: Royal Inniskilling Fusiliers. Unit: 8ᵗʰ Bn. Date of death: 1 March 1917.

Service No: 25292. Born in Bray Co. Wicklow. Died at home.

ASHMORE, William: Rank: Private. Regiment or Service: East Lancashire Regiment. Unit: 8ᵗʰ Bn. He was previously with the Liverpool Regiment where his number was 37256. Date of death: 16 November 1916. Service No: 32166. Born in Blessington, Wicklow. Enlisted in Liverpool while living in Walton in Lancashire. Killed in action. Grave or Memorial Reference: B.10. Cemetery; Frankfurt Trench British Cemetery, Beaumont Hamel in France.

AUSTIN, Joseph: Rank: Private. Regiment or Service: Highland Light Infantry. Unit: 18ᵗʰ (Glasgow Yeomanry) Bn. He was previously with the East Yorkshire Regiment where his number was 3057. Date of death: 26 March 1918. Service No: 202610. Born in Arklow, Co. Wicklow. Enlisted in Hull in Yorkshire. Killed in action. Grave or Memorial Reference: He has no known grave but is listed on Panel 72 on the Pozieres Memorial in France.

B

BAILEY, Patrick: Rank: Lance Corporal. Regiment or Service: Royal Dublin Fusiliers. Unit: 2nd Bn. Date of death: 22 May 1915. Age at death: 19. Service No: 11641. Born in Clonmore, Co. Wicklow. Enlisted in Carlow. Killed in action.

Supplementary information: Son of Christopher and Margaret Bailey, of Arnold, Coolkenno, Tullow, Co. Carlow. Grave or Memorial Reference: He has no known grave but is listed on Panel 44 and 46 on the Ypres (Menin Gate) Memorial in Belgium.

BAIRD, Robert: Rank: Lance Corporal. Regiment or Service: Royal Dublin Fusiliers. Unit: 8th Bn. Date of death: 29 April 1916. Service No: 16520. Born in Wicklow. Enlisted in Dublin while living in Broomhall. Co. Wicklow. Died of wounds.

Supplementary information: Son of Mrs K.M. Baird, of Broomhall, Co. Wicklow. Grave or Memorial Reference: I.J.27. Cemetery: Noeux-Les-Mines Communal Cemetery in France.

BAKER, C.: Rank: Corporal. Regiment or Service: Royal Dublin Fusiliers. Date of death: 6 February 1919. Service No: 20378. Grave or Memorial Reference: South. 3MM. 36 East. Cemetery: Arklow Cemetery, Co. Wicklow.

BAKER, Walter Henry: Rank: Second Lieutenant (TP). Regiment or Service: Machine Gun Corps (Infantry). Unit: 36th Bn. Date of death: 20 October 1918. Died of wounds. Age at death: 24.

Supplementary information: Son of the Revd H.F. Baker and Mrs C.H. Baker, of Co. Wicklow, Ireland. Grave or Memorial Reference: II.B.11. Cemetery: Harlebeke New British Cemetery in Belgium.

BALL-ACTON, Reginald Thomas Annesley: Rank: Captain and Major. Regiment or Service: King's Own Yorkshire Light Infantry. Unit: 7th Bn. Date of death: 22 May 1915.

Supplementary information: Younger brother of **ACTON, Charles Annesley** also died in

The gravestone of C. Baker.

the First World War. Killed in action. Age at death: 38. From De Ruvigny's Roll of Honour: son of the late Col. Charles Ball-Acton, C.B., The King's Own (Yorkshire Light Infantry), by his wife, Georgina Cecilia, second daughter of George Annesley (Viscount Valentia Coll); and grandson of Lieut-Col William Acton, of West Aston, Co, Wicklow, J.P., D.L., M.P. and brother to Major C.A. Acton (q.v.). Born: Wicklow, 2 October 1877. Educated in Rugby School; Oxford Military College, Cowley, and the Royal Military College Sandhurst. Gazetted 2nd Lieut, King's Own (Yorkshire Light Infantry) 22 December 1897. Promoted to Lieutenant 26 March, 1899. Captain 6 August 1914, and Major 3 March 1916. Served with the 2nd Battalion (105th Foot) in the South African War, April, 1900–2 (Queen's Medal with three clasps, and King's Medal with two clasps). Resigned his commission soon after the termination of the war, and took up farming in South Africa and the Argentine. Joined the Special Reserve of Officers in about 1912. Rejoined his regiment at the outbreak of War in August 1914. He went to France in December and was wounded at the end of January 1915 and invalided home. He was subsequently with the 7th Battalion, at Hall for a year, returning to France in March 1916, and was killed in action near Ypres 22 May following. Buried in St Jean Cemetery there. On this occasion Major Ball-Acton had volunteered to go out with some men on patrol duty. On their return, two were absent, and he immediately ordered to go and look for them, and in doing so was twice wounded, the second time fatally, 2nd Lieut Bond and Private Garnet brought him back at great risk, thinking he was alive. Lieut Bond was awarded the Military Cross for his conduct. He married at Iron Acton, Co. Gloucester, 17 April 1913 to Isabel (Kilmacurragh, Rathdrum, Co. Wicklow), second daughter of the late Revd William Richmond, Vicar of Rockhampton, Co. Gloucester. They had a son, Charles, born 25 April 1914. Grave or Memorial Reference: He has no known grave but is listed on Sp memorial 9 in White House Cemetery, St Jean-Les-Ypres in Belgium.

BARR, Charles: (Served under the name **Charles Russell**). Rank: Rifleman. Regiment or Service: Royal Irish Rifles. Unit: 1st Bn. He was previously with the North Irish Horse where his number was 2416. Date of death: 24 March 1918. Age at death: 19. Service No: 20187. Born in Malton, Yorks. Enlisted in Bray, Co. Wicklow while living in Rathdrum, Co.

Wicklow. Killed in action. Grave or Memorial Reference: He has no known grave but is listed on the Pozieres Memorial in France.

BARRETT, John: Rank: Private. Regiment or Service: Royal Dublin Fusiliers. Unit: 2nd Bn. Date of death: 24 October 1918. Service No: 15566. Age at death: 24. Born in Stratford, Co. Wicklow. Enlisted in Carlow while living in Stratford-on-Slaney. Died of wounds.

Supplementary information: Son of James and Margaret Barrett, of Stratford-on-Slaney, Co. Wicklow. Grave or Memorial Reference: III. A. 4. Cemetery; Belgrade Cemetery, Belgium.

BARRINGTON, Richard M.: Rank: Private. Regiment or Service: Royal Inniskilling Fusiliers. Unit: 9th Bn. Date of death: 1 July 1916, first day of the Battle of the Somme. Service No: 17579. Born in Bray, Co. Wicklow. Enlisted in Finner Camp, Co. Donegal. Killed in action. Grave or Memorial Reference: He has no known grave but is listed on Pier and Face DA and 5 B on the Thiepval Memorial in France.

BARTON, Charles Erskine: Rank: Captain. Regiment or Service: Royal Irish Rifles. Unit: 4th Bn. Attached to the 2nd Bn. Age at Death; 35. Date of Death: 23 August 1918. Supplementary information from Jimmy Taylor: Second son of Charles William Barton, Glendalough House, Annamoe, Co. Wicklow. BLGI. Husband of Norah Grace Deane Barton. Brother of T.E. Barton. Educated at St Columba's College, Dublin. His elder brother, Robert Childers Barton (1881–1975), resigned his commission at the time of the 1916 Rising. He was Sinn Féin MP for West Wicklow 1918–22, Minister for Agriculture in the First Dáil (1919–21), and was a delegate and signatory of the Anglo-Irish Treaty in 1921. Their cousin, Robert Erskine Childers (1870–1922), author of *The Riddle of the Sands*, brought a shipment of arms from Germany for the Irish Volunteers in July 1914. He served in the Royal Navy during the war and was elected to Dáil Éireann in 1921 and appointed secretary to the Irish delegation that negotiated the Treaty. During the Civil War he was arrested at Glendalough House estate, court-martialled for possession of a revolver and executed by the Free State Forces. His son, Erskine Hamilton Childers (1905–1974), was later elected President of Ireland.

Promoted Lt. 17 September 1914. From the *Free Press* 11 December 1915,

Capt. Barton first served as a Second Lieutenant in the 3rd Royal Scots Fusiliers (Militia) from 1902 to 1904. He volunteered on the outbreak of the present war in August 1914 and was gazetted First Lieutenant in the 4th Bn Royal Irish Rifles. He went to the front in April where he served with the 1st Royal Irish Fusiliers till June 26th when he was invalided home suffering from gas poisoning. He was promoted Captain on 1st October 1915 and is now at Carrickfergus pending his recall to the front.

Returned to France during 1916. The war diary does not say when he joined 2nd RIR but it mentions that he was in hospital 16 January 1917. Gassed 14 August 1918 and died at No. 5 British Red Cross Hospital 23 August 1918. Age 35. From *Irish Life*, 27 September 1918: 'Capt. C. Erskine Barton … resided at Ruane, New Ross, and was a magistrate for the County of Wexford.' Effects to his widow at 7 Prince of Wales Terrace, Bray, Co. Wicklow.

Supplementary information: Son of the late C.W. Barton, D.L, of Glendalough House, Annamoe, Co. Wicklow. Husband of Norah Deane Barton, of 4 Mount Pleasant Villas, Bray. Died of wounds. From an article in the *Enniscorthy Guardian,*

Captain C Erskine Barton, RIR, formerly of Ruane Cottage, New Ross, died of the 23rd inst, at the age of 36 at an hospital at the Base, in France, from gas poisoning. He had been resident at Ruane Cottage since about 1910, volunteered for the war in August 1914, and went to France in May 1915, being subsequently invalided home from gas poisoning. He had only returned to the front a few weeks when he was again severely gassed on the 14th of the present month. He had been through several engagements, including the battle of Hill 60. He was the second son of the late Mr Charles W Barton of Glendalough House, Annamoe, Co Wicklow, and his younger brother; Lieut Thos E Barton, fell in action in 1916.

Captain Barton, who was a Magristrate for the Co. Wexford, used to sit at the Arthurstown petty sessions when residing at Ruane Cottage. He was a former member of the New Ross Agricultural Show Society, and took a practical interest in fowl, having exhibited some fine specimens at the shows. In politics he was a follower of Sir Edward Carson, and was for some time secretary of the Wexford Unionist Association, and his experience with the ways of political life was shown in the storm which surrounded his name in 1914, when he incautiously committed himself to the fiction of Catholic intolerance in South Wexford. This pronouncement produced an indignant protest, and a public meeting of repudiation was held at Ballykelly in the district where he was residing at the time when the matter was exposed and evidence of the privilige enjoyed by him was given by his Catholic neighbours referred to. He joined the New Ross Corps of the National Volunteers a short time previous to volunteering for the war. Grave or Memorial Reference: II.D.41. Cemetery; Terlincthun British Cemetery, Wimille in France.

BARTON, Thomas Eyre: Rank: 2 Lt. Regiment or Service: Royal Irish Rifles. Unit; 2nd Bn, also listed as 14th Battalion attached to the 2nd Battalion. Date of Death: 16 July 1916. Supplementary information from Jimmy Taylor, brother of C.E. Barton. Joined the Royal Naval Armoured Car Division in October 1914. Served as a Petty Officer. Discharged 11 Novemeber 1915 upon disbandment of the Corps. Applied for a commission 23 Novemeber 1915. Joined 2nd RIR 21 May 1916. Killed in action 16 July 1916. He was the third and youngest son of the late Charles

William Barton by his wife, Agnes Alexandra Frances, daughter of the Revd Charles Childers, of Nice, France; Canon of Gibraltar. Born in Glendalough House 15 August 1884. Educated Fettes College, Edinburgh, and Trinity Hall, Cambridge; joined the Royal Naval Air Service October 1914, and served with the Armoured Car Section in Gallipoli; was invalided home in November 1915, with fever. Gazetted 2/Lt. Royal Irish Rifles 14 December; went to France 15 May 1916.'

A WO telegram to his home on 16 July 1916 advised that he was slightly wounded at duty and requested details of his next of kin. Another telegram sent on 19 July 1916 notified that he was missing from 16 July. His identity disc was recovered but nothing else. Died intestate. Next of kin was his mother. Siblings were Frances (39), Dulcibella (37), Robert (36), Charles (34), all at the same address. The senior next of kin was later shown as his brother Robert. WO advised, 8 April 1920, that Barton had been exhumed from a point just north-west of Ovillers and reburied in Ovillers Military Cemetery, Somme. His Company Commander wrote of him that he was very popular with all ranks; the idol of the men, the life of the Company mess and that his courage was magnificent. Grave or Memorial Reference: IX.K.8. Cemetery, Ovillers Military

Cemetery in France.

Witness statements: 5266 Rfn J. Graham, a/Cpl No. 1 Platoon, at Horton County of London War Hospital, Epsom. On 16 July they went over and were held up by barbed wire. He saw Barton dead about 50 yards from their trenches. 1369 Rfn J. O'Brien, A Coy, at Havre Hospital. He saw Barton killed instantly by machine gun fire about midnight 16 July. 7747 Rfn J. O'Sullivan, B Coy Machine Gun Section, saw Barton hit by shrapnel 9 July 1916 in the trenches (see above). Barton shouted 'Go ahead boys'. He didn't see Barton again. Someone else told him Barton was killed the same day. 7446 Sgt W. Hall said they advanced about three minutes past one on Sunday morning, 16 July. We opened fire with machine guns and so lay down until orders came to charge. Then we all got up and cheered and were away. Lt. Barton fell dead almost at once.' 4420 CSM W. Toal saw Barton killed by a shell that knocked him into a shell hole.

BATE, Thomas: Rank: Lieutenant. Regiment or Service: Royal Welsh Fusiliers. Unit: 1/5th and also listed as 5th (Flintshire)Bn (Territorial). Date of death: 26 March 1917 also listed as 26 May 1917. Age at death: 26 also listed as 27. Killed in action in Gaza.

Supplementary information: From De Ruvigny's Roll of Honour. Second and only surviving son of Thomas Bate, of Kelsterton, Co. Flint, and his wife Perenna, daughter of William Owen of Blessington, Co. Wicklow. Born: Kelsterton, 1 July 1890. Educated: Fonthill, East Grinstead and Shrewsbury. He took up farming in Australia after leaving school. He returned home, and having a commission in the Royal Welsh Fusiliers (T.F.) in the early months of 1914, continued with them on the outbreak of war, and with them trained in England till early July 1915. He subsequently went with them to Gallipoli, served with the Egyptian Expeditionary Force in Egypt and Palestine, and was killed in action near Gaza 26 March 1917.

His Colonel wrote,

He died in a noble manner, leading and encouraging his men in the attack on the Turkish position on 26th March. All who were near him during the attack bear witness as to his gallant conduct throughout this day up to the time of his death. He was always to the fore, and showed an utter disregard to his own personal safety ... He was a fine fighting soldier and a favourite with all ranks. I have put his name forward for recommendation, and I hope it will go through. You have every reason to feel intensely proud of him.

The gravestone of Alexander Beard on the left.

His servant added,

> He died a hero, if ever there was one. He was one of our best officers; his old platoon loved him. I lost my best friend when I lost Capt, Bate; I shall never forget him as long as I live. His first thought was about his men, and himself later. I never had a better master.

He was mentioned in Despatches (*London Gazette*, 22 May 1917) for gallant and distinguished service in the field. Grave or Memorial Reference: He has no known grave but is listed on panels 20 to 22 on the Jerusalem Memorial in Israel.

BAYLE, Joseph: Rank: Sergeant. Regiment or Service: Royal Inniskilling Fusiliers. Unit: 9th Bn. Date of death: 21 March 1916. Age at Death: 27. Service No: 13492. Born in Baltinglass, Co. Wicklow. Enlisted in Dublin. Died of wounds.

Supplementary information: Son of Mrs Elizabeth Bayle, of 15 Bath Avenue, Sandymount, Dublin. Grave or Memorial Reference: A.9. Cemetery: Gezaincourt Communal Cemetery Extension, Somme in France.

BEARD, Alexander Sherlock: Rank: Sergeant/Observer. Regiment or Service: Royal Air Force. V. R. Date of death: 24 February 1942. Age at death 32. Service No: 1378465.

Supplementary information: Son of Alexander Charles and Esther Beard of Seaford. Husband of Daisy Beard of Seaford. Lost over the Irish Republic. The aircraft they were flying was a Lockheed Hudson V (Long Range) and had a four man crew. It crashed into the Irish Sea during terrible weather and the bodies of two of the crew (Sgt Jack Rostern 1068192 and Sgt Alexander Sherlock Beard) were picked up by a fishing vessel just off Cahore Point. One other body was found after the war. He spent from 1924 to 1929 at the Fleur De Lys house in Hurstpierpoint College and is listed on the Hurstpierpoint College Memorial.

From an article written in 2005 by his daughter Patricia Sherlock-Beard for the BBC,

> My father was a motorcycle policeman in the Metropolitan Police at that time and I can remember that there was a poison gas scare in the area when he was called out to help the local police forces. My mother and I together with some neighbours sat in our gas masks for three and one half hours until my father came home and said that the scare had

been caused by a petrol spillage in the road. It seemed that the siren was always sounding, and one day, on my way to school, a Stuka dive bomber appeared out of the sky and machine-gunned us as we went along the road. After this, my father decided it would be better for my mother and I to move in with my grandfather and grandmother in Seaford, Sussex and we went to stay there in early 1940. My father ... although being in a reserved occupation, decided that he wanted to do something more active to help with the War effort and he joined the Royal Air Force as a volunteer reservist, against my mother's wishes.

He was then 31 years old, so older than most of those who were joining up. He was sent for training to Hamilton, Canada and was there for nine months. On his return he joined Coastal Command as a Sergeant Observer/Navigator and carried out several sorties. However, during a sortie in bad weather over the Irish Sea in 1942 his plane ended up in the sea and he was killed. Only the pilot and my father's bodies were found by local Irish fishermen and they were buried in a military grave in Cork Cemetery. The other members of the crew were never found.

This news really devastated my mother and I was almost inconsolable – my father having always meant so much to me and I was the only child. I don't really think my mother quite understood how I felt, or perhaps she thought, as a child of eight, I would probably get over his loss before she did. I have always missed him and found it difficult to grow up without his gentle guidance.

In 1943, my mother's brother who was in the Royal Navy, having survived being torpedoed and spending 28 days in an open lifeboat with 30 others, was killed in a motor-cycle accident so our last serving family member, my uncle by marriage to my aunt, who was also in the Royal Navy, in HMS *Erebus* was the only person who returned at the end of the War.

Grave or Memorial Reference: Prot. Ground. Joint Grave E.75. Cemetery: Arklow Cemetery, Co. Wicklow.

BEHAN, John Joseph: Rank: Corporal. Regiment or Service: Royal Irish Rifles. Unit: 2nd Bn. Date of death: 23 April 1916. Service No: 8615. Born in Baltinglass, Co. Wicklow. Enlisted in Dublin while living in Dover. Killed in action. Grave or Memorial Reference: I. F. 8. Cemetery; Ecoivres Military

Cemetery, Mont-St-Eloi in France.

BEHAN, William John Thomas: Rank: Corporal. Regiment or Service: Royal Air Force. Unit: (serving in HMS *Illustrious*). Age at death: 25. Date of death: 10 January 1941. Service No: 534795.

Supplementary information: Son of William and Evelyn Behan, of Greystones, Co. Wicklow. On 10 January 1941 HMS. *Illustrious* was attacked while escorting a convoy east of Sicily by Axis Savoia-Marchetti SM. 79 and Ju-87 'Stuka' dive-bombers, being hit by eight bombs and suffering extensive damage, destroying her sick bay and ward room, and killing many. The aircraft carrier was heavily damaged by German dive bombers when the armoured flight deck was penetrated by a bomb, that and six other bomb hits, put her out of action until the following December. Grave or Memorial Reference: He has no known grave but is listed on Panel 2, Column 2 on the Malta Memorial, Floriana, Malta.

BELL, Robert: Rank: Private. Regiment or Service: Royal Dublin Fusiliers. Unit: 2nd Bn. Date of death: 24 May 1915. Service No: 8501 and 85001. Born in Templemore. Enlisted in Dublin while living in Magherymore, Co. Wicklow. Killed in action. Age at death: 18.

Supplementary information: Son of Mr and Mrs William Bell, of Magherymore, Wicklow. Grave or Memorial Reference: He has no known grave but is listed on Panel 44 and 46 on the Ypres (Menin Gate) Memorial in Belgium.

BENSON, Arthur George: Rank: Corporal. Regiment or Service: Royal Dublin Fusiliers. Unit: 2nd Bn. Date of death: 18 November 1918. Service No: 13097. Age at death: 19. Born in Shinrone, Co. Offaly. Enlisted in Dublin while living in Shinrone. Died of wounds.

Supplementary information: Son of James and Catherine Benson, of 4 Sutton Villas, Dargle Road, Bray, Co. Wicklow. Native of Bellevue, Shimroe, King's County. Grave or Memorial Reference: S.III. J.6. Cemetery: St Sever Cemetery Extension, Rouen in France.

BERGIN, John: Rank: Ordinary Seaman. Regiment or Service: Mercantile Marine. Ship: SS *Walter Ulric* (Carnarvon). Date of death: 29 March 1917.

Supplementary information: Son of Mrs Elizabeth Bergin, of Dunbur, Co. Wicklow. Grave or Memorial Reference: He has no known grave but is listed on the Tower Hill Memorial in the UK.

BERGIN, Patrick: Rank: Able Seaman. Regiment or Service: Mercantile Marine. Ship: SS *Walter Ulric* (Carnarvon). Date of death: 29 March 1917.

Supplementary information: Son of Mrs Elizabeth Bergin, of Dunbur, Co. Wicklow. Grave or Memorial Reference: He has no known grave but is listed on the Tower Hill Memorial in the UK.

BERRY, Edward Fleetwood: Rank: Captain. Regiment or Service: 9th Gurkha Rifles. Indian Army. Unit: Adjt. 2nd Bn. attd. 1st Bn. Date of death: 17 April 1916. Age at death: 27. Born 23 May 1889. He won the Military Cross and is listed in the *London Gazette*.

Supplementary information: Son of Mary Fleetwood Berry (*née* Chatterton), of Kilgarran, Enniskerry, Co. Wicklow, and the late Ven. James Fleetwood Berry, B.D, Archdeacon of Tuam. Edward Fleetwood Berry. Born: 23 May 1888 in Sligo. Baptized at Calry, Co. Sligo. Died of wounds received in Mesopotamia on 17 April 1916. He left school in 1906 and passed into Sandhurst; 2nd Lt. Wiltshire Regiment 1907. Became Lt. in 1909 and transferred to the Indian Army Goorka Rifles in 1909. In Burma

Rifles in 1914. and was A.D.C. to Lord Carmichael, Governor of Bengal; also served in the Great War in France and Mesopotamia. Awarded the Military Cross for 'brilliant dash and leadership' at Neuve Chapelle on 10 March 1915. From *Families From King's County and County Westmeath, Ireland,*

Only son of James and Mary. Served in the Wiltshire Regt. & Goorka Rifles and was A.D.C. to Lord Carmichael, Governor of Bengal, also served in the Great War in France and Mesopotamia, and was killed April 17 or 18, 1916 aged 27.

Grave or Memorial Reference: He has no known grave but is listed on Panel 51 of the Basra memorial in Iraq. He is also listed on the Great War memorial Cross in St Nicholas Collegiate Church of Ireland, Church Lane in Galway.

BIRD, Harold Sebastain: Rank: Ordinary Seaman. Regiment or Service: Merchant Navy. Unit: SS *Langleegorse* (Newcastle-on-Tyne). Age at death: 25. Date of death: 23 January 1941. The ship was sunk by a Focke-Wulf Condor aircraft 200 miles off the Irish coast while *en route* from Durban to London. There were no survivors.

Supplementary information: Son of William and Teresa Bird. Husband of Monica Josephine Bird, of Wicklow. Grave or Memorial Reference: He has no known grave but is listed on Panel 63 of the Tower Hill Memorial, UK.

BOLTON, John Charles: Rank: Sergeant. Regiment or Service: Royal Irish Regiment. Unit: 7th Bn. CWGC says his unit was the South Irish Horse where his number was 1198. He won the Military Medal and is listed in the *London Gazette*. Date of death: 21 March 1918. Age at death: 26. Service No: 25039. Born in Dunganstown, Co. Wicklow. Enlisted in Dublin while living in Rathnew, Co. Wicklow. Killed in action.

Supplementary information: Son of James and Annie Bolton, of Kilcandra, Rathdrum, Co. Wicklow. Enlisted May, 1915. Grave or Memorial Reference: He has no known grave but is listed on Panels 30 and 31 on the Pozieres Memorial in France.

BOYCE, Edward: Rank: Private. Regiment or Service: Royal Dublin Fusiliers. Unit: 8th Bn. Date of death: 29 April 1916. Age at death: 35. Service No: 14538. Born in Rathnew, Co. Wicklow. Enlisted in Wicklow. Killed in action.

Supplementary information: Son of Edward and Margaret Boyce, of Rathnew, Co. Wicklow. Grave or

Memorial Reference: He has no known grave but is listed on Panel 127 to 129 on the Loos Memorial in France.

BOYD, Thomas Evelyn: Rank: Private. Regiment or Service: Royal Dublin Fusiliers. Unit: 10th Bn. Date of death: 25 February 1918. Age at death: 20. Service No: 26537. Born in Bray, Co. Wicklow. Enlisted in Dublin while living in Bray, Co. Wicklow.

Supplementary information: Son of Mr and Mrs Walter Boyd, of Ravenna, Bray, Co. Wicklow. Grave or Memorial Reference: VI.D.24. Cemetery: Cologne Southern Cemetery, Germany.

BOWYER, Clifford Charles John: Rank: Squadron Leader (Pilot). Regiment or Service: Royal Air Force Volunteer Reserve. Unit: 15 Sqdn. Age at death: 21. Date of death: 14 May 1943. Service No: 118812.

Supplementary information: Son of Percy George and Vera May Bowyer, of Greystones, Co. Wicklow. Flying Stirling III BK704 LS-Z during Operation Bochum they took off 0014 hrs Mildenhall. Coned at 11,000 feet and hit by flak. Exploded and crashed 01:30 hrs at Barlo 6km NNE of Bocholt. Bowyer was buried on 17 May. His grave is now in the Reichwald

Forest Cemetery. At twenty-one he was one of the youngest Squadron Leader pilots killed on bomber operations in 1943. He is also mentioned in 'Bomber Command Losses'. Vol. 4 W R. Chorley. Grave or Memorial Reference: 21.B.15. Cemetery: Reichswald Forest War Cemetery, Rheinberg in Germany.

BRADSHAW, James: Rank: Private. Regiment or Service: Royal Inniskilling Fusiliers. Unit: 9th Bn. Date of death: 16 August 1917. Age at death: 22. Service No: 13493. Born in Wicklow, Co. Wicklow. Enlisted in Dublin. Killed in action.

Supplementary information: Son of James and Hannah E. Bradshaw, of Bally McSimon, Glenealy, Co. Wicklow. Grave or Memorial Reference: He has no known grave but is listed on Panel 70 to 72 on the Tyne Cot Memorial in Belgium.

BRADY, Edward: Rank: Private. Regiment or Service: Leinster Regiment. Unit: 7th Bn. Date of death: 1 November 1915. Service No: 3508. Born in Bray, Co. Wicklow. Enlisted in Dublin while living in Dublin. Died at home. Grave or Memorial Reference: Old Ground in the South east corner (5103) Cemetery: Kilbarrack Cemetery in Sutton, Dublin.

BREAN, Joseph: Rank: Private. Regiment or Service: Royal Army Service Corps, Army Service Corps Unit: 19th Remount Squadron. Date of death: 26 October 1918. Service No: R4/087389. Enlisted in Bristol while living in Baltinglass, Co. Wicklow.

Supplementary information: Son of Mrs Anne Higgins (formerly Brean), of Colin Moore, Co. Kildare. Grave or Memorial Reference: I.D.8. Cemetery: Arquata Scrivia Communal Cemetery Extension in Italy.

BREEN, Patrick: Rank: Lance Corporal. Regiment or Service: Royal Dublin Fusiliers. Unit: 8th Bn. Date of death: 27 April 1916. Age at death: 21. Service No: 14265. Born in Bray, Co. Wicklow. Enlisted in Bray. Killed in action.

Supplementary information: Son of James and Mary Breen, of 92 Boghall Cottages, Bray, Co. Wicklow. Grave or Memorial Reference: He has no known grave but is listed on Panel 127 to 129 on the Loos Memorial in France.

BREEN, Patrick: Rank: Sergeant. Regiment or Service: Royal Irish Regiment. Unit: 7th (South Irish Horse) Bn. He was previously with the Royal Dublin Fusiliers where his number was 10205. Date of death: 8 April 1918. Service No:

12047. Born in Avoca, Co. Wicklow. Enlisted in Dublin while living in Avoca. Died of wounds. Grave or Memorial Reference: II.A.8. Cemetery: Hautmont Communal Cemetery in in France.

BRERTON, George S.: Rank: Private (Lance Corporal). Regiment or Service: Royal Irish Fusiliers. Unit: 1st Garrison Bn. He was previously with the Royal Irish Regiment where his number was 19313. Date of death: 15 April 1917. Age at death: 42. Service No: 5536. Born in Baltinglass, Co. Wicklow. Enlisted in Liverpool while living in Baltinglass, Co. Wicklow. Died at Sea.

Supplementary information: Son of William and Bella Brereton, of Baltinglass, Co. Wicklow. Served in the South African Campaign and in the Natal Rebellion (1906) with Durban Light Inf. Grave or Memorial Reference: He has no known grave but is listed on Mikra Memorial in Greece.

BRESTLAUN, Owen: Rank: Private. Regiment or Service: Royal Dublin Fusiliers. Unit: 1st Bn. Date of death: 29 June 1915. Age at death: 28. Service No: 10053. Born in Carnew. Enlisted in Carlow while living in Taney, Co. Carlow. Killed in action in Gallipoli.

Supplementary information: Son

of the late Daniel Brestlaun, of Ballyellis, Gorey, Co. Wexford, and of Bessie McGuinness (formerly Brestlaun), of Ardoyne, Tullow, Co. Carlow. Grave or Memorial Reference: He has no known grave but is listed on Panel 190 to 196 on the Helles Memorial in Turkey.

BREWSTER, John C.: Rank: Private. Regiment or Service: Irish Guards. Unit: 1st Bn. Date of death: 11 July 1915. Service No: Listed as 5008 and 3008. Born in Dublin. Enlisted in Dublin. Killed in action.

Supplementary information: Son of Mr J.C. Brewster, of Wingates, Bray, Co. Wicklow. Grave or Memorial Reference: II.C.2. Cemetery: Cuinchy Communal Cemetery in France.

BRIEN, James: Rank: Sailor. Regiment or Service; Mercantile Marine. Unit: SS *Cardiff*. Date of death: 10 February 1918.

Supplementary information: Son of George and Mary Brien, of 8 Abbey Street, Arklow, Co. Wicklow. Grave or Memorial Reference: He has no known grave but is listed on the Tower Hill Memorial in the UK.

BRIEN, Joseph: Rank: Private. Regiment or Service: Royal

Irish Fusiliers. Unit: 9th (North Irish Horse) Bn. Date of death: 3 October 1918. Age at death: 20. Service No: 42455. Formerly he was with the Royal Irish Rifles where his number was 4451. Born in Bray, Co. Wicklow. Enlisted in Dublin while living in Bray. Killed in action.

Supplementary information: Son of Michael and Mary Brien, of 11 Ravenswell Row, Bray, Wicklow. Grave or Memorial Reference: IV.F.26. Cemetery: Dadizele New British Cemetery in Belgium.

BRIEN, Michael: Rank: Private. Regiment or Service: Royal Irish Fusiliers. Unit: 8th Bn. Date of death: 10 August 1916. Age at death: 20. Service No: 10734. Born in Bray, Co. Wicklow. Enlisted in Bray. Killed in action.

Supplementary information: Son of Michael and Mary Brien, of 11 Ravenswell Row, Bray, Co. Wicklow. Grave or Memorial Reference: H.4. Cemetery, Bois-Carre Military Cemetery, Haisnes in France.

BRIEN, Michael: Rank: Able Seaman. Regiment or Service: Mercantile Marine. Unit: SS *Astoria* (London). Date of death: 9 October 1916. Age at death: 26. Astoria was sunk by German submarine number U46, 120 nm.

North-east for Vardö (Norway) in the western part of Barent Sea. Astoria was loaded with copper, leather and engine parts from from New York to Arkhangelsk.

Supplementary information: Son of Matthew and Catherine Brien (*née* Byrne), of 7 Fair Green, Arklow, Co. Wicklow. Born at Arklow. Grave or Memorial Reference: He has no known grave but is listed on the Tower Hill Memorial in the UK.

BRIEN, Phelim: Rank: Rifleman. Regiment or Service: Royal Irish Rifles. Unit: 1st Bn. Date of death: 14 November 1916. Age at death: 20. Service No: 3958. Born in Bray, Co. Wicklow. Enlisted in Clonmel while living in Shankill, Co. Dublin. Killed in action.

Supplementary information: Son of Thomas and Lizzie Brien, of 11 Mavenswell Row, Bray, Co. Wicklow. Grave or Memorial Reference: He has no known grave but is listed on Pier and Face 15 A and 15 B on the Thiepval Memorial in France.

BRIEN, Thomas: Rank: Private. Regiment or Service: Royal Dublin Fusiliers. Unit: 1st Bn. Date of death: 28 December 1915. Age at death: 38. Service No: 22321. Born in Roundwood, Co. Wicklow. Enlisted in Naas while living in

Blessington. Killed in action in Gallipoli.

Supplementary information: Son of Thomas Brien, of Roundwood, Co. Wicklow. Husband of Bridget Brien, of Burgage, Blessington, Co. Wicklow. Grave or Memorial Reference: II.E.2. Cemetery, Twentv Tree Copse Cemetery in Turkey.

BRIEN, Thomas: Rank: Private. Regiment or Service: Royal Dublin Fusiliers. Unit: 1st Bn. Date of death: 24 March 1918. Service No: 19900. Enlisted in Dublin while living in Bray, Co. Wicklow. Died of wounds. Grave or Memorial Reference: 3. Cemetery, Rosieres British Cemetery in France.

BRINE, Michael: Rank: Lance Corporal. Regiment or Service: Irish Guards. Unit: 1st Bn. He won the D. C. M. and is listed in the London Gazette. Date of death: 5 May 1915. Age at death: 23. Service No: 3975. Born in Baltinglass, Co. Wicklow. Enlisted in Athlone, Co. Westmeath. Died of wounds. Grave or Memorial Reference: IV.B.78. Cemetery, Bethurne Town Cemetery in France.

BRINKLEY, William: Rank: Private. Regiment or Service:

Royal Field Artillery. Unit: 82nd Battery. Date of death: 6 July 1915. Service No: 91581.

Supplementary information: Husband of Teresa Brinkley, of Moneystown, Co. Wicklow. Grave or Memorial Reference: He has no known grave but is listed on Face 1 of the Kirkee Memorial in India.

BRISCOE, Henry Whitby: Rank: Private. Rank: Second Lieutenant (TP). Regiment or Service: Royal Irish Fusiliers. Unit: 3rd Garrison Bn. Age at death: 43. Date of death: 15 April 1917. Died. Regiment or Service: Royal Dublin Fusiliers. Unit: 1st Bn.

Supplementary information: Son of Arthur Wellesley Briscoe, of Leinster Road, Rathmines, Dublin. Husband of Mary Zoe Briscoe, of 6 Duncairn Terrace, Bray, Co. Wicklow. A civil servant (Irish Land Commission), barrister-at-law. Grave or Memorial Reference: He has no known grave but is listed on the Mikra Memorial Memorial in Greece.

BRODERICK, Patrick: Rank: Lance Corporal. Regiment or Service: Royal Dublin Fusiliers. Unit: B Company, 9th Bn. Date of death: 16 August 1917. Age at death: 22. Service No: 12974. Born in Newtownmountkennedy, Co.

Wicklow. Enlisted in Dublin while living in Newtownmountkennedy, Co. Wicklow. Killed in action.

Supplementary information: Son of John and Annie Brodrick, of Newtown, Mountkennedy, Co. Wicklow. Grave or Memorial Reference: He has no known grave but is listed on Panel 144 to 145 on the Tyne Cot Memorial in Belgium.

BROE, Thomas: Rank: Private. Regiment or Service: Royal Dublin Fusiliers. Unit: 6th Bn. Date of death: 5 October 1917. Service No: 26411. Born in Lacken, Blessington. Enlisted in Dublin. Killed in action. Grave or Memorial Reference: XIV. B.9. Cemetery: Cement House Cemetery in Belgium.

BROOKE, Henry Hastings: Rank: Major. Regiment or Service: Connaught Rangers. Unit: 4th Bn. Age at death: 37.

Supplementary information: Son of Frank Brooke. Husband of Frances Mary Brooke (*née* Bernard), of 28 Collingham Place, Earl's Court, London. Born at Ardeen, Co. Wicklow. From a Wicklow newspaper article of the time,

Captain H Brooke. Connaught Rangers, who was so badly wounded at the front has arrived at his fathers place at Ardeen, Shillelagh. Everyone is exceedingly glad to know that the gallant Captain who has sacrificed so much for his country, at whose disposal he so ungrudgingly placed his services when the war broke out, is in good health, but alas! Is very much feared that the bullet which passed through his temples did its nefarious work too well, and it is very much feared he has lost the sight of bith eyes.

Grave or Memorial Reference: 1891. Cemetery: Sandown-Shanklin (Shanklin) Cemetery UK.

BROOKS, Joseph: Rank: Acting Corporal. Regiment or Service: Royal Dublin Fusiliers. Unit: 9th Bn. Date of death: 28 September 1918. Service No: 24680. Born in Wicklow. Enlisted in Dublin while living in Greenock. Died at home. No burial details available.

BROWN, Mervyn Gamble: Rank: Serjeant. Regiment or Service: Royal Artillery. Unit: 24 Bty, 9H.A.A. Regt. Date of death: 2 May 1946. Service No: 1452072.

Supplementary information: Son of William Frederick and Lila Molly Brown, of Enniskillen. Husband of Patricia Lucy Brown, of Bray, Co. Wicklow. Grave or Memorial Reference: Sec. 1. Grave 132. Cemetery: Breandrum Cemetery, Enniskillen, Co. Fermanagh.

BROWNE, Dominick Augustus: Rank: Captain. Regiment or Service: Royal Irish Rifles. Unit: Adjt to the 1st Bn. Date of death: 1 July 1916 (first day of the Battle of the Somme). Age at death: 28. Killed in action.

Supplementary information: Son of the late Frank and Mary Browne, of Killadreenan, Co. Wicklow. Grave or Memorial Reference: He has no known grave but is listed on Face 15 A and 15 B on the Thiepval Memorial in France.

BROWNE, Patrick: Rank: Private. Regiment or Service: Royal Dublin Fusiliers. Unit: 8th Bn. Date of death: 27 April 1916. Service No: 14532. Born in Rathnew, Co. Wicklow. Enlisted in Wicklow. Killed in action (missing). Age at death: 29. Grave or Memorial Reference: He has no known grave but is listed on Panel 127 to 129 the Loos Memorial in France.

BROWNE, Peter Raleigh Howe: Rank: Second Lieutenant. Regiment or Service: Royal Irish

Fusiliers. Unit: 1st Bn. Age at death: 22. Date of death: 24 May 1940. Service No: 74702.

Supplementary information: Son of Cyril Edward and Alice Christina Browne, of Bray, Co. Wicklow. Grave or Memorial Reference: Plot 10. Row B. Grave 2. Cemetery: Longuenesse (St Omer) Souvenir Cemetery. Pas de Calais, France.

BRUCE, William John: Rank: Private. Regiment or Service: Irish Guards. Unit: 1st Bn. Date of death: 29 June 1917. Service No: 4446. Born in Derraloney, Co. Wicklow. Enlisted in Tralee, Co. Kerry. Killed in action.

Supplementary information: Son of William and Ann Bruce, of Deralossery, Glendalough, Co. Wicklow. Grave or Memorial Reference: Plot 3. Row G. Grave 3. Cemetery; Ferme-Olivier Cemetery in Belgium.

BRYAN, Edward: Rank: Sergeant. Regiment or Service: East Yorkshire Regiment. Unit: 6th Bn. Date of death: 8 December 1915. Age at death: 41. Service No: 3/7807. Born in St Andrews, Co. Wicklow. Enlisted in Richmond while living in Stockton-on-Tees. Died in the Dardinelles.

Supplementary information: Son of Richard and Esther J. Bryan, of 6 Mason's Court, Stockton-on-Tees.

Grave or Memorial Reference: A.52. Cemetery: Alexandria (Chatby) Military and War Memorial Cemetery in Egypt.

BRYAN, William: Rank: Private. Regiment or Service: Leinster Regiment. Unit: 1st Bn. Date of death: 15 March 1915. Age at death: 38. Service No: 3811. Born in Bray, Co. Wicklow. Enlisted in Dublin. Killed in action.

Supplementary information: Son of the late Mr and Mrs Michael Bryan. Husband of Mary Jane Quinn (formerly Bryan) of Shankhill, Co. Dublin. Grave or Memorial Reference: He has no known grave but is listed on Panel 44 on the Ypres (Menin Gate) Memorial in Belgium.

BUCKLEY, William: Rank: Private. Regiment or Service: Royal Irish Regiment. Unit: 7th Bn. He was previously with the South Irish Horse where his number was 1299. Age at death: 29 (age also listed as 30). Date of death: 6 August 1918. Service No: 25059. Born in Enniskerry, Co. Wicklow. Enlisted in Dublin while living in Enniskerry. Died as a prisoner of war in Valenciennes in France.

Supplementary information: Son of Francis and Georgina Buckley, of Enniskerry, Co. Wicklow. Grave or Memorial Reference:

V.E.9. Cemetery; Valenciennes (St Roch) Communal Cemetery in France.

BURKE, James: Rank: Fusilier. Regiment or Service: Royal Inniskilling Fusiliers. Unit: 1st Bn. Age at death: 23. Date of death: 15 September 1942. Service No: 6979437.

Supplementary information: Son of Thomas and Dorothy Burke, of Wicklow. Enlisted while living in Tyrone. Grave or Memorial Reference: 3.C.5. Cemetery: Delhi War Cemetery in India.

BURKE, John: Rank: Lance Corporal. Regiment or Service: Royal Dublin Fusiliers. Unit: 9th Bn. Date of death: 11 September 1916. Age at death: 36. Service No: 12369. Born in Newtownmountkennedy, Co. Wicklow. Enlisted in Dublin while living in Newtownmountkennedy, Co. Wicklow. Died of wounds.

Supplementary information: Husband of M. Burke, of Newtownmountkennedy, Co. Wicklow. Grave or Memorial Reference: X.D.2. Cemetery; Etaples Military Cemetery in France.

BURNE, Arthur Edward Thomas: Rank: Lance Corporal.

Arthur Edward Thomas Burne.

Regiment or Service: Australian Infantry, A.I.F. Unit: 49th Bn and 9th Bn, 12th Reinforcement. Date of death: 23. Service No: 3700. Born in Bally Reane, (birth location also listed as Rathdrum) Co. Wicklow.

Supplementary information: Educated: Grammer School, Co. Wicklow. Age on entering Australia: 18. Enlisted on 15 January 1915 in Toowoomba. Occupation on enlistment: Labourer. Height: 5'5.7". Weight: 150lbs, Eyes: brown. Hair: brown. Complexion: fair. Religious Denomination: Methodist. Next of kin: Mother: Mrs Margeret L. Burne, Lucklands, Oakey, Queensland. Unit embarked from Brisbane, Queensland, on board HMAT A50 *Itonus* on 30 December 1915. Father: Thomas Burne. Killed in action on 12 October 1916. Served in Egypt and the Western Front. Allotted to and proceeded to join the 49th Bn, Zeitoun, Egypt. 29 February 1916: reverts to ranks. 18 March 1916. Embarked, Alexandria, to join the British Expeditionary Force, 5 June 1916: disembarked, Marseilles, France. 12 June 1916: appointed Lance Corporal. 6 September 1916. Won the Military Medal and is listed in the Commonwelath Gazette No 62, dated 19 April 1917 on page 924, position 28. Dated 19 April 1917: 'At POZIERES, who on the night of 13 August, 1916, went out under a heavy barrage to recon-noitre the enemy's position. They took shelter in shell holes during the whole day and returned during night of 14/15th instant with valuable information regarding enemy's positions.' Also listed in the *London Gazette*, position 28, dated 16 November 1917. Brother: 4742 Private Charles Radford Burne. 15th Bn, killed in action, 11 April 1917. Also entitled to the British War Medal and the Victory Medal.

A letter from the Base Records Office, dated 27 December 1917 states;

Dear Madam.

It is with feelings of admiration at the gallantry of a brave Australian soldier who nobly laid down his life in the service of our King and Country, that I am directed by the Honourable The Minister to forward to you, as the next-of-kin of the late 3700 Lance Corporal A. E. T. Burne, 49th Battalion, Australian Imperial Force, the Military Medal which His Majesty the King has been graciously pleased to award to that gallant soldier for conspicuous bravery and devotion to duty while serving with the Australian Imperial Expeditionary Force.

I am also to ask that you accept his deep personal sympathy in the loss which, not only you, but the Australian Army, has sustained by the death of Lance Corporal A. E. T. Burne, whose magnificent conduct of the field of battle helped to earn for our Australian soldiers a fame which will endure as long as memory lasts.

I shall be obliged if you will kindly let me know whether it comes safely to hand by signing and returning the receipt slip.

Yours faithfully.
Officer, I. C. Base Records.

Grave or Memorial Reference: Plot III, Row F, Grave No. 2. Ridgewood Military Cemetery, Voormezeele, Belgium. He is also listed on panel 147 of the Roll of Honour on the the Australian War Memorial.

BURNE, Charles Radford: Rank: Private. Regiment or Service: Australian Infantry, A.I.F. Unit: 15th Bn. 15th Reinforcement. Originally reported missing but after a Court of Inquiry on 2 November 1917 that was changed to Killed in action in Bullecourt. Date of death: 11 April 1917. Age at Death. 22. Service No: 4742. Served in Tel-El-Kebir, Heliopolis, Egypt, Alexandria, Bulford, Folkstone, England and the famous Bull Ring in France. Born in Ballyreane, Co. Wicklow. Educated in Rathdrum National School, Co. Wicklow. Enlisted in Brisbane,

Queensland on 28 September 1915 in Brisbane while living in Lucklands, Queensland. Religious Denomination: Methodist. Age on arrival in Australia: 17. Occupation on enlistment: Axeman. Height: 5'7". Embarked, from Brisbane, aged 21, Queensland, on board HMAT A73 *Commonwealth* on 28 March 1916. Next of kin listed as mother, Mrs Margaret L. Burne, Lucklands, Oakey, Queensland (Father deceased). Killed in action at Bullecourt.

Supplementary information: Son of Thomas William and Margaret Laetetia Burne. Born in Co. Wicklow. Brother of Arthur Edward Thomas Burne.

A letter from his Mother to the Officer in charge of Base records states;

Dear Sir.

My son Charlie was seen on Apr 11th 1917 at Bullecourt "Mowing down Germans with a machine gun" was the report from a Sergeant George Sillars of the 15th Bn who has since been killed. Another Sergeant of the 15th Bn, Richard Chary says the Sergeant of my sons platoon Sergeant Thomas Bofort who was made prisoners on that 11th might know about him. I am writing to Victoria Barracks in Brisbane for his address. Will write again if he can give me any information. I still sometimes think that my boy maybe alive; I feel very grateful to all those who have instituted these steps. Believe me.

Yours Faithfully.
Margaret L Burne.

His war medals and death plaque were sent to his Mother in 1921. Grave or Memorial Reference. He has no known grave but is listed on the Australian National Memorial, Villiers-Bretonneux in France.

BURNE/BYRNE, John William: Rank: Private. Regiment or Service: Royal Irish Fusiliers. Unit: 4th Bn. Age at death: 40. Date of death: 11 December 1918. Service No: 7125.

Supplementary information: Son of Charles Byrne, of 6 New Cottages, Killincarrig, Delgany. Grave or Memorial Reference: In North-West part. Cemetery: Delgany (Christ Church) Church of Ireland Churchyard, Co. Wicklow.

BURNE, Maurice: Rank: Private. Regiment or Service: Irish Guards. Unit: 1st Bn. Date of death: 4 August 1915. Service No: 4237. Born in Arklow, Co. Wicklow. Enlisted in Liverpool in Lancashire while living in Altrincham, Cheshire.

Supplementary information: From

De Ruvigny's Roll of Honour. Third son of Maurice Burne, of Co. Wicklow, by his wife, Elizabeth (21 Springfield Road, Bangor, Co. Down), daughter, of the late David Madders, of Arklow. Born Ballyraine, Arklow, Co. Wicklow 27 November, 1890. Educated at Skibbereen, Co. Cork. He was an Under-Gardener to the Marquis of Waterford, at Curraghmore, Portlaw, Co. Waterford. Enlisted at Liverpool, 22 October 1912. He served with the Expeditionary Force in France, from August 1914. He was twice wounded, the latter time severely, and was killed in action at Givenchy 4 August 1915. Grave or Memorial Reference: I.E.6. Cemetery: Guards Cemetery, Windy Corner, Cuinchy in France.

BUTLER, Philip: Rank: Private. Regiment or Service: Royal Irish Regiment. Unit: 2nd Bn. Date of death: 19 October 1914. Service No: 4391. Born in Newtownbarry, Co. Kilkenny. Enlisted in Graiguenamanagh, Co. Kilkenny while living in Tinahely, Co. Wicklow. Killed in action. He has no known grave but is listed on Panel 11 and 12. on the Le Touret Memorial in France.

BYRNE, Denis: Rank: Private. Regiment or Service: Royal Irish Fusiliers. Unit: listed as 7th/8th and 8th Bn. He was previously with the Royal Dublin Fusiliers where his number was 20387. Date of death: 10 August 1917. Service No: 22900. Born in Aughrim, Co. Wicklow. Enlisted in Bray, Co. Wicklow while living in Aughrim. Killed in action. Grave or Memorial Reference: He has no known grave but is listed on Panel 42 on the Ypres (Menin Gate) Memorial in Belgium.

BYRNE, Edward: Rank: Temp 2Lt. Regiment or Service: Duke of Cornwalls Light Infantry. Unit: 6th Battalion. 23 August 1917. Killed in action.

Supplementary information: From De Ruvigny's Roll of Honour: eldest son of the late Henry Byrne, of Dunlavin, County Wicklow, by his wife Mary, daughter of Andrew Halpin and nephew of Patrick Byrne Ex-Superintendant of the Dublin Metropolitan Police. Born in Dunlavin, County Wicklow, 8 December 1886. Educated: De La Salle College, Waterford; Leeds University and London University, was subsequently employed as teacher under London City Council. Gazetted: 2nd Lieutenant, Duke of Cornwall's Light Infantry from the London University, O.T.C. 9 October 1915. Trained at Weymouth and Wareham and served with the Expeditionary Force in France and

The gravestone of John William Burne.

Flanders from 9 September 1916, took part in the fighting on the Somme, the battle of Arras and the fighting around Ypres. Was killed in action at Inverness Copse 23 August 1917, while leading his platoon into action. His Colonel wrote, 'He was killed instantaneously by a rifle bullet through the head whilst leading his platoon very gallantly. His loss is mourned by all ranks, by whom he was universally liked and admired.' Grave or Memorial Reference: He has no known grave but is listed on Panel 80 to 82 and 163A on the Tyne Cot Memorial in Belgium.

BYRNE, Edward: Rank: Private. Regiment or Service: Royal Dublin Fusiliers. Unit: 1st Bn. Date of death: 4 June 1915. Age at death: 22. Service No: 8531. Born in Newcastle, Co. Wicklow.

Enlisted in Dublin while living in Newcastle. Killed in action in Gallipoli.

Supplementary information: Son of Patrick and Bridget Byrne, of O'Reilly Cottage, Newcastle, Co. Wicklow. Grave or Memorial Reference: He has no known grave but is listed on Panel 190 to 196 on the Helles Memorial in Turkey.

BYRNE, George: Rank: Private. Regiment or Service: Royal Inniskilling Fusiliers. Unit: 7th Bn. Date of death: 25 April 1916. Age at death: 23. Service No: 24914. Born in Newtown Wicklow. Enlisted in Seaforth while living in Newtown. Died of wounds.

Supplementary information: Son of George Byrne, of Tittour, Newtownmountkennedy, Co. Wicklow. Grave or Memorial Reference: I.C.17. Cemetery,

Edward Byrne.

Philosophe Military Cemetery, Mazingarbe in France.

BYRNE, James: Rank: Lance Corporal. Regiment or Service: Royal Dublin Fusiliers. Unit: 2nd Bn. Date of death: 23 October 1916. Age at death: 29. Service No: 20346. Born in Blackrock, Co. Dublin. Enlisted in Bray while living in Aughrim, Co. Wicklow. Killed in action.

Supplementary information: Son of James and Elizabeth Byrne of Sweetmount, Churchtown, Dundrum, Co. Dublin. Grave or Memorial Reference: XV. M.5. Cemetery, Ovillers Military Cemetery in France.

BYRNE, James: Rank: Private. Regiment or Service: Royal Munster Fusiliers. Unit: 2nd Bn. Date of death: 6 September 1914. Service No: 7309. Born in Wicklow. Enlisted in Armagh while living in Dublin. Died of wounds. Grave or Memorial Reference: He has no known grave but is listed on the La-Ferte-Sous-Jouarre Memorial in France.

BYRNE, James: Rank: Private. Regiment or Service: Royal Irish Fusiliers. Unit: 8th Bn. He was previously with the Royal Irish Regiment where his number was 3602. Date of death: 22 May 1916. Service No: 22001. Born in Bray, Co. Wicklow. Enlisted in Bray. Killed in action.

Supplementary information: Son of Mrs Maria Byrne, of 12 Captains Avenue, Bray, Co. Wicklow. Grave or Memorial Reference: III. K. 16. Cemetery, St Patrick's Cemetery, Loos in France.

BYRNE, James: Rank: Lance Corporal. Regiment or Service: Royal Munster Fusiliers. Unit: 2nd Bn. He was previously with the Royal Dublin Fusiliers where his number was 20244. Date of death: 21 March 1918. Age at death: 35. Service No: 18109. Born in Ashford, Co. Wicklow. Enlisted in Dublin while living in Dublin.

Supplementary information: Son of John and Catherine Byrne; husband of Martha Byrne, of Mountain View Cottage, Kill-o-grange, Blackrock, Co. Dublin. Killed in action. Grave or Memorial Reference: He has no known grave but is listed on Panel 78 and 79 on the Pozieres Memorial in France.

BYRNE, James: Rank: Able Seaman. Regiment or Service: Merchant Navy. Unit: M.V. *Athelfoam* (Liverpool), Age at death: 39. Date of death: 22 October 1944.

Supplementary information: Son

of Charles and Ann Byrne (*née* Penstion), of Arklow. Grave or Memorial Reference: R.C. Ground. Grave NN. 45. James Byrne was the only casualty on the M.V. *Athelfoam* that year. Circumstances regarding his death are not available. Cemetery: Arklow Cemetery in Co. Wicklow.

BYRNE, James: (also listed as **James AUGUSTINE**): Rank: Gunner. Regiment or Service: Royal Garrison Artillery. Unit: 12th Heavy Battery. Date of death: 31 July 1916. Age at death: 32 also listed as 35. Service No: 22820. Born in Rathdrum, Co. Wicklow. Enlisted in Dublin while living in Wicklow. Killed in action.

Supplementary information: Son of James and Anne Byrne, of Glasmarget, Rathdrum, Co. Wicklow. Grave or Memorial Reference: II.Q.6. Cemetery; Danzig Alley British Cemetery, Mametz in France.

BYRNE, John: Rank: Private. Regiment or Service: Royal Army Medical Corps. Unit: 97th Field Ambulance. Date of death: 15 August 1917. Service No: 68413. Born in Kilcoole, Co. Wicklow. Enlisted in Dublin. Killed in action. Grave or Memorial Reference; II.G.30. Cemetery, Coxyde Military Cemetery in France.

BYRNE, Joseph: Rank: Lance Corporal. Regiment or Service: Royal Inniskilling Fusiliers. Unit: 11th Bn. Date of death: 16 August 1917. Service No: 28427. Born in Tinahely, Co. Wicklow. Enlisted in Omagh while living in Tinahely. Killed in action. He has no known grave but is listed on Panel 70 to 72 on the Tyne Cot Memorial in Belgium.

BYRNE, Joseph: Rank: Acting Sergeant. Regiment or Service: Royal Dublin Fusiliers. Unit: 6th Bn. Date of death: 9 December 1915. Service No: 13288. Born in Bray, Co. Wicklow. Enlisted in Dublin while living in Bray. Killed in action in the Balkans. Grave or Memorial Reference: He has no known grave but is listed on Doiran Memorial in Greece.

BYRNE/BURNE, John William: Rank: Private. Regiment or Service: Royal Irish Fusiliers. Unit: 4th Bn. Age at death: 40. Date of death: 11 December 1918. Service No: 7125.

Supplementary information: Son of Charles Byrne, of 6 New Cottages, Killincarrig, Delgany. Grave or Memorial Reference: In north-west part. Cemetery: Delgany (Christ Church) Church of Ireland Churchyard, Co. Wicklow. See page 39.

BYRNE, Martin: Rank: Gunner. Regiment or Service: Royal Horse Artillery and Royal Field Artillery. Unit: 53rd Battery, 2nd Brigade. Date of death: 25 September 1916. Service No: 34415. Born in Bray. Enlisted in Bray. Killed in action. Grave or Memorial Reference: XXIII.C.8. Cemetery: Delville Wood Cemetery, Longueval in France.

BYRNE, Michael: Rank: Acting Sergeant. Regiment or Service: Royal Dublin Fusiliers. Unit: 9th Bn. Date of death: 8 August 1917. Service No: 7213. Born in Rathdrum, Co. Wicklow. Enlisted in Naas while living in Rathdrum. Killed in action. He has no known grave but is listed on Panel 44 and 46 on the Ypres (Menin Gate) Memorial in Belgium.

BYRNE, Michael Joseph: Rank: Corporal and Acting Corporal. Regiment or Service: Royal Inniskilling Fusiliers. Unit: 9th Bn. Date of death: 29 March 1918. Age at death: 28. Service No:. 12/28428. Born in Rathmines, Dublin. Enlisted in Wicklow. Killed in action.
Supplementary information: Son of Thomas P. and Mary Byrne. Born at Tinahely, Co. Wicklow. Grave or Memorial Reference: II.D.27.

Cemetery; Ham British Cemetery, Muille-Villette in France.

BYRNE, Patrick: Rank: A/ C. S. M. Regiment or Service: Leinster Regiment. Unit: 7th Bn. Date of death: 31 July 1917. Service No: 1288. Born in Dublin. Enlisted in Dublin while living in Arklow. Killed in action. Grave or Memorial Reference: B.20. Cemetery: Potijze Chateau Lawn Cemetery in Belgium.

BYRNE, Patrick: Rank: Fusilier. Regiment or Service: Royal Inniskilling Fusiliers. Unit: 1st Bn. Age at death: 26. Date of death: 18 April 1942. Service No: 6977612
Supplementary information: Son of Patrick and Alice Byrne, of Wicklow. Enlisted while living in Tyrone. Grave or Memorial Reference: He has no known grave but is listed on Face 11 on the Rangoon Memorial in Myanmar.

BYRNE, Patrick: Rank: Private. Regiment or Service: Royal Dublin Fusiliers. Unit: 1st Bn. Date of death: 1 July 1916, first day of the battle of the Somme. Age at death: 39. Service No: 24591. Born in Ballyconnell, Co. Wicklow. Enlisted in Wicklow while living in Garryhoe, Co. Wicklow. Killed in action.
Supplementary information: Son

of Patrick Byrne. Enlisted in 1915. Grave or Memorial Reference: He has no known grave but is listed on Pier and Face 16C. on the Thiepval Memorial in France.

BYRNE, Patrick: Rank: Private. Regiment or Service: Irish Guards. Unit: 1st Bn. Date of death: 15 January 1917. Age at death: 28. Service No: 9921. Born in Tinahely. Enlisted in Wicklow. Died of wounds.

Supplementary information: Son of John and Anne Byrne, of Ballyknocker, Shillelagh, Co. Wicklow. Grave or Memorial Reference: VI.D.12A. Cemetery, Wimereux Communal Cemetery in France.

BYRNE, Patrick: Rank: Sapper. Regiment or Service: Corps of Royal Engineers. Unit: 175th Tunnelling Company, R.E. Date of death: 6 March 1917. Age at death: 41. Service No: 157759. Born in Rathvilla, Co. Wicklow. Enlisted in Hamilton, Lanarkshire while living in Glenboig, Lanarkshire. Killed in action.

Supplementary information: Son of Patrick and Bridget Byrne, of Kiltegan, Co. Wicklow; husband of Anna Maria Byrne, of 242 Annathill, Glenboig, Lanarkshire. Grave or Memorial Reference: M. 17. Cemetery; Aveluy Communal

Cemetry Extension in France.

BYRNE, Patrick: Rank: Private. Regiment or Service: Royal Dublin Fusiliers. Unit: 'F' Coy. 3rd Bn. Date of death: 17 June 1916. Age at death: 39. Service No: 22571. Born in Kingstown in Dublin. Enlisted in Lianelly while living in Kingsown. Killed in action.

Supplementary information: Son of John and Margaret Byrne, of Co. Wicklow. Grave or Memorial Reference: III.F.1. Cemetery, St Patricks Cemetery, Loos in France.

BYRNE, Peter: Rank: Private. Regiment or Service: Royal Dublin Fusiliers. Unit: 1st Bn, transferred to the Labour Corps where his number was 398098. Date of death: 25 November 1918. Age at death: 34. Service No: 3/20362.

Supplementary information: Son of Morgan Byrne. Husband of Mary Byrne, of 14 Cottage, Kilcoole, Co. Wicklow. Grave or Memorial Reference: Grave or Memorial Reference: III.F.20. Cemetery: Awoingt British Cemetery in France.

BYRNE, Peter: Rank: Lance Corporal. Regiment or Service: Irish Guards. Unit: 2nd Bn. Date of death: 20 June 1916. Age at death: 20. Service No: 6723. Born in Wexford,

Co. Wexford. Enlisted in Dublin while living in Ballinacarrig, Co. Wicklow. Killed in action.

Supplementary information: Son of Peter and Mary Byrne, of Ballinacarrig, Co. Wicklow. Grave or Memorial Reference: He has no known grave but is listed on Panel 11 on the Ypres (Menin Gate) Memorial in Belgium.

BYRNE, Robert: Rank: Lance Corporal. Regiment or Service: Irish Guards. Unit: 2nd Bn. Date of death: 27 September 1916. Service No: 7033. Born in Rathdrum, Co. Wicklow. Enlisted in Bray, Co. Wicklow. Killed 'by a shell'. Grave or Memorial Reference: III.W.3. Cemetery: Guards Cemetery, Lesboeufs in France.

BYRNE, Simon: Rank: Private. Regiment or Service: Royal Irish Fusiliers. Unit: 1st Bn. Date of death: 3 May 1917. Service No: 21740. Born in Barrindarrig, Co. Wicklow. Enlisted in Bray while living in Kilbridge, Co. Kildare. Killed in action.

Supplementary information: Son of Terence and Eliza Byrne, of Ballard, Kilbride, Wicklow. Grave or Memorial Reference: He has no known grave but is listed on Bay 9 the Arras Memorial in France.

BYRNE, Simon: Rank: Private. Regiment or Service: Royal Irish Fusiliers. Unit: 2nd Garrison Battalion. Previously he was with the Royal Dublin Fusiliers where his number was 20350. Date of death: 30 October 1917. Age at death: 45. Service No: 1052 and G-1052. Born in Hacketstown, Co. Carlow. Enlisted in Wicklow while living in Rathdrum, Co. Wicklow. Died in Salonika.

Supplementary information: Son of Cornelius and Kate Byrne. Husband of Annie Byrne, of Shroughmore, Avoca, Co. Wicklow. Grave or Memorial Reference: 139. Cemetery; Mikra British Cemetery, Kalamaria in Greece.

BYRNE, Thomas: Rank: Private. Regiment or Service: Royal Dublin Fusiliers. Unit: 9th Bn. Age at death: 24. Date of death: 30 July 1916. Service No: 15601. Born in Dublin. Enlisted in Dublin. Died of wounds.

Supplementary information: Son of Thomas and Annie Byrne, of Kilcommon, Tinahely, Co. Wicklow. Grave or Memorial Reference: V.G.62. Cemetery: Bethune Town Cemetery in France.

BYRNE, Timothy: Rank: Private. Regiment or Service: Canadian Infantry (Central Ontario Regiment). Unit: 54th Bn.

Date of death: 3 April 1917. Age at death: 32. Service No: 761237. Born 18 December 1882 in Arklow, Co. Wicklow Enlisted on 6 April 1916 in Vancouver while living in 146 E Vancouver, B. C. Occupation on enlistment; Sailor. Height: 5'7½". Complexion: fresh. Eyes: grey. Hair: auburn. Religion: Roman Catholic. Next of kin listed as his sister Miss Susan Byrne, Sanderson Villa, Arklow.

Supplementary information: Son of John and Sarah Byrne, of 11 Abbey Street, Arklow, Co. Wicklow. Grave or Memorial Reference: He has no known grave but is listed on the Vimy Memorial in France.

BYRNE, William: Rank: Lance Corporal. Regiment or Service: Royal Dublin Fusiliers. Unit: 8th Bn. Date of death: 6 September 1916. Age at death: 22. Service No: 5080. Born in Rathnew, Co. Wicklow. Enlisted in Wicklow. Killed in action. Grave or Memorial Reference: He has no known grave but is listed on Pier and Face 16 C. on the Thiepval Memorial in France.

BYRNE, William: Rank: Private. Regiment or Service: Irish Guards. Unit: 1st Bn. Age at death: 29. Date of death: 1 December 1914. Age at death: 29. Service No: 2894. Born

William Byrne, Irish Guards.

in Killivaney, Co. Wexford. Enlisted in Gorey, Co. Wexford. Killed in action.

Supplementary information: Son of Tobias and Mary Byrne, of Ballythomas, Tinahely, Co. Wicklow. Grave or Memorial Reference: He has no known grave but is listed on Panel 11 on the Ypres (Menin Gate) Memorial in Belgium.

BYRNE, William: Rank: Pte. Regiment or Service: Canterbury Regiment. New Zealand Expeditionary Force. Date of Death: 26 November 1918. Service No.: 13870. Age at death: 44.

Supplementary information: Born in Wicklow. Served on the Western Front. Information taken from the Nominal Roll of the New Zealand Expeditionary Force. First Known Rank: Private. Occupation before enlistment: Clerk. Next of kin: Mrs M. Byrne (wife), Thames Street, Oamaru, New Zealand. Body on Embarkation: New Zealand Expeditionary force. Embarkation Unit: 40th. Reinforcements B

Company. Embarkation Date: 10 July 1918. Place of embarkation: Wellington, New Zealand. Transport: HMNZT 107. Vessel: *Tahiti*. Destination: Plymouth, England. Nominal Roll Number: 86. Page on Nominal Roll: 8. Grave or Memorial Reference: Block 22B. Lot 13. Cemetery: Christchurch (Sydenham) Cemetery, New Zealand.

BYRNE, William Joseph: Rank: Private. Regiment or Service: Royal Irish Fusiliers. Unit: 5th Bn. Date of death: 7 November 1917. Age at death: 30. Service No: 12615. Born in Wicklow. Enlisted in Warrington in Lancashire while living in Bray, Co. Wicklow. Killed in action in Egypt.

Supplementary information: Son of Elizabeth Byrne, of Earl of Meath's Cottages, Windgates, Bray, Co. Wicklow, and the late Richard Byrne. Grave or Memorial Reference: XX. B. 14. Cemetery, Gaza War Cemetery in Israel.

C

CAHILL, Patrick: Rank: Private and Lance Corporal. Regiment or Service: Royal Guards. Unit: 1st Bn. Date of death: 30 December 1914. Age at death: 24. Service No: 4340. Born in Kilcullen, Co. Kildare. Enlisted in Naas while living in Dunlavin, Co. Wicklow. Died of wounds.

Supplementary information: Son of Patrick and Mary Cahill, of Grangebeg, Dunlavin, Co. Wicklow. Grave or Memorial Reference: I.E.15. Cemetery, Le Touret Military Cemetery, Richebourg-L'Avoue in France.

CAHILL, Thomas: Rank: Private. Regiment or Service: Royal Irish Regiment. Unit: 2nd Bn. Date of death: 21 October 1914. Service No: 8596. Born in Barnderry Co. Wicklow. Enlisted in Naas while living in Wicklow. Killed in action. Grave or Memorial Reference: I.742. Cemetery, Villeneuve-St Georges Old Communal Cemetery 18 Kms south of Paris in France.

CAMPBELL, Peter: Rank: Private. Regiment or Service: Royal Dublin Fusiliers. Unit: 1st Bn. Date of death: 4 September 1918. Service No: 27195. Born in Kilquade, Co. Wicklow. Enlisted in Bray while living in Greystones. Killed in action. Grave or Memorial Reference: II.M.13. Cemetery, Trois Arbres, Cemetery in Steenwerck in France.

CANAVAN, William: Rank: Seaman. Regiment or Service: Royal Naval Reserve. Unit: H.M.P M.S. *Nepaulin*. Age at death: 22. Date of death: 20 April 1917. Service No: 4845A.

Supplementary information: Son of Michael Canavan, of Sea Lane, Arklow. Grave or Memorial Reference: 23. Memorial: Plymouth Naval Memorial, UK. He is also listed in the Dover Patrol Book of Rememberance.

CAREY, John: Rank: Private. Regiment or Service; Argyll and Southerland Highlanders. Unit: 10th Bn. Date of death: 29 September 1915. Age at death: 25. Service No: S/1771. Born in Newton, Co. Wicklow. Enlisted in Stirling while living in Dublin. Died of wounds.

War medals.

Supplementary information: Son of Philip and Mary Carey, of Castle Lane, Kilgobbin, Sandyford, Co. Dublin. Grave or Memorial Reference: II.C.5. Cemetery, St Venent Communal Cemetery in France.

CAREY, Michael: Rank: Lance Corporal. Regiment or Service: Royal Irish Fusiliers. Unit: 6th Bn. Date of death: 15 August 1915. Age at death: 18. Service No: 12830. Born in Kilmacanogue, Co. Wicklow. Enlisted in Dublin while living in Kilmacanogue, Co. Wicklow. Killed in action in Gallipoli.

Supplementary information: Son of James and Esther Carey, of 4 Yankey Terrace, Newtown Park, Blackrock, Co. Dublin. Grave or Memorial Reference: He has no known grave but is listed on Panel 178 to 180 on the Helles Memorial in Turkey.

CARPENDALE, Maxwell Montague: Rank: Major. Indian Army. Regiment or Service: 36th Jacob's Horse. Age at death: 35. Date of death: 14 October 1918.

Supplementary information: Son of Mrs E.H. Carpendale, of Sydenham Villas, Bray, Co. Wicklow, and the late Col. Montague Maxwell Carpendale (36th Jacob's Horse). Husband of Catherine Carleton Carpendale. Occupation: Officer in the 36th Jacob's Horse in the Indian Army. He is also listed on the War Memorial Rathmichael Church, Shankhill, Dublin and the War Memorial, Bray. Death: 14 October 1918. Killed in action at Damascus, Syria. Maxwell is honoured on the War Memorial and Roll of Honour at Rathmichael Church on Rathmichael Road, in Shankhill, County Dublin, on the Bray War Memorial on Quinsborough Road in Bray, County Wicklow, and on the Great War Memorial, in Christ Church, Church Road, Bray. Grave or Memorial Reference: A.18. Cemetery, Damascus Commonwealth War Cemetery in Syria.

CARROLL, William: Rank: Lance Corporal. Regiment or Service: Royal Irish Fusiliers. Unit: 1ˢᵗ Bn. Formerly he was with the Hussars of the line where his number was 13136. Date of death:18 April 1918. Service No: 18958. Born in Dundrum, Co. Dublin (Ireland's Memorial Records records Dundrum, Co. Wicklow). Enlisted in Dublin. Killed in action. Age at death: 31.

Supplementary information: Son of William and Jemima Carroll, of 43 Lennox Street, Dublin. Grave or Memorial Reference: He has no known grave but is listed on Panel 141 to 142 on the Tyne Cot Memorial in Belgium.

CARTWRIGHT, Kathleen Maud: Rank: Private. Regiment or Service: Auxiliary Territorial Service. Date of death: 11 September 1943. Service No: W-279743.

Supplementary information: Daughter of James J. and Mary Jane Gorry, of Bray, Co. Wicklow. St Patrick's Sec. Grave B. L. 88. Grave or Memorial Reference: (Screen Wall. Panel 1). Cemetery: Glasnevin (or Prospect) Cemetery in Dublin.

CASEMENT, Roger: Rank: Lieutenant Colonel. Regiment or Service: Royal Field Artillery. Age at death: 53. Date of death: 21 December 1917.

Supplementary information: Husband of Catherine Isabel Casement, (daughter of Colonel Tottenham of Ballycurry) of Cloragh House, Ashford, Co. Wicklow. Grave or Memorial Reference: About 10 yards south-west of Church door. Cemetery: Killiskey Church of Ireland Churchyard, one mile outside Ashford, Co. Wicklow.

CASH, James: Rank: Rifleman. Regiment or Service: Rifle Brigade. Unit: 2ⁿᵈ Bn. Date of death: 27 May 1918. Service No: 6623. Born in Straffan, Co. Kildare. Enlisted in Dublin while living in Dublin. Killed in action.

Supplementary information: Son of Thomas and Mary Cash (*née* Delayney), of Grangecon, Co. Wicklow; husband of Julia Cash, of 9 Upper Digges Street, Dublin. Grave or Memorial Reference: He has no known grave but is listed on the Soissons Memorial in France.

CATHEART/CATHCART, Arthur: Rank: Sergeant. Regiment or Service: Essex Regiment. Unit: 1ˢᵗ Bn. Date of death: 6 June 1915. Service No: 7461. Born in Stebbing in Essex. Enlisted in Warley in Essex while living in Bray, Co. Wicklow. Killed

The gravestone of Roger Casement.

in action in Gallipoli.

Supplementary information: Son of Mr and Mrs Walter Cathcart, of 2 Pleasant Cottages, Shenfield Common, Brentwood, Essex; husband of Adelaide Mary Cathcart, of 9 Fitzwilliam Terrace, Bray, Co. Wicklow. Grave or Memorial Reference: He has no known grave but is listed on Panel 144 to 150 or 229 to 233 on the Helles Memorial in Turkey.

Height: 5' 11". Complexion: fair. Eyes: brown. Hair: light. Religion: Church of Ireland. Next of kin listed as Mary Chamney.

Supplementary information: Son of John and Mary Chamney, of Monahullen, Shillelagh, Co. Wicklow, Ireland. Grave or Memorial Reference: He has no known grave but is listed on Panel 30 and 32 on the Ypres (Menin Gate) Memorial in Belgium.

CHAMNEY, Henry: Rank: Private. Regiment or Service: 5th Canadian Mounted Rifles (Quebec Regiment). Date of death: 2 June 1916. Age at death: 26. Service No: 112194. Born 27 February 1891 in Shillelagh, Co. Wicklow. Enlisted on 21 January 1915 in Ingersoll. Occupation on enlistment: farmer.

CHASTY, Richard: Rank: Lance Corporal. Regiment or Service: Royal Inniskilling Fusiliers. Unit: 1st Bn. Date of death: 8 September 1915. Service No: 9834. Born in Strangford, Co. Down. Enlisted in Dublin while living in Bray. Died of wounds at home. Grave or Memorial Reference: C. E. 1721.

Richard C. Chasty.

Supplementary information: From De Ruvigny's Roll of Honour. Son of James Chasty, Caretaker for the High School, 40 Harcourt Street, Dublin, Naval Pensioner of 38 years. Husband of Clara Lucretia, daughter, of Samuel How. Born: Portaferry, Co. Down 24 August 1893. Educated: Stragford, Lower Moville, Co. Donegal, and Shanaher Belmullet, Co. Mayo National Schools. Enlisted in the Royal Inniskilling Fusiliers about 25 September 1909. He was wounded in action at the Dardinelles, 22 May 1915, and died at Netley Hospital, 7 September 1915. Cemetery: Netley Military Cemetery behind the Royal Victoria Hospital, Hampshire.

CHRISTIE, James: Rank: Private. Regiment or Service: Royal Dublin Fusiliers. Unit: 1st Bn. Date of death: 29 August 1915. Service No: 8878. Born in Dunlavin, Co. Wicklow. Enlisted in Carlow while living in Dunlavin. Died of wounds in Gallipoli. Grave or Memorial Reference: He has no known grave but is listed on Panel 190 to 196 on the Helles Memorial in Turkey.

CLANCY, James: Rank: Corporal. Regiment or Service: Royal Irish Rifles. Unit: 2nd Bn. Date of death: 23 November 1917.

Age at death: 23 also listed as 24. Service No: 9406. Born in Arklow, Co. Wicklow. Enlisted in Kilsyth in Stirlingshire. Killed in action.

Supplementary information: Son of William and Alice Clancy, of Rock Big, Arklow, Co. Wicklow. Grave or Memorial Reference: He has no known grave but is listed on Panel 10 on the Cambrai Memorial in France.

CLARE, James: Rank: Private. Regiment or Service: Royal Dublin Fusiliers. Unit: 1st Bn. Date of death: 17 June 1915. Service No: 10393. Born in Ashford, Co. Wicklow. Enlisted in Dublin while living in Rathnew, Co. Wicklow. Died of wounds in Gallipoli. Grave or Memorial Reference: I. C. 67. Cemetery: East Mudros Military Cemetery in Greece.

CLARE, Patrick: Rank: Private. Regiment or Service: Royal Dublin Fusiliers Unit: 3rd Bn. Date of death: 1 March 1916 Service No: 20358. Enlisted in Wicklow. Died at home.

Note: Seamus and Jodie Burnell intensively searched this cemetery early in the year without finding Private Clare's grave. Deciding it was worth one final look Seamus and his brother Paul, who is a paramedic with Dublin Fire Brigade and also an ex-Irish

The gravestone of Patrick Clare.

Army man went to have a search. It could not be located this time either. Now Paul is a spiritual guy and in his mind he appealed to a higher power for aid and was immediately strongly drawn to one particular overgrown area. He beat down the high grass and Private Clare's headstone appeared from the entanglement. If it were not for Paul the image you see above would not have been possible. Grave or Memorial Reference: Near south-west corner. Cemetery: Kilcommon Cemetery, Co. Wicklow.

CLARKE, Ciaran Anthony: Rank: Leading Aircraftman. Regiment or Service: Royal Air Force Volunteer Reserve. Age at death: 33. Date of death: 18 November 1941 Service No: 1377842.

Supplementary information: Son of Joseph A. and Frances Clarke (*née* Doyle), of Bray, Co. Wicklow. Grave or Memorial Reference: Grave O. 42. Cemetery: Little Bray (St Peter's) Catholic Cemetery, Co. Wicklow.

CLEARY, John: Rank: Private. Regiment or Service: Royal Dublin Fusiliers. Unit: 'D' Company, 9th Bn. Date of death: 27 April 1916. Age at death: 29. Service No: 21526. Born in Bray, Co. Wicklow. Enlisted in Bray. Killed in action.

Supplementary information: Son of the late William and Margaret Cleary, of 7 Railway Terrace, Bray; husband of Elizabeth Cleary, of Bowden Cottage, Bray, Co. Wicklow. Grave or Memorial Reference: He has no known grave but is listed on Panel 127 to 129 on the Loos Memorial in France.

CLEARY, John: Rank: Corporal. Regiment or Service: Army Service Corps, and Royal Army Service Corps. Date of death: 16 February 1918. Age at death: 37. Service No: M2-099325. Born in Dublin. Enlisted in Dublin while living in Dublin. Died at home.

Supplementary information: Husband of A. Cleary, of Friar's Hill, Wicklow. Grave or Memorial Reference: Grave or Memorial Reference: Dublin. MA. 25. Cemetery; Glasnevin (or Prospect) Cemetery, in Dublin.

CLUCAS, Robert: Rank: Private. Regiment or Service: Royal Inniskilling Fusiliers. Unit: 7th Bn. Date of death: 27 April 1916. Age at death: 18. Service No: 26329. Born in Shankhill, Co. Antrim. Enlisted in Belfast. Killed in action.

Supplementary information: Son of Thomas and Sarah Clucas, of 3 Purcell's Terrace, Bray, Co. Wicklow.

This First World War Death Plaque was also known as the Widow's Penny. It was given to the next of kin.

Grave or Memorial Reference: He has no known grave but is listed on Panel 60 the Loos Memorial in France.

COATES, Henry: Rank: Private. Regiment or Service: Australian Infantry. Unit: A. I. F. 2–3 M. G. Bn. Age at death: 23. Date of death: 15 June 1945. Service No: NX15812.

Supplementary information: Son of Mrs Maud Coates, of Greystones, Co. Wicklow. Grave or Memorial Reference: K.D.7. Cemetery: Lae War Cemetery in Papua New Guinea.

COCHRANE, William Lindley Bloomer: Rank: Pilot Officer. Regiment or Service: Royal Air Force Volunteer Reserve. Age at death: 21. Date of death: 2 November 1940. Service No: 74596.

Supplementary information: Son of William Lindley Bloomer Cochrane and Margaret Winifred Cochrane, of Bray, Co. Wicklow.

Grave or Memorial Reference: Row 2. Grave 7. Cemetery: North Weald Bassett (St Andrew) Churchyard in the UK. The church and surrounding churchyard adjoin North Weald Bassett Aerodrome, a Royal Air Force Operational Station during the 1939–1945 War. 'The churchyard was used for war time burials by this station and also by the R. A. F. Station at Stapleford Tawney, some six miles away. In January 1945, a 'V' rocket fell on a hangar at Stapleford Tawney, killing ten men belonging to the R.A.F. and the R.A.F. Regiment, nine of whom are buried in the churchyard'. (from the CWGC).

COFFEY, Joseph: Rank: Private. Regiment or Service: Royal Irish Regiment. Unit: 2nd Bn. He was previously with the Royal Dublin Fusiliers where his number was 20011. Date of death: 21 August 1918. Service No: 12005. Born in Colchester in Essex. Enlisted in Cork while living in Bray, Co.

Wicklow. Killed in action. Grave or Memorial Reference: He has no known grave but is listed on Panel 5 of the Vis-En-Artois memorial in France.

COLEMAN, Samuel: Rank: Private. Regiment or Service: Royal Dublin Fusiliers. Unit: 1st Bn. Formerly he was with the Royal Irish Regiment where his number was 10019. Date of death: 28 October 1916. Service No: 43104. Born in Carlow. Enlisted in Carlow. Died of wounds.

Supplementary information: Husband of Mary Coleman, of Spratstown, Colbinstown, Co. Wicklow. Grave or Memorial Reference: VIII.E.7. Cemetery: Etaples Military Cemetery in France.

COLGAN, Alexander: Rank: Private. Regiment or Service: Royal Dublin Fusiliers. Unit: 2nd Bn. Date of death: 1 July 1916, first day of the battle of the Somme. Age at death: 21. Service No: 20280. Born in Merrion, Dublin. Enlisted in Bray while living in Kilpedder, Co. Wicklow. Killed in action.

Supplementary information: Son of William and Susan Colgan, of Booterstown, Co. Dublin. Grave or Memorial Reference: I.D.62. Cemetery: Sucrerie Military Cemetery in France.

COLLINS, Francis John: Rank: Lieutenant Commander. Regiment or Service: Royal Indian Marines. Secondary Regiment: Royal Engineers. Secondary Unit: attd. Inland Water Transport. Date of death: 25 March 1917. Age at death: 37 (age also listed as 35). Killed by 'accident in discharge of his duty' on the river Tigris.

Supplementary information: Son of Bernard J. and Teresa M. Collins, of 6 Beresford Terrace, Ferrybank, Arklow, Co. Wicklow. Born in Carnew. Grave or Memorial Reference: IV.J.3. Cemetery: Basra War Cemetery in Iraq.

COLOMB, George Lushington: Rank: Lieutneant and Second Lieutenant. Regiment or Service: London Regiment and RFC (70 Squadron). Unit: 4th (City of London) Battalion (Royal Fusiliers). Date of death: 22 November 1916. Date of birth, 26 July 1889. Age at death: 27. Killed in action.

Supplementary information: Son of Mr William and Mrs Maud Colomb, of Rossleigh, Greyfriars, Co. Wicklow. Native of Athlone. Brother of Mervyn William Colomb. Native of Greystones, Co. Wicklow.

From the Haileybury Register 1862–1983 Hailey 1903–06.

Observer (formerly 4 Bn, London Regt)

His pilot was wounded - Lt R. Gilby

Lt George Lushington Colomb, the second child of Mrs Maud and Mr William R. Colomb of Rossleigh, Greystones Ireland. He and his brother Mervyn were educated at Haileybury and both enlisted in the London Rgt on the outbreak of war. They fought as non-commissioned officers at Ypres and Neuve Chappelle where they were both wounded. Mervyn who had just received his commission died of his wounds. George received his D. S. M. for his gallentry in rescuing wounded comrades, at the same time he received his commission. After serving for some time at the depot at home he joined the R. F. C. He had been at the front for five weeks and had taken part in one successful engagement when his machine met with an accident which caused his death, he died at the age of 27 November 22nd 1916.

He is also listed on the Kenilworth Warwickshire War Memorial in Warwickshire, UK. Grave or Memorial Reference: I.G.17. Cemetery: Gezaincourt Communal Cemetery Extension, Somme in France.

COLOMB, Mervyn William:

Rank: Second Lieutenant. Regiment or Service: 4th Battalion London Regiment (Royal Fusiliers) (Territorial). Date of death: 11 May 1915.

Supplementary information: Son of Mr William and Mrs Maud Colomb of Rossleigh, Greystones, Co. Wicklow. Resided at Kentall, Warwick Road, Kenilworth. Brother of George Lushington Colomb.

From the Kenilworth, Warwickshire War Memorial.

Second Lieutenant, 4th (Battalion London Regiment) Royal Fusiliers). Wounded near Ypres, died in England 11 May 1915. Buried in Aldershot Military Cemetery, Hampshire. AF. 1869 Son of Mr William and Mrs Maud Colomb of Rossleigh, Greystones, Co. Wicklow. Resided at Kentall, Warwick Road, Kenilworth. Brother of George Lushington Colomb.

From the Haylebury Register; 1862–1984;

MERVYN WILLIAM COLOMB, Second Lieutenant 4th Battalion, London Regiment (Royal Fusiliers) who died on Tuesday 11 May 1915. Additional Information: Son of William and Maud Colomb, of Rossleigh, Greystones, Co. Wicklow.

Cemetery: ALDERSHOT MILITARY CEMETERY Hampshire, United Kingdom Grave or Reference Panel Number: AF. 1869. Brother G. L. Colomb. Killed in action 22 November 1916 Haileybury Register 1862–1983 Hailey 1901–4 born 22 January 1887 Died of wounds 7 May 1915.

He is also listed on the Wye College Roll of Honour. Grave or Memorial Reference: AF. 1869. Cemetery: Aldershot Military Cemetery, Hampshire. UK.

COMERTON, Patrick: Rank: Able Seaman. Regiment or Service: Merchant Navy Unit: SS *Newbury* (London). Age at death: 49. Date of death: 5 September 1941.

Supplementary information: Son of James and Mary Comerton. Husband of Mary Ellen Comerton, of Arklow, Co. Wicklow. Grave or Memorial Reference: He has no known grave but is listed on Panel 72 on the Tower Hill Memorial, UK.

CONNELL, Francis: Rank: Private. Regiment or Service: South Lancashire Regiment. Unit: 2nd Bn. Date of death: 24 October 1914. Age at death: 29. Service No: 7196. Born in Baltinglass, Co. Wicklow. Enlisted

in Dublin while living in Kiltegan, Co. Wicklow. Killed in action.

Supplementary information: Son of Richard and Mary Connell, of Kiltegan, Baltinglass, Co. Wicklow. He has no known grave but is listed on Panel 23 on the Le Touret Memorial in France.

CONNOR, George: Rank: Sergeant. Regiment or Service: Royal Dublin Fusiliers. Unit: 6th Bn. Date of death: between 2 October 1916 and 4 October 1916. Service No: 16367. Born in Wicklow. Enlisted in Naas while living in Rathnew, Co. Wicklow. Killed in action. Grave or Memorial Reference: II. C. 6. Cemetery: Struma Military Cemetery in Greece.

CONNOR, John: Rank: Private. Regiment or Service: Royal Dublin Fusiliers. Unit: 1st Bn. Date of death: 12 August 1917. Age at death: 20. Service No: 8504. Born in Bray, Co. Wicklow. Enlisted in Dublin while living in Bray. Died of wounds.

Supplementary information: Son of John and Jane Connor, of Bray, Co. Wicklow. Also served at Gallipoli and in Egypt. Grave or Memorial Reference: V.D. 11. Cemetery: Artillery Wood Cemetery in France.

CONNOR, Joseph: Rank: Private. Regiment or Service: Royal Irish Regiment. Unit: 1st Garrison Battalion attached to the 86th Trench Mortar Battery. He was previously with the Royal Munster Fusiliers where his number was 7933. Date of death: 3 July 1917. Age at death: 20. Service No: 5550. Born in Kilbride, Co. Wicklow. Enlisted in Kilbride. Died in Egypt. Grave or Memorial Reference: H.68. Cemetery, Cairo War Memorial Cemetery in Egypt.

CONNOR, Martin: Rank: Sergeant. Regiment or Service: South Lancashire Regiment. Unit: 6th Bn. Date of death: 10 August 1915. Service No: 10458. Born in Ashford, Co. Wicklow. Enlisted in Warrington in Lancashire while living in Ashford. Killed in action in Gallipoli. Grave or Memorial Reference: He has no known grave but is listed on Panel 139 to 140 on the Helles Memorial in Turkey.

CONNORS, James: Rank: Ordinary Seaman. Regiment or Service: Merchant Navy. Unit: S. S. *Amlwch Rose* (Liverpool). Age at death: 23. Date of death: 6 December 1940.
Supplementary information: Son of John Connors and of Mary Connors (*née* Kelly), of Arklow,

Co. Wicklow. Grave or Memorial Reference: He has no known grave but is listed on Panel 8 on the Tower Hill Memorial, UK.

CONRON, Patrick: Rank: Private. Regiment or Service: Irish Guards. Unit: 1st Bn. Date of death: 30 March 1918. Service No: 12259. Born in Knockinirgan, Co. Wicklow. Enlisted in Glasgow in Lanarkshire. Killed in action. Grave or Memorial Reference: I.V.J.7. Cemetery; Douchy-les-Ayette British Cemetery in France.

CONROY, Michael: Rank: Private. Regiment or Service: Irish Guards. Unit: 2nd Bn. Date of death: 31 July 1917. Age at death: 35. Service No: 7313. Born in Crossbridge, Co. Wicklow. Enlisted in Dublin. Killed in action.
Supplementary information: Son of Martin and Margaret Conroy, of Muskeagh, Tinahely, Co. Wicklow. Grave or Memorial Reference: I.B.5. Cemetery; Artillery Wood Cemetery in France.

CONVY, Michael: Rank: Sergeant. Regiment or Service: Kings Liverpool Regiment. Unit: 4th Bn. Date of death: 26 September 1917. Service No: 8646. Born in Clara, Kings County. Enlisted in Warrington while living in Clara.

Killed in action.

Supplementary information: Son of Patrick and Mary Ann Convy. Husband of Elizabeth Convy, of 9 Abbeyview, Bray, Co. Wicklow. Grave or Memorial Reference: He has no known grave but is listed on Panel 31 to 34 and 162 and 162A and 163A the Tyne Cot Memorial in Belgium.

CONWAY, William: Rank: Lance Corporal. Regiment or Service: Connaught Rangers. Unit: 6th Bn. Date of death: 9 December 1916. Age at death: 27. Service No: 9694. Born in Baltinglass, Co. Wicklow. Enlisted in Naas while living in Baltinglass. Killed in action.

Supplementary information: Son of Peter and Annie Conway, of Baltinglass, Co. Wicklow. Grave or Memorial Reference: G.15.

Cemetery: Pond Farm Cemetery in Belgium.

COOLING, John Joseph: Rank: Private. Regiment or Service: Australian Infantry. AIF. Unit: 2nd Bn, B Comany. Date of death: 9 August 1915. Service No: 379. Born in Delgany and birth also listed as Windgates, Bray, Co. Wicklow. He went to school in the National School in Bray. He was nineteen years old when he entered Australia. Enlisted aged 23 on 24 August 1914 in Randwick, New South Wales. Religion: R.C. Occupation on enlistment: labourer. Marital Status: single. Weight: 182lbs, Complexion: fresh. Eyes: brown. Hair: dark. Height: 5'9". Next of kin listed as Richard Cooling, Wyngate Brae, Co. Wicklow. Parents: John and Sarah

Casualty form of John Joseph Cooling.

Cooling. Native of Windgate, Bray, Co. Wicklow, Ireland. Killed in action in Lone Pine, Gallipoli. Age at death: 24.

Supplementary information: Unit embarked from Sydney, New South Wales, on board transport A23 *Suffolk* on 18 October 1914. Wounded in action, 25–30 April 1915; admitted to Kasr El Aini Hospital, Cairo, 1 May 1915. Discharged to Convalescent Hospital, Helouan, 24 May 1915; rejoined unit at Gallipoli, 13 July 1915. Reported missing in action, 7–14 August 1915. Subsequently reported killed in action, 6–9 August 1915. Australian War Memorial Embarkation Number. Entitled to the 1914–15 Star, British War Medal and the Victory Medal. From De Ruvigny's Roll of Honour: second son of John Joseph Cooling of Windgates, Co. Wicklow by his wife Sarah, daughter of Thomas Boyd. Born Windgates, 31 January 1891. Educated in Bray National School. He went to Australia in 1910 and settled in Sydney. On the outbreak of war he volunteered and joined the Commonwealth Expeditionary Force in September 1914, leaving for Egypt with the first contingent. He was severely wounded on 26 April during the historic landing at the Dardinelles and was invalided back to Cairn, but rejoined his unit in July. Shortly afterwards he was reported as missing and later was officially stated to have been killed in action between 8 and 9 of August, 1915. Grave or Memorial Reference: He has no known grave but is listed on Special Memorial C.22 on the Lone Pine Memorial in Turkey.

COOPER, Alfred M.: Rank: Private. Regiment or Service: Royal Inniskilling Fusiliers. Unit: 9th Bn. Date of death: 3 July 1916. Age at death: 19. Service No: 13502. Born in Balbriggan, Co. Dublin. Enlisted in Dublin while living in Bray. Died of wounds.

Supplementary information: Son of John and Mary Cooper, of 5 Westbourne Terrace, Bray, Co. Wicklow. Grave or Memorial Reference: Plot 2. Row B. Grave 9. Cemetery: Forceville Communal Cemetery and Extension in France.

COSTELLO, George: Rank: Private. Regiment or Service: Queens Own Cameron Highlanders. Unit: 1st Bn. Date of death: 24 October 1914. Service No: 9274. Born in Bray, Co. Wicklow. Enlisted in Inverness, Inverness-Shire while living in Kirkcaldy, Fifeshire. Killed in action. Grave or Memorial Reference: He has no known grave but is listed on Panel 38 and 40 on the Ypres (Menin Gate) Memorial in Belgium.

COURTENAY, Michael Hudson: Rank: Lieutenant Colonel. Regiment or Service: Royal Garrison Artillery. Unit: Cdg. 1st Heavy Bde. Date of death: 4 January 1916. Age at death: 48. Awards: Twice Mentioned in Despatches. Died of wounds during the siege of Kut. Killed in action.

Supplementary information: Son of William and Elizabeth Courtenay, J.P. Husband of Laura Courtenay, of 19 Craigerne Rd, Blackheath. Born at Woodmount, Arklow, Co. Wicklow. Grave or Memorial Reference: K. 15. Cemetery: Kut War Cemetery in Iraq.

COYLE, John: Rank: Private. Regiment or Service: Leinster Regiment. Unit: 2nd Bn. Date of death: 2 October 1914. Service No: 7395. Born in Kilcool, Co. Wicklow. Enlisted in Glasgow. Killed in action. Grave or Memorial Reference: He has no known grave but is listed on Panel 10 on Ploegsteert Memorial in Belgium.

CRAIG, William Hedley: Rank: 2nd Lieutenant. Regiment or Service: Royal Air Force & Army. Unit: 30th Squadron Royal Flying Corps and Royal Engineers. Date of death: 15 April 1917. Age at death: 27. Born in Bray, Co. Wicklow and native of Greystones. Religious denomination: Church of Ireland. Observer (formerly 4 Bn, London Regt). The pilot was Lt R Gilby and he survived the action. While attached to the 70th Sqdn in a Strutter serial A1917 22. 11. 16, 2nd Lt Craig was killed in action during air combat.

Supplementary information: Educated in St Stephen's Green School. Son of Thomas Craig, solicitor from Novara House, Bray, Co. Wicklow. Next of kin listed as Mrs Craig of 'Kenmare' Orwell Park, Dublin and Thomas Craig, of Novara House Bray, Co. Wicklow. 2lt H.W. Craig was flying as observer in BE 2c 4149 of No. 30 Sqn RFC, flown by 2Lt charles leigh Pickering when both airmen were killed in action in Mesopotamia on 15 April 1917. The airmen were on a reconnaissance mission over basra when they were shot down near Samara. Hauptmann Hans Schüz from FA2 was creditied with a victory. It was the eighth of his eventual ten The German pilot conducted the burial of the two downed airmen. Grave or Memorial Reference: XIV.K.14. Cemetery: Baghdad (North Gate) War Cemetery, Iraq. He is also named in the University of Dublin War List.

CRIMMIN/CRIMEEN, Denis: Rank: Private. Regiment

The Crimmin Brothers.

or Service: Royal Dublin Fusiliers. Unit: 1st Bn. Date of death: 26 April 1915. Service No: 9819. Born in Rathvilly, Co. Carlow. Enlisted in Naas while living in Ferrybank, Co. Wicklow. Joined the Army in 1907. Killed in action in Gallipoli. He had two brothers who also served, Thomas in the Royal Navy and William in the Royal Field Artillery. Grave or Memorial Reference: D.13. V Beach Cemetery in Turkey.

CRITCHLEY, Joseph: Rank: Private. Regiment or Service: Royal Dublin Fusiliers. Unit: 2nd Bn. Date of death: 23 October 1916. Service No: 20312. Born in Castlemacaden, Co. Wicklow. Enlisted in Wicklow while living in Avoca, Co. Wicklow. Killed in action. Grave or Memorial Reference: He has no known grave but is listed on Pier and Face 16C. on the Thiepval Memorial in France.

CROFTON, Edward Vivian Morgan: Rank: Lieutenant. Regiment or Service: Royal Engineers. Unit: 61st Field Coy. Date of death: 14 July 1917. Age at death: 28. Killed in action.

Supplementary information: Son of Edward Hugh Robert Crofton, of Marlton House, Wicklow, by his wife, Wilhelmina Francis Westropp Harrison, daughter, of William John Harrison Moreland, of Raheen Manor Co. Clare and a great-grandson of Sir Hugh Crofton, of Mohill Castle, Co. Leitrim. Born: 24 June 1889, Dublin. Underwent training at Chatham; afterwards served with a Field Coy, at Gibraltar; returned home in July 1914. He was stationed at Chatham; he assisted in training 62nd Field Coy. He served with the Expeditionary Force in France and Flanders from May, 1915; took part in the operations in the Ypres salient and was invalided home suffering from shell concussion. He rejoined his regiment at Chatham on his recovery in March, 1916, and again went to France, August 1916; was killed in action, 14 July 1917 near Vlerstraat. Buried there.

His Commanding Officer wrote;

> He was a very gallant officer and a loyal friend, hard working and conscientious, always ready to carry through any work, even in difficult circumstances. The following incident is typical. Before the attack of 9 April, 1917, your son was responsible for laying out certain assembly trenches in no mans land, and a covering party had been arranged for, but had failed to get into position; nevertheless, your son, at great personal risk, went out and correctly laid out and finally dug the trenches; he did this with great fearlessness and efficiency, and one of his N.C.O's received the Military Medal for this very work. His loss will be much felt and his place hard to fill.

and a brother officer, wrote, 'Your son had been one of the brave men who have sacrificed everything for the sake of his principles; he was always admired and popular among us and we all feel his loss, both as a fine soldier and a fine man.' Another also wrote; 'Your son's sense of duty led him to get away from the job he had at the Base and come to the front. Many men would have preferred to have stayed at the Base at the expense of their better feelings,' and another; 'Your son was one of the most fearless officers I have met.' Grave or Memorial Reference: II.D.10. Cemetery; Klein-Vierstraat British Cemetery in Belgium.

CROOKE, John Joseph: Rank: Private. Regiment or Service: Royal Munster Fusiliers. Unit: 1st Bn. Date of death: 21 August 1915. Service No: 10357. Born in Queenstown, Co. Cork. Enlisted in Tralee, Co. Kerry while living in Arklow, Co. Wicklow. Killed in action in Gallipoli. Grave or Memorial Reference: He has no known grave but is listed on Panel 185 to 190 on the Helles Memorial in Turkey.

CROSS, Patrick: Rank: Rifleman. Regiment or Service: Royal Irish Rifles. Unit: 1st Bn. Date of death: 25. 12 March 1915. Service No: 8955. Born in Dublin. Enlisted in Dublin while living in Rathdrum, Co. Wicklow. Killed in action. *Supplementary information:* Son of Richard Cross, of Clara Wood,

Rathdrum, Co. Wicklow. Grave or Memorial Reference: He has no known grave but is listed on Panel 42 and 43 on the Le Touret Memorial in France.

CROW, Albert Edgar: (also down as Albert Edward). Rank: Guardsman. Regiment or Service: Grenadier Guards. Unit: 2ⁿᵈ Bn. Date of death: 16 September 1916. Service No: 21726. Born in Wicklow. Enlisted in Cardiff. Killed in action. Grave or Memorial Reference: He has no known grave but is listed on Pier and Face 8 D on the Thiepval Memorial in France.

CROWLEY, Michael: Rank: Private. Regiment or Service: Royal Dublin Fusiliers. Unit: 7ᵗʰ Bn. Date of death: 3 October 1916. Service No: 25181 and 5/25181. Born in Rathdrum, Co. Wicklow. Enlisted in Wicklow. Killed in action in the Balkans. Grave or Memorial Reference: II.C.7. Cemetery: Struma Military Cemetery in Greece.

CULBERT, Patrick: Rank: Private. Regiment or Service: Royal Dublin Fusiliers. Unit: 1ˢᵗ Bn. Date of death: 15 June 1915. Service No: 17959. Born in Kilkenny. Enlisted in Inverkeithling while

living in Wicklow. Died of wounds. Killed in action in Gallipoli. Grave or Memorial Reference: XI.E.10. Cemetery: Twelve Tree Copse Cemetery in Turkey.

CULLAGH, Timothy: Rank: Fusilier. Regiment or Service: Royal Inniskilling Fusiliers. Unit: 6th Bn. Age at death: 25. Date of death: 13 June 1944. Service No: 6148440. Enlisted while living in Belfast.
Supplementary information: Son of Ellen Cullagh. Husband of Mary Cullagh, of Newtownmountkennedy, Co. Wicklow. Grave or Memorial Reference: I.C.14. Cemetery: Orvieto War Cemetery in the Province of Terni, Italy.

CULLEN, Edward: Rank: Private. Regiment or Service: Machine Gun Corps. Unit: Infantry and 16ᵗʰ Coy. He was previously with the Royal Dublin Fusiliers where his number was 20190. Date of death: 21 March 1918. Age at death: 21. Service No: 74025. Born in Newtown, Co. Wicklow. Enlisted in Wicklow. Killed in action.
Supplementary information: Son of Simon and Mary Cullen, of Newtownmountkennedy, Co. Wicklow. Grave or Memorial Reference: He has no known grave but is listed on Panel 90 to 93 on

the Pozieres Memorial in France.

CULLEN, Hugh James: Rank: Private. Regiment or Service: Royal Dublin Fusiliers. Unit: 10th Bn. Date of death: 30 November 1917. Age at death: 27. Service No: 29073. Born in Wicklow. Enlisted in London while living in Pimlico in Middlesex. Died of wounds.

Supplementary information: Son of Patrick and Brigid Cullen, of Ballenfoyle, Knockenarrigan. Husband of Helen Mary Cullen, of Ballenfoyle, Knockenarrigan, Dunlavin, Co. Wicklow. Grave or Memorial Reference: H.5. Cemetery: St Leger British Cemetery in France.

CULLEN, James: Rank: Private. Regiment or Service: Royal Munster Fusiliers. Unit: 1st Bn. Date of death: 28 April 1915. Service No: 8916. Born in Kilquade, Co. Wicklow. Enlisted in Dublin while living in Timore, Co. Wicklow. Died of wounds in Gallipoli. Grave or Memorial Reference: He has no known grave but is listed on Panel 185 to 190 on the Helles Memorial in Turkey.

CULLEN, John: Rank: Private. Regiment or Service: Loyal North Lancashire Regiment. Unit: 1st Bn. Date of death: 31 October 1914. Age at death: 31. Service No: 7065. Born in Bray, Co. Wicklow. Enlisted in Preston while living in Liverpool. Killed in action.

Supplementary information: Husband of the late Sarah Cullen. Grave or Memorial Reference: He has no known grave but is listed on Panel 41 and 43 on the Ypres (Menin Gate) Memorial in Belgium.

CULLEN, John: Rank: Private. Regiment or Service: Irish Guards. Unit: 1st Bn. Date of death: 1 November 1914. Age at death: 20. Service No: 4322. Born in Ballahara, Co. Wicklow. Enlisted in Dublin. Killed in action.

Supplementary information: Son of James and Annie Cullen, of Ballyhara Cottage, Wicklow. Grave or Memorial Reference: He has no known grave but is listed on Panel 11 on the Ypres (Menin Gate) Memorial in Belgium.

CULLEN, Patrick: Rank: Private. Regiment or Service: Irish Guards. Unit: 1st Bn. Date of death: 6 September 1914. Age at death: 20. Service No: 4321. Born in Ballahara, Co. Wicklow. Enlisted in Dublin. Killed in action.

Supplementary information: Son of James and Anne Cullen of Ballyhara, Wicklow. Grave or

Memorial Reference: IV. D. 4/5. Cemetery: Montreuil-Aux-Lions British Cemetery in France.

CULLEN, Patrick: Rank: Lance Corporal. Regiment or Service: Royal Dublin Fusiliers. Unit: Y Company, 1st Bn. Date of death: 1 March 1917. Age at death: 30. Service No: 8535. Born in Newcastle, Co. Wicklow. Enlisted in Newcastle, Co. Wicklow. Killed in action.

Supplementary information: Son of Michael and Bridget Cullen, of Timore, Newcastle, Co. Wicklow.

Grave or Memorial Reference: VI.C.2. Cemetery: Sailly-Saillisel British Cemetery in France.

CUMMINS, David: Rank: Private. Regiment or Service: Royal Dublin Fusiliers. Unit: 8th Bn. Date of death: 29 April 1916. Service No: 18803. Born in Blessington in Wicklow. Enlisted in Dublin while living in Wicklow. Died of Gas Poisoning. Age at death: 36. Grave or Memorial Reference: III.H.54. Cemetery: Bethune Town Cemetery in France.

D

DALTON, Edward: Rank: Private. Regiment or Service: Royal Dublin Fusiliers. Unit: 2ⁿᵈ Bn. Date of death: 5 April 1916. Service No: 19130. Born in Bray, Co. Wicklow. Enlisted in Bray. Killed in action. Grave or Memorial Reference: C. 11. Cemetery: Bois-Carre Military Cemetery in Haisnes, France.

DALTON, Michael: Rank: Private. Regiment or Service: Royal Dublin Fusiliers. Unit: 5ᵗʰ Bn. Date of death: 23 May 1916. Service No: 15143. Born in Newcastle, Co. Wicklow. Enlisted in Dublin while living in Newtownmountkennedy, Co. Wicklow. Died at home.
Supplementary information: Husband of Mrs A. Dalton, of Newtownmountkennedy, Co. Wicklow. Grave or Memorial Reference: 593. Cemetery: Curragh Military Cemetery in Kildare.

DALY, Christopher: Rank: Lance Corporal. Regiment or Service: Royal Dublin Fusiliers. Unit: 8ᵗʰ Bn. Date of death: 29 April 1916. Service No: 14448.

Born in Ashford, Co. Wicklow. Enlisted in Dublin while living in Ashford. Killed in action. Grave or Memorial Reference: He has no known grave but is listed on Panel 127 to 129 on the Loos Memorial in France.

DALY, Robert: Rank: Private. Regiment or Service: Leinster Regiment. Unit: 2nd Bn. Date of death: 13 May 1915. Age at death: 28. Service No: 7701. Born in Rathnew, Co. Wicklow. Enlisted in Wicklow. Died from pneumonia while a prisoner of war in Germany.
Supplementary information: Son of Christopher and Anne Daly, of Blessington, Co. Wicklow. Native of Rathnew, Co. Wicklow. Grave or Memorial Reference: III. K. 11. Cemetery: Niederzwhren Cemetery in Germany.

DANN, John Robinson: Rank: Private. Regiment or Service: Machine Gun Corps (Infantry). Unit: 113ᵗʰ Coy. He was previously with the Royal Highlanders where his number was 4801.

Date of death: 31 July 1917. Age at death: 23. Service No: 60507. Born in Newcastle, Co. Wicklow. Enlisted in Dublin while living in Greystones. Killed in action.

Supplementary information: Son of Mrs S. Dann, of Kilpedder, Greystones, Co. Wicklow, and the late Mr A. Dann. Grave or Memorial Reference: He has no known grave but is listed on Panel 56 on the Ypres (Menin Gate) Memorial in Belgium.

DARCY, Daniel: Also down as **DARCY, O.** Rank: Private. Regiment or Service: Household Cavalry and Cavalry of the Line. Unit: 6th Dragoons (Inniskillings). Date of death: 15 February 1918. Age at death: 39. Service No: 21029. Born in Tramore, Waterford. Enlisted in Waterford while living in Kiltegan, Co. Wicklow.

Supplementary information: Son of James Darcy. Husband of Kate Darcy, of Feddang Kiltegan, Co. Wicklow. Grave or Memorial Reference: VI.J.29. Cemetery: Tincourt New British Cemetery in France.

DARLEY, Arthur Tudor: Rank: Commander. Regiment or Service: Royal Navy Unit: H.M.S. *Good Hope.* Date of death: 1 November 1914. Age at death: 38.

Supplementary information:

Husband of Charlotte Sinclair Hunt, (formerly Darley), of Wraysbury House, Emsworth, Hants. From Diamond Jubilee Review: As an Acting Sub-Lieutenant Darley was appointed to command Torpedo-Boat 53 on 15 June 1897. He is commemorated on a plaque in the grounds of St James Church, North Street, Elmsworth in Hampshire, UK. From De Revigny's Roll of Honour: Elder son of Wellington Darley, of Violet Hill Bray, Co. Wicklow by his wife Anna Frances, daughter of Richard Tudor. Born Glenouthwel, Rathfarnam, Co. Dublin, 29 August 1876. Educated at Cheam and Stubbingham House, Fareham, Hants. He joined the Brittanica in 1890, passing in seventh out of fifty-seven candidates. He was promoted to Midshipman, 15 March 1893. Sub Lieutenant 15 September 1896. Lieutenant 15 December 1898; and Commander 31 December 1909. In January 1910 he was appointed Flag Commander to Admiral Winslow; Commander in Chief on the China Station, and in June 1912 was one of the first fifteen commanders selected for special appointment to the newly formed War Squadron In March 1914, he was temporarily appointed to R.M.S. *Good Hope*, while waiting to take up and appointment to the Flagship of the China Squadron, and was killed in the naval action of Coronel on the coast of Chili,

1 November 1914. He married at Christchurch Cathedral, Dublin, November 1910, (Wray- Bury House, Emsworth, Hants) eldest daughter of Major General Edward Sinclair May. C.B., C,M. G. Commanding the Lucknow Division, India and left a son and a daughter; Arthur Tudor born (posthumous) 5 December 1914, and Evelyn Elizabeth, born 25 December 1911. Grave or Memorial Reference: He has no known grave but is listed on Portsmouth Memorial, UK.

DARLEY, John Evelyn Carmichael: Rank: Lieutenant Colonel. Regiment or Service: 4th (Queen's Own) Hussars. Date of death: 31 March 1918. Age at death: 38. Killed in action.

Supplementary information: Son of Wellongton Darley, of Violet Hill, Bray, Co. Wicklow, J.P., by his wife, Anna Frances, daughter, of Richard Tudor; and brother to Commander A.T. Darley, Royal Navy (q.v). Born in Dublin, 14 April 1879. Educated at Eton. Gazetted 2nd Lieut, 5th Lancers, 15 November 1899. Promoted to Lieutenant, 3 October, 1900. Captain 25 December 1901, major June 1913, and Lieutenant. Colonel April 1916. Served with the regiment in the South African War (1900–02) and was severly wounded during the persuit of Kritzinger in January 1902; in the previous December. He had been specially promoted Captain, and transferred to the 4th Hussars as a reward for services in South Africa (Queen's Medal with three clasps, and King's Medal with two clasps) served in India and again in South Africa. Acted as A.D.C. to General Sir Archibald Hunter, Governor of Gibraltar from 1910 to 1913. Served with the Expeditionary Force in France and Flanders from 15 August 1914; took part in the retreat from Mons and in the First and Second Battles of Ypres. 4 November 1914, and 17 April 1915. In April 1916, became Lieutenant-Colonel of his regiment; during the operations near Cambrai in November 1917. He commanded the dismounted Cavalry Brigade in Bourlon Wood and was killed in action on Moreuil Ridge, south-east of Amiens, 31 March 1918. Buried at Thennes. He was mentioned in Despatches (*London Gazette*, 20 May, 1918) by F.M. Sir Douglas Haig, for gallant and distinguished service in the field, and received the Mons medal. Grave or Memorial Reference: B.13. Cemetery: Moreuil Communal Cemetery Allied Extension in France. See page 78.

DARLINGTON, The Revd Charles Arnold: Rank: Chaplain. Regiment or Service: Royal Naval

Volunteer Reserve. Unit: H.M.S. *Drake*. Age at death: 30 Date of death: 5 November 1943.

Supplementary information: Son of Charles Horace John and Frances Ellen Darlington, of Enniskerry, Co. Wicklow. Grave or Memorial Reference: Sec. C. Cons. Grave 18139. Cemetery: Plymouth (Weston Hills) Cemetery, UK.

DARLINGTON, John Thomas: Rank: Private. Regiment or Service: Royal Inniskilling Fusiliers. Unit: 8th Bn. Formerly he was with the Royal Dublin Fusiliers where his number was 21627. Date of death: 27 May 1916. Age at death: 35. Service No: 26630. Born in Drumcondra in Dublin. Enlisted in Dublin. Died.

Supplementary information: Son of Joseph Edward and Alice Anne Darlington, of 4 Alexandra Terrace, Bray, Co. Wicklow. Grave or Memorial Reference: I.E.17. Cemetery: Etreat Churchyard in France.

DAWSON, Thomas: Rank: Private. Regiment or Service: Royal Irish Fusiliers. Unit: 2nd Bn Date of death: 17 May 1916. Age at death: 26. Service No: 10579. Born in Bray. Enlisted in Dublin while living in Bray. Died in Salonika. Grave or Memorial Reference: 1401. Cemetery; Mikra British Cemetery, Kalamaria in Greece.

DAY, John Edward: Rank: Captain and Temporary Captain. Regiment or Service: Royal Irish Regiment. Unit: 'A' Coy. 6th Bn. Age at death: 22. Date of death: 6 April 1917. Died of Wounds.

Supplementary information: Son of the Very Revd Maurice W. Day and Katherine L. F. Day of Culloden, Bray, Co. Wicklow. Born at Newport, Co. Tipperary. From the Day memorial, Christ Church Cathedral(COI), Henrietta Street, Waterford. Son of Kathlene Louisa Frances, daughter, of the late Charles Garfit, J.P. Born: St John's Rectory, Newport, Co. Tipperary, 1 December 1894. Educated Hamilton House, Marlborough College and Trinity College, Dublin. Gazetted 2nd Lt, Royal Irish Regt, 15 August, 1914. Promoted to Lieutenant 30 November following, and Captain 6 April 1916, served with the Expeditionary Force in France from 18 December 1915, was severely wounded, 8 April 1916. Returned to France in September and died 6 April 1917 from wounds received in action while in command of a raid near Wytschaete. Buried in Bailleul. Brigardier-General Pereira, commanding the 47th Infantry Division wrote,

He was such a splendid young officer in every way. I have always had the highest opinion of a trust him, and I feel that his place cannot be filled. He was absolutely fearless, and led his men into action with splendid coolness. Besides being a gallant, capable and most conscientious officer, he was beloved by his men. Thanks in great measure to him, the operation was completely successful.

and Major Hutcheson;

Everyone of us loved your son most dearly, and we all feel your loss, and will do so for a long time. He will never be forgotten in the regiment. Your son was senior officer in the attack, and was leading the regiment on the night of the 5th. The attack was a very great success. The regiment has received the congratulations from the Army and the Corps Commanders. There is no doubt had he lived he would have received honours for his gallant behaviour.

From the Day Memorial, Christ Church Cathedral(COI), Henrietta Street, Waterford;

Sic itur ad astra.

In loving memory of
the very Revd Maurice William
Day: M.A.
Dean of this Cathedral : and
Rector of Holy Trinity Parish

1913-1916.
Who dies at Courtmacsherry
Co. Cork
August 29 1916: Aged 58 years.
Also of his sons.
Maurice Charles Day B.A.
Seniors Scholar Trinity College.
Cambridge: Bell University
Scholar.
1911: Wrangler 1913: Lieutenant.
13th Rajputs: Killed in Action at
Tanga: German East Africe
Nov 3 1914: Aged 23 years and
John Edward Day
Captain 6th (service) Battalion
The Royal Irish Regimwnt:
Died of wounds received in
action
Near Whyschaete: On Good
Friday April 6 1917: Aged 22
years
This tablet is placed here by
Katherine L.F. Day: Wife and
Mother.

Grave or Memorial Reference: III.B.60. Cemetery: Bailleul Communal Cemetery Extension (Nord) in France.

DELAMERE, John William: Rank: Private. Regiment or Service: Canadian Infantry (Saskatchewan Regiment). Unit: 28th Bn. Date of death: 15 September 1916. Age at death: 28. Service No: 311860. Born 12 July 1887 in Dublin. Enlisted on 5 January 1815 Winnipeg while

75

living in the Manitoba Hotel in Winnipeg. Occupation on enlistment; Farmer. Height; 5'5½". Complexion: flush. Eyes: blue. Hair: dark. Religion: Presbyterian.

Supplementary information: Son of John Delamere, of Calary, Co. Wicklow. Grave or Memorial Reference: He has no known grave but is listed on the Vimy Memorial in France.

DELAMERE, Samuel: Rank: Private. Regiment or Service: Canadian Infantry (Alberta Regiment). Unit: 31st Bn. Date of death: 4 May 1917. Age at death: 34. Service No: 115838. Born: 22 January 1885 in Dublin. Enlisted: 17 January 1917 in Portage Le Prairie while living in Rutland, Sask. Occupation on enlistment: farmer. Height: 5'5". Complexion: ruddy. Eyes: blue. Hair: dark brown. Religion: Church of Ireland. Next of kin listed as Mrs M. Delamere (Mother) of Rutland Sask.

Supplementary information: Son of Matthew and Elizabeth Delamere, of Calary, Co. Wicklow. Grave or Memorial Reference: III. A.8. Cemetery: Barlin Communal Cemetery Extension in France.

DELANEY, Thomas: Rank: Lance Corporal. Regiment or Service: Royal Engineers. Age at death: 51. Date of death: 28 January 1940. Service No: 1857927.

Supplementary information: Son of Daniel and Mary Jane Delaney. Husband of Esther Delaney, of Bray, Co. Wicklow. Grave or Memorial Reference: Sec. 50. Grave 15898. Cemetery: Margate Cemetery, Kent, UK.

DELANEY, William: Rank: Private. Regiment or Service: Royal Irish Fusiliers. Unit: 8th Bn. He was previously with the Connaught Rangers where his number was 4121. Date of death: 6 September 1916. Age at death: 19. Service No: 21052. Born in Barndarrig, Co. Wicklow. Enlisted in Dublin while living in Rathdrum, Co. Wicklow. Killed in action.

Supplementary information: Son of Peter and Elizabeth Delaney. Grave or Memorial Reference: He has no known grave but is listed on Pier and Face 16C. on the Thiepval Memorial in France.

DEMPSEY, Simon: Rank: Lance Corporal. Regiment or Service: Irish Guards. Unit: 1st Bn. Date of death: 9 June 1915. Killed in action. Service No: 6282. Born in Wexford, Co. Wexford. Enlisted in Dublin. See page 78.

Supplementary information: Brother of Thomas Dempsey, of 'Mountain View', Castle Street,

Bray, Co. Wicklow.
From the *Wicklow People*,

There has been keen regret felt in Bray last week when news was received that Mr Simon Dempsey, brother of Mr Thomas Dempsey, Dargle Road, had been killed at the front. For a number of years Mr Simon Dempsey worked with his brother at Messrs Donnehys Coach Factory, Little Bray and enjoyed an immense share of popularity. He subsequently returned to Wexford and joined the R. I. C. seven years ago. Grave or Memorial Reference: D. 44. Cemetery: Cambrin Churchyard Extension in France.

DERRY, Joseph: Rank: Private. Regiment or Service: Leicestershire Regiment. Unit: 11th Bn. Date of death: 22 March 1918. Service No: 23193. Born in Arklow, Co. Wicklow. Enlisted in Leicester while living in Narborough in Leics. Killed in action in Dadizeele. Grave or Memorial Reference: He has no known grave but is listed on Bay 5 on the Arras Memorial in France.

DEVEREUX, George Patrick: Rank: Private. Regiment or Service: Labour Corps. He was previously with the Cheshire Regiment where his number was 21532. Date of death: 19 May 1918. Age at Deathm 49. Service No: 53092. Born in Bray, Co. Wicklow. Enlisted in Birmingham. Died at home.

Supplementary information: Son of Patrick and Sarah Devereux. Husband of Annie Devereux, of 6/84, Great Lister Street, Birmingham. Grave or Memorial Reference: Screen Wall. 74.024499. Cemetery: Birmingham (Witton) Cemetery, UK.

DEVINE, Thomas: Rank: Corporal. Regiment or Service: Royal Dublin Fusiliers. Unit: 2nd Bn. Date of death: 1 July 16, first day of the battle of the Somme. Age at death: 45. Service No: 14596. Born in Baltinglass, Co. Wicklow. Enlisted in Dublin while living in Lucan, Co. Dublin. Killed in action.

Supplementary information: Son of Mr and Mrs Patrick Devine, of Stratford-on-Slaney, Co. Wicklow. Husband of Mary Devine of Donard, Co. Wicklow. Grave or Memorial Reference: He has no known grave but is listed on Pier and Face 16 C. on the Thiepval Memorial in France.

DICKENSON, Joseph: Rank: Master. Regiment or Service:

Simon Dempsey.

John Evelyn Darley.

Mercantile Marine. Unit: SS *Alacrity*. Mined off Lowestoft, mines laid by UC 5. On 27 of April 1916 German Submarine mine-layer UC 5 ran aground on the Shipwash Shoal and was stuck fast. The crew were taken prisoner by the HMS *Shelldrake* and UC 5 was taken back to England to display how German mine-layers worked. It was later scrapped. UC 5 was responsible to the loss of twenty-nine ships including the death of the thirteen man crew of Belfast built SS *Alracrity*. Date of death: 30 March 1916.

Supplementary information: Son of the late Master Michael Dickinson and Mrs Mary Ann Dickinson, of Arklow, Co. Wicklow. Husband of Frances Sherwood Dickinson, of 6 Belvidere Place, Dublin. He has no known grave but is listed on the Tower Hill Memorial UK.

DIXON, James: Rank: Gunner. Regiment or Service: Royal Horse Artillery and Royal Field Artillery. Unit: 61st Howitzer Bty. Date of death: 23 April 1916. Age at death: 36. Service No: 4364. Born in Kilquide, Wicklow. Enlisted in Wigan, Lancs. Died at home.

Supplementary information: Son of Mrs Mary Dixon, of Stylebawn, Delgany, Co. Wicklow. Grave or Memorial Reference: 24. 149. Cemetery: Nowrich Cemeteru, Norfolk UK.

DOLAN, Thomas: Rank: Private. Regiment or Service: Royal Dublin Fusiliers. Unit: 1st Bn. Date of death: 29 June 1915. Service No: 17821. Born in Rathdrum, Co. Wicklow. Enlisted in Hamilton while living in Nacherty, Uddington. Killed in action in Gallipoli. Grave or Memorial Reference: He has no known grave but is listed on Panel 190 to 196 on the Helles Memorial in Turkey.

DONOHOE, John James: Rank: Private. Regiment or Service: Irish Guards. Unit: 2nd Bn and 3rd Res. Bn. Age at death: 22. Date of death: 22 November 1917. Service No: 10741. Born in Galway, enlisted in Galway while living in Ferrybank, Co. Wicklow. Killed in action.

Supplementary information: Son of Andrew Donohoe, of Cabul House, Ferrybank, Arklow. Grave or Memorial Reference: North. 2 L. 25 East. Cemetery: Arklow Cemetery, Co. Wicklow.

DOODY, Joseph: Rank: Private. Regiment or Service: Royal Dublin Fusiliers. Unit: 10th Bn. He was previously with the Army Service Corps where his number was 66696. Date of death: 28 May 1917. Age at death: 23. Service No: 28962. Born in Baltinglass, Co. Wicklow. Enlisted in Bristol while living in Baltinglass, Co. Wicklow. Killed in action.

Supplementary information: Son of the late James and Bridget Doody, of Clough, Baltinglass; husband of Hannagh Doody (*née* Donnelly), of Ranheen, Baltinglass, Co. Wicklow. Grave or Memorial Reference: Grave or Memorial Reference: He has no known grave but is listed on Bay 9 on the Arras Memorial in France.

DOOLAN, Thomas: Rank: Private. Regiment or Service: Royal Army Service Corps. Date of death: 8 October 1915. Service No: M2/079522. Born in Dublin. Enlisted in Dublin while living in Bray, Co. Wicklow. Died at home. Grave or Memorial Reference: Prot. ground 4. D. 2157. Cemetery: Rathnew Cemetery, Co. Wicklow.

DOOLITTLE, Thomas: Rank: Sergeant. Regiment or Service: Royal Dublin Fusiliers. Unit: 9th Bn. Date of death: 8 August 1917. Service No: 8036. Born in Wicklow. Enlisted in Dublin while living in Wicklow. Killed in action. Grave or Memorial Reference: He has no known grave but is listed on Panel 44 and 46 on the Ypres (Menin Gate) Memorial in Belgium.

DOONER, Stephen: Rank: Corporal. Regiment or Service: Royal Dublin Fusiliers. Unit: 9th Bn. Date of death: 9 September 1916. Age at death: 21. Service No: 18036. Born in Rathnew, Co. Wicklow. Enlisted in Dublin while living in Greystones. Killed in action.

Supplementary information: Son of James and Rose Dooner, of 22 James Avenue, Clonliffe Road, Dublin. Grave or Memorial Reference: He has no known grave but is listed on Pier and Face 16C on the Thiepval Memorial in France.

DORAN, Myles: Rank: Stoker. Regiment or Service: Royal Naval Reserve Unit: HMS *Goliath*. Date of death: 13 May 1015. Service No: 2578S.

Supplementary information: Son of Patrick and Elizabeth Doran, of Carnew, Co. Wicklow. Husband of Nora Hatton (formerly Doran), of 17 King's Down Road, Abram, Platt Bridge, Wigan. On 13 May 1915 sunk by three torpedoes fired from the Turkish torpedo boat *Muavenet* which was manned by a German crew at the time. 570 of her complement were lost. Extracts from *Naval Review vol IV* (Naval Society) about *Goliath*.

The Goliath while acting as right flank ship was torpedoed

The gravestone of James Donohoe.

and sunk by an enemy torpedo boat, which under cover of a fog, slipped down the Straits, passed our destroyer patrol, fired her torpedoes, and escaped. There was a large loss of life. The casemate-doors jambed and imprisoned many of the guns' crews. An enemy 'enclair' wireless message was intercepted, which stated that a British transport had been sunk by three torpedoes.

Grave or Memorial Reference: 8. Memorial: Plymouth Naval Memoril UK.

DORAN, Patrick: Rank: Private. Regiment or Service: Royal Munster Fusiliers. Unit: 2nd Bn. Date of death: 29 May 1916. Service No: 7660. Born in Wicklow. Died of Bronchitis contracted at Ypres in Arklow. Grave or Memorial Reference: South 3HH, 20 East. Arklow Cemetery.

DORNIN, Thomas: Rank: Private. Regiment or Service: Royal Dublin Fusiliers. Unit: 9th Bn. Date of death: 7 May 1916. Service No: 18937. Born in Bray, Co. Wicklow. Enlisted in Dublin while living in Bray. Died. Grave or Memorial Reference: V.C. 20. Cemetery: Bethune Town Cemetery in France.

DOWDALL, James: Rank: Private. Regiment or Service: King's Own Scottish Borderers. Unit: 1st/5th Bn. He was previously with the Royal Irish Regiment where his number was 3605. Date of death: 8 October 1918. Age at death: 25. Service No: 31165. Born in Bray, Co. Wicklow. Enlisted in Bray, while living in Bray. Killed in action.

Supplementary information: Nephew of Patrick Dowdall. Native of Bray. Grave or Memorial Reference: III.K. 10. Cemetery: Oxford Road Cemetery in Belgium.

DOWLING, George Thomas: Rank: Private. Regiment or Service: Leinster Regiment. Unit: 2nd Bn. 25 February 1915. Age at death: 36. Service No: 7201. Born in Arkow. Enlisted in Fermoy, Co. Cork. Killed in action.

Supplementary information: Son of Mortimer Evan Dowling; husband of Norah Dowling, of Ahern, Conna, Co. Cork. Native of Arklow, Co. Wicklow. Grave or Memorial Reference: A. 11. Cemetery: Ferme Buterne Military Cemetery in France.

DOWSE, Richard Henry: Rank: Chief Engineer. Regiment or Service: Mercantile Marine. Unit: SS *Towneley* (Newcastle).

Date of death: 2 February 1918. Age at death: 48.

Supplementary information: Richard Henry Dowse was born on 12 October 1868 at Camolin, Wexford. Son of Mary Dowse (*née* Halahan), of St John's Vicarage, York Road, Kingstown, Dublin, and the late Richard Henry Dowse who appeared on the 1911 census at Scholarstown, Rathfarnham. Born at Carnew, Co. Wicklow. SS *Towneley* was a 2.476 grt defensively armed British Merchant steamer was torpedoed without warning by a German torpedo from submarine U-46 on the 31 January 1918, 18 miles NE¼E from Trevose Head, North Cornwall. Six lives were lost including Master. Vessel was *en route* from Devonport for Barry Roads. Owned by Burnett & Co., Newcastle. U-46 was one of the few German submarines to survive the war after sinking thousands of tons of British Naval and Mercantile Marine ships. He has no known grave but is listed on the Tower Hill Memorial, UK and St Johns Mounttown Memorial in Monkstown Parish Church, Dublin.

DOWZER, Robert: Rank: Sergeant (Flt. Engr.). Regiment or Service: Royal Air. Force Volunteer Reserve. Unit: 196 Sqdn. Age at death: 20. Date of death: 4 February 1944. Service No: 1795818.

Supplementary information: Son of Joseph and Elizabeth Dowzer, of Tinahely, Co. Wicklow. Grave or Memorial Reference: Row G. Grave 3. Cemetery: Lyon (La Doua) French National Cemetery, Rhone in France.

DOYLE, Alexander: Rank: Private. Regiment or Service: Royal Dublin Fusiliers. Unit: 8th Bn. Date of death: 17 September 1916. Age at death: 43. Service No: 14051. Born in Rathnew, Co. Wicklow. Enlisted in Dublin while living in Greystones. Died of wounds.

Supplementary information: Brother of Elizabeth Duffy, of Rathnew, Co. Wicklow. Grave or Memorial Reference: X.E.1. Cemetery: Etaples Military Cemetery in France.

DOYLE, Charles: Rank: Cook. Regiment or Service: Mercantile Marine. Unit: SV *Brandon* (Barrow-in-Furness). Date of death: 24 March 1917. Age at death: 17.

Supplementary information: Son of Thomas Doyle, of 6, Ashwood Walk, Wexford Rd, Arklow, Co. Wicklow, and the late Jane Doyle (*née* Hogan). Grave or Memorial Reference: He has no known grave but is listed on the Tower Hill Memorial, UK.

The gravestone of Patrick Doran.

DOYLE, Denis Patrick: Rank: Private. Regiment or Service: Royal Munster Fusiliers. Unit: 6th Bn. Date of death: 7 April 1917. Age at death: 22. Service No: 5976. Enlisted in Dublin while living in Ashford, Co. Wicklow. Died of wounds in Greek Macedonia.

Supplementary information: Son of Andrew and Mary Doyle, of Ballyknocken, Ashford, Co. Wicklow. Grave or Memorial Reference: E.EA.A.612. Cemetery: Addolorata Cemetery in Malta.

DOYLE, Denis: Rank: Private. Regiment or Service: Irish Guards. Unit: 1st Bn. Date of death: 1 November 1914. Age at death: 21. Service No: 4003. Born in Bray, Co. Wicklow. Enlisted in Dublin while living in Dublin. Killed in action.

Supplementary information: Son of Michael and Margaret Doyle, of Golden Ball, Kilteman, Co. Dublin. He has no known grave but is listed on Panel 11 on the Ypres (Menin Gate) Memorial in Belgium.

DOYLE, Douglas Robert: Rank: Pilot Officer (Nav.). Regiment or Service: Royal Air Force Volunteer Reserve. Date of death: 19 April 1944. Service No: 154086. Grave or Memorial Reference: Family plot. Cemetery: Greystones (Redford) Cemetery, Co. Wickow.

DOYLE, Francis: Rank: Sergt. Regiment or Service: Royal Garrison Artillery. Unit: 146th Siege Battery. Date of death: 23 March 1918. Service No: 282247. Born in Monkwearmouth Durham. Enlisted in Wicklow while living in Rearcross, Co. Wicklow. Died of wounds. Grave or Memorial Reference: XXXI.H.1. Cemetery: Etaples Military Cemetery in France.

DOYLE, Hugh: Rank: Private. Regiment or Service: Royal Dublin Fusiliers. Unit: 9th Bn. Date of death: 21 September 1917. Service No: 24595. Born in Rathnew, Co. Wicklow. Enlisted in Wicklow while living in Rathnew. Killed in action. He has no known grave but is listed on Special Memorial 5 in Croisilles British Cemetery in France.

DOYLE, James: Rank: Private. Regiment or Service: Royal Irish Regiment. Unit: 2nd Bn. Date of death: 21 March 1918. Service No: 15020. Formerly he was with the Royal Dublin Fusiliers where his number was 25964. Born in Killamote, Co. Wicklow. Enlisted in Naas, Co. Kildare while living in Duncormick, Co. Wexford. Killed in action. Grave or Memorial Reference: He has no known grave but is listed on

Panel 31 and 31 on the Pozieres Memorial in France.

DOYLE, James: Rank: Lance Corporal. Regiment or Service: Royal Dublin Fusiliers. Unit: 2nd Bn. Date of death: 25 May 1915. Age at death: 22. Service No: 9012. Born in Dublin. Enlisted in Wicklow while living in Ballylusk, Co. Wicklow. Died of wounds.

Supplementary information: Son of Jane Doyle, of Ballylusk, Ashford, Co. Wicklow. Grave or Memorial Reference: II. B. 5. Cemetery: Hazebrouck Communal Cemetery in France.

DOYLE, James: Rank: Private. Regiment or Service: Royal Dublin Fusiliers. Unit: 8th Bn. Date of death: 27 April 1916. Service No: 15653. Born in Bray, Co. Wicklow. Enlisted in Bray. Killed in action. Grave or Memorial Reference: He has no known grave but is listed on Panel 127 to 129 on the Loos Memorial in France.

DOYLE, John: Rank: Private. Regiment or Service: Royal Dublin Fusiliers. Unit: 8th Bn. Date of death: 6 July 1916. Age at death: 22. Service No: 20205. Born in Kilmacanague, Co. Wicklow. Enlisted in Bray, Co. Wicklow. Killed in action.

Supplementary information: Foster son of Mary Giles, of Kilmurray, Bray, Co. Wicklow. Grave or Memorial Reference: F.4. Cemetery: Bois-Carre Military Cemetery in Haisnes, France.

DOYLE, John: Rank: Private. Regiment or Service: East Yorkshire Regiment. Unit: 6th Bn. Date of death: 21 August 1915. Service No: 12232. Born in Greystones, Co. Wicklow. Enlisted in Dublin. Killed in action in the Dardinelles. Grave or Memorial Reference: He has no known grave but is listed on Panel 51 to 54 on the Helles Memorial in Turkey.

DOYLE, John: Rank: Sailor. Regiment or Service: Merchant Navy. Unit: SS *Barbara Marie* (Newcastle-on-Tyne). Age at death: 22. Date of death: 12 June 1940.

Supplementary information: Son of John and Elizabeth Doyle, of Arklow, Co. Wicklow. Grave or Memorial Reference: He has no known grave but is listed on Panel 13 on the Tower Hill Memorial, UK.

DOYLE, Martin Kevin: Rank: Rifleman. Regiment or Service: Rifle Brigade. Unit: 9th Bn. Date of death: 3 May 1917. Service No: S/26092. Born in Shillelagh, Co. Wicklow. Enlisted in Dartford in Kent while living in Lugduff, Co. Wicklow. Killed in action. Grave or Memorial Reference: He has no known grave but is listed in Bay 9 of the Arras Memorial in France.

DOYLE, Michael: Rank: Private. Regiment or Service: Royal Irish Regiment. Unit: 7th Bn. Date of death: 21 March 1918. Age at death: 30. Service No: 4435. Born in Tomacork. Enlisted in Gorey while living in Carnew. Killed in action.

Supplementary information: Son of James Doyle, of Collatton Row, Carnew, Co. Wicklow. Grave or Memorial Reference: He has no known grave but is listed on Panel 30 and 31 on the Pozieres Memorial in France

DOYLE, Owen: Rank: Pionéer. Regiment or Service: Corps of Royal Engineers. Unit: 'J' Special Company, R. E. He was previously with the Royal Dublin Fusiliers where his number was 3/20383. Date of death: 23 October 1917. Service No: 129038. Born in Greystones, Co. Wicklow. Enlisted in Greystones. Died of wounds. Grave or Memorial Reference: II.L.2. Cemetery: Bucquoy Road Cemetery, Ficheux in France.

DOYLE, Patrick: Rank: Private. Regiment or Service: Royal Dublin Fusiliers. Unit: 8th Bn. Date of death: 29 April 1916. Age at death: 18. Service No: 22498. Born in Rathfarnham, Co. Dublin. Enlisted in Naas while living in Baltinglass. Killed in action.

Supplementary information: Son Son of Jim and Marget Doyle. Grave or Memorial Reference: He has no known grave but is listed on Panel 127 to 129 on the Loos Memorial in France.

DOYLE, Patrick: Rank: Private. Regiment or Service: Royal Dublin Fusiliers. Unit: 2nd Bn. Date of death: 12 November 1914. Service No: 6423. Born in Baltinglass, Co. Wicklow. Enlisted in Dublin. Killed in action. Grave or Memorial Reference: IX.B.80. Cemetery: Cite Bonjean Military Cemetery, Armentieres in France.

DOYLE, Patrick: Rank: Sergeant. Regiment or Service: Machine Gun Corps. Unit: Infantry and 86th Company. Formerly he was with the Royal Dublin Fusiliers where his number was 11187. Date of death: 20 April 1917. Age at death: 22. Service No: 21004. Born in Blacklion, Co. Wicklow. Enlisted in Dublin while living in Kilcoole. Died of wounds.

Supplementary information: He

was mentioned in despatches and was the son of Patrick Doyle, 22 Cottage, Kilcoole, Delgany, Co. Wicklow. Grave or Memorial Reference: XXX.A.32. Cemetery; Cabaret-Rouge British Cemetery, Souchez in France.

DOYLE, Peter: Rank: Private. Regiment or Service: Royal Dublin Fusiliers. Unit: D Company, 9th Bn. Date of death: 16 August 1917. Age at death: 32. Service No: 13781. Born in Wicklow. Enlisted in Dublin while living in Wicklow. Killed in action.

Supplementary information: Son of John and Sarah Doyle, of Ball Alley, Wicklow. He has no known grave but is listed on Panel 144 to 145 on the Tyne Cot Memorial in Belgium.

DOYLE, Thomas: Rank: Lance Corporal. Regiment or Service: Royal Irish Rifles. Unit: 1st Bn. Date of death: 10 March 1915. Age at death: 27. Service No: 8100. Born in Newtownmountkennedy, Co. Wicklow. Enlisted in Dublin. Killed in action.

Supplementary information: Son of Thomas and Bridget Doyle, of 22 Lower Clanbrassil, Dublin. Native of Kilmurry, Co. Wicklow. Grave or Memorial Reference: IV.A.6. Cemetery: Guards Cemetery, Windy Corner in France.

DOYLE, William Christopher: Rank: Private. Regiment or Service: Northumberland Fusiliers. Unit: 3rd Bn (Special Reserve). Date of death: 11 May 1915. Age at death: 32. Service No: 110. Born in Arklow, Co. Wicklow. Enlisted in Dublin. Died of wounds at home. Son of Michael Anne Doyle, of Clifton Terrace, Ranelagh Road, Dublin. Grave or Memorial Reference: R.U.34. Cemetery: Newcastle-Upon-Tyne (St Andrew's and Jesmond) Cemetery, UK.

DROUGHT, George Thomas Acton: Rank: Major. Regiment or Service: Royal Field Artillery. Age at death: 34. Date of death: 15 June 1915.

Supplementary information: Husband of Louise L. Palmer (formerly Drought), of Ash Priors, Cheltenham, Gloucs. Grave or Memorial Reference: In near left corner. Cemetery: Glenealy Church of Ireland Churchyard, Co. Wicklow.

DRURY, Michael: Rank: Private. Regiment or Service: Royal Army Service Corps and also listed as Army Service Corps. Mechanical Transport, Secondary Regiment, Royal Garrison Artillery. Attached to the 481st Siege Battery. Date of death: 3 July 1918. Service No:

M/28280. Born in Rathnew, enlisted in Dublin while living in Finchley. Died. Grave or Memorial Reference: LXVII. F. 18. Cemetery: Etaples Military Cemetery in France.

DUFFY, James: Rank: Private. Regiment or Service: Royal Dublin Fusiliers. Unit: 2nd Bn. Date of death: 1 July 1916, first day of the Battle of the Somme. Service No: 20191. Born in Killadreenan, Newtownmountkennedy, Co. Wicklow. Enlisted in Wicklow. Killed in action. Grave or Memorial Reference: He has no known grave but is listed on Pier and Face 16C on the Thiepval Memorial in France.

DUGGAN, George Grant: Rank: Captain. Regiment or Service: Royal Irish Fusiliers. Unit: 5th Bn. Date of death: 16 August 1915. Age at death: 29.

Supplementary information: Son of George and Emilie Duggan, of Ferney, Greystones, Co. Wicklow. Husband of Dorothy Duggan, of Glenvar, St Kevin's Park, Rathgar, Dublin. B.A, Trinity College, Dublin. Member of the Dublin University Athletic Union; also an Irish International cross country runner. As part of the 10th Irish Division in Gallipoli he died of wounds during the fight for Kislagh Dagh and is mentioned in the book *The Irish at the Front* by Michael McDonagh. His brother Lt **Duggan J.R.** 5th Bn, Royal Irish Regiment died (age at death 20) the same day in the Dardinelles. His son **DUGGAN, Dermot Harry Tuthill** during the Second World War on H.M.S. *Ardent* where he was a surgeon.

Supplementary information from De Ruvigny's Roll of Honour: Capt Royal Irish Fusiliers. Third son of George Duggan of 5 College Steet, Dublin & Ferney, Greystones, Co. Wicklow. Manager, Provincial Bank of Ireland, Ltd, Dublin. Mother: Emilie Asenath, daughter of Colonel Charles Coote Grant, late Bedfordshire Regt. (died 23 August 1914). Born Birr, King's Co., 12 April 1886. Educated: High School, and Trinity College, Dublin, where he graduated with a B.A. in 1908. On leaving, he entered the service of the Irish Lights Commissioners. He was one of the original members of the Dublin University O.T.C. and was one of the first N.C.O. to be appointed, being promoted Corpl. In 1910. The following year he was one of small body of N.C.O. and Cadets specially selected for exceptional efficiency and smartness, to attend the coronation. He subsequently received a commission on the unattached list (T.F.) for service with the D.U.O.T.C, and was promoted Lieut. 8 February

Advertisment for Sunlight Soap.

1913. He qualified at the School of Musketry, Hythe, in March 1914, and was appointed to the command of a platoon in the School of Instruction for officers of the new Armies established in Trinity College in September. of the same year.

On the temporary closing of this school, in about the middle of April 1914 he joined the 5th Battn. Royal Irish Fusiliers as Lieut, and was at once promoted to the command of a company, with the rank of temporary Captain on 28 October 1914. He left with his regiement for the Dardanelles,

early in July 1915. He took part in the landing at Sulva Bay, 6 August 1915, and was severely wounded in the fighting there during the following ten days in Ridge over the Bay. He died the same day on board HMS hospital ship *Gloucester Castle*. Buried that night in the Egean Sea. His youngest brother fell in action there the same day

Capt. Duggan, of a bright and genial disposition, was one of the finest long-distance runners that Trinity College has ever possessed, and it would be no light task to compile a list of his many triumphs in the College Park, with the D.U. Harriers, in inter-University and in International contests. For several years he organised the College Races, and managed the affairs of the Dublin University Athletic Union with conspicuous success. But his greatest work was, undoubtedly, the inauguration of Trinity Week, an enterprise to which he devoted himself heart and soul, and of the original Committee of which he was the foremost member. He was also a former Scoutmaster of the 6th South County Dublin (Lesson Park) troop; a member of the Executive of the County Dublin Association and an active member of the Sea Scout Committee, in whose interests he worked until the outbreak of war. He was the only child of the late Henry Johnson, of Oaklands, Upper Assam, and had two sons: George Villiers Grant, born: 31 May 1911; and Dermot Harry Tuthill, born 5 July 1912. Brother of John Rowswell Duggan below. Grave or Memorial Reference: He has no known grave but is listed on Panel 178 to 180 on the Helles Memorial in Turkey and he is also commemorated on a marble plaque on the walls of the reading room in Trinity College, Dublin.

DUGGAN, James: Rank: Private. Regiment or Service: Royal Irish Regiment. Unit: 6th Bn. Date of death: 18 October 1916. Age at death: 19. Service No: 11247. Born in Baltinglass, Co. Wicklow. Enlisted in Clonmel, Co. Tipperary while living in Baltinglass. Killed in action.

Supplementary information: Son of Margaret Duggan, of Main Street, Baltinglass, Co. Wicklow, and the late Charles Duggan. Employed at G.P.O. Balunglass. Grave or Memorial Reference: He has no known grave but is listed on Panel 33 on the Ypres (Menin Gate) Memorial in Belgium.

DUGGAN, John ROWSELL: Rank: Lieutenant. Regiment or Service: The Royal Irish Regt. 5th Bn. Unit: 5th Battn. (Pioneers) Brother of George Grant Duggan above.

Supplementary information: from De Ruvigny's Roll of Honour. Son of George Duggan, of 5 College Street. Dublin and Fernay Greystones, Co. Wicklow. Manager Provincial Bank of Ireland, Ltd, Dublin. Mother: Emilie Asenath, daughter. of Col. Charles Coote Grant, late Bedfordshire Regt. Born in Dublin, 31 October 1894. Educated in The High School, Dublin, where he won a 1st Class Scholarship, and passed into Trinity College in 1912. There he joined the Medical School and became, like his brother, a prominent Member of the O.T.C. On the outbreak of war he relinquished his medical studies and was gazetted 2nd Lieut, 5th Royal Irish Regt, 15 August 1914, and promoted Lieut, 28 January. 1915. He left with his regt. for the Dardanelles early in July 1915, as part of the 10th Division, and was killed in action on the Karakol Dagh Spur. above Sulva Bay, 16 August 1915. He was at first reported wounded and missing and no officer saw him fall, but the Medical Officer of the Dressing Station at Sulva Bay, to whom Lieut. Duggan went when shot through his left wrist and with shrapnel injury to face and side, told him he should go to the Hospital Ship. He said his men were without an officer so he rejoined them in the firing line, and the subsequent story is briefly told by his Sergt. P J Nolan (on whose testimony his death was officially reported). 'He left the firing line, had his wounds dressed and returned shortly afterwards, where he was hit in the face with an explosive bullet and killed.' To his father, Sergt. Nolan wrote: 'Your son could have saved his own life, but he was always good to his men and he died encouraging them to fight till the last'. His Colonel, Earl of Granard, wrote,

I am sorry to tell you that your son has been missing since 10 August. He went with his company into action our that date, and we have not seen him since. I have enquired from several of the men of his company and they all tell me that he was wounded whilst gallantly leading his men. I sincerely hope that he is a prisoner, and it is always a consolation to know that the Turks treat their prisoners with the greatest consideration. I have now soldiered for a great many years and can honestly say that I never came across a better subaltern; and as regards his social qualifications, he was beloved by all ranks of the regt.

Lieut. Duggan was a noted rifle shot and won many medals and prizes, including Daily Express and Lord Roberts Medals; Adjutants cup of Trinity College, O.T.C, and he was presented with a rifle for the highest aggregate score in Leinster Schools, 1912. Lieutenant J. R. Duggan was killed on 16 August n Gallipoli, aged 30. Two brothers of these officers, Mr Duggan's second and fourth sons, are in the Naval Service, one being in the Transport Department at Whitehall and the other an assistant paymaster in a battleship. He has no known grave but is commemorated on special memorial 9 in AZMAK Cemetery in Suvla, Turkey and he is also commemorated on a marble plaque on the walls of the reading room in Trinity College.

John Rowsell Duggan.

DUNNE, Edward Patrick: Rank: Private. Regiment or Service: Royal Irish Fusiliers. Unit: 1st Bn. Date of death: 6 July 1915. Age at death: 34. Service No: 8950. Born in Tinahely, Co. Wicklow. Enlisted in Waterford while living in Ballytruckle. Killed in action.

Supplementary information: Son of Mr and Mrs Patrick Dunne, of Waterford. Grave or Memorial Reference: III.D.10. Cemetery: Artillery Wood Cemetery in Belgium.

DUNNE, James: Rank: Private. Regiment or Service: Leinster Regiment. Unit: 1st Bn. Date of death: 14 February 1915. Age at death: 23. Service No: 3385.

Born in Baltinglass, Co. Wicklow. Enlisted in Fermoy, Co. Cork. Killed in action.

Supplementary information: Son of Henry Dunne, of Fontslawn, Athy, Co. Kildare. He has no known grave but is listed on Panel 44 on the Ypres (Menin Gate) Memorial in Belgium.

DUNNE, Thomas: Rank: Private. Regiment or Service: Welsh Regiment. Unit: 8th Pionéer Bn. Date of death: 26 December 1917. Service No: 12585. Born in Blessington, Co. Wicklow. Enlisted in Neath. Died in Mesopotamia. Grave or Memorial Reference: I.B.10. Cemetery: Baghdad (North Gate) War Cemetery in Iraq.

First World War enlistment posters.

WITH THE

IRISH CANADIAN RANGERS
199TH OVERSEAS BATTALION

91 STANLEY STREET   MONTREAL

Lt-Col. H. J. TRIHEY, O.C.

Have You any women folk worth defending?

Remember the Women of Belgium

JOIN TO-DAY

VICTORY

PUT

YOUR BACK

INTO IT AND HELP
TO GIVE
THE FINAL PUSH

Sign the Enlistment Form.

"FAITH, THERE'S NO WAN COULD BE BOLDER"

Come on Boys!

JOIN THE

IRISH CANADIAN
OVERSEAS BATTALION RANGERS

Headquarters   Under
91 STANLEY ST.   Lt. Col. H. J. TRIHEY
MONTREAL.

E

EAGAR, William George Massy: Rank: Captain. Regiment or Service: Royal Munster Fusiliers. Unit: 3rd Bn. attd. 1st Bn. Date of death: 21 August 1915. Age at death: 23. Killed in action.

Supplementary information: Son of W. J. A. and Ida J. Eagar, of 'Iveragh' Church Road, Greystones, Co. Wicklow. Grave or Memorial Reference: He has no known grave but is listed on Panel 185 to 190 on the Helles Memorial in Turkey. Grave or Memorial Reference: He has no known grave but is listed on Panel 185 to 190 on the Helles Memorial in Turkey.

EAGLETON/EGLETON, Thomas: Rank: Lance Corporal. Regiment or Service: Irish Guards. Unit: 2nd Battalion. Date of death:5 December 1917. Ireland's Memorial Records give his date of death as 17 December 1917. Service No:6379. Born in Birr, King's County. Enlisted in Birr, King's County. Died of wounds. Age at death: 23. Service Numer; 6379. Irish Guards. 2nd Battalion.

Supplementary information: From De Ruvigny's Roll of Honour. Son of Michael Eagleton, Newbridge Street, Birr, Kings County by his wife Bridget, daughter of Thomas McGuinness of County Kilkenny. Born 26 April 1894. Educated Presentation Brothers School, Birr. He was a shop assistant. He enlisted 2 January 1915. Served with the Expeditionary Force in France and Flanders from 1 May 1916 and was killed in action on the Somme 5 December 1915. Buried 5½ north-east of Combles. His Captain wrote; 'He was deeply regretted by the NCOs and men of No 1 Coy.' He was awarded the Military Medal in November 1917, for bravery in discharge of duty and is listed in the London Gazette. Grave or Memorial Reference: V.D.17. Cemetery: Rocquigny-Equancourt Road British Cemetery, Equancourt in France.

EARL, F. R.: Rank: Private. Regiment or Service: Royal Army Service Corps. Unit: 614th M.T. Coy. (Edinburgh).

Secondary Regiment: Royal Inniskilling Fusiliers. Date of death: 9 February 1919. Service No: M/397696.

Supplementary information: Son of John Loftus Earl, of Co. Wicklow, and the late Sarah Earl. Grave or Memorial Reference: D.6. Cemetery: Edinburgh (Comely Bank) Cemetery UK.

EDGE, HENRY Edward: (Listed in Soldiers died in the Great war as Harry Edge). Rank: Private. Regiment or Service: Royal Dublin Fusiliers. Unit: 10th Bn. Date of death:14 February 1916. Age at death: 17. Service No: 25345. Born in Rathdrum. Enlisted in Wicklow. Died from a fall from his horse during training in Dublin.

Supplementary information: Son of David Edge of Ballinderry, Rathdrum. Grave or Memorial Reference: In the north-east part. Cemetery: Rathdrum, (St Saviour) Church of Ireland Churchyard, Co. Wicklow.

EDWARDS, Alan Jack Denis: Rank: Corporal. Regiment or Service: Royal Army Medical Corps. Age at death: 29. Date of death: 3 May 1942. Service No: 7346413.

Supplementary information: Husband of Dorothy Edwards, of Bray, Co. Wicklow. Born in Manchester and enlisted while living in Manchester. Grave or Memorial Reference: He has no known grave but is listed on face 18 on the Rangoon Memorial in Taukkyan War Cemetery in Burma.

EDWARDS, Charles: Rank: Rifleman. Regiment or Service: Rifle Brigade. Unit: 6th Bn. Date of death: 26 March 1918. Service No: B/941. Born in Bray, Co. Wicklow. Enlisted in London while living in Peckham, Surrey. Died at home. Burial information is not available at this time.

ELLIS, Patrick: Rank: Private. Regiment or Service: Royal Dublin Fusiliers. Unit: 2nd Bn. Date of death: 7 November 1917. Service No: 20318. Born in Rathnew, Co. Wicklow. Enlisted in Wicklow. Killed in action. Age at death: 28. Grave or Memorial Reference: II.B.7. Cemetery: Croiselles British Cemetery in France.

ELMITT, Austin Joyce: Rank: Captain and Acting Captain. Regiment or Service: Welsh Regiment. Unit: 17th First Glamorgan (Bantham) Bn. Date of death: 24 November 1917.

The gravestone of Henry Edge.

Age at death: 20. Killed in action at Burlon Wood. He won the Military Cross and is listed in the *London Gazette*.

Supplementary information: Son of Austina Winifred Elmitt, of 3 Milward Terrace, Meath Rd, Bray, Co. Wicklow, and Lt. Col. George E.B. Elmitt. Grave or Memorial Reference: He has no known grave but is listed on Panel 7 on the Cambrai Memorial, Louveral in France and is also mentioned on the Bray memorial.

ELMITT, George Carleton Brooksby: Rank: Second Lieutenant. Regiment or Service: Royal Irish Rifles. Unit: 7ᵗʰ Bn. Date of death: 16 August 1917. Age at death: 19. Killed in action.

Supplementary information: Son of Austina W. Elmitt, of 3 Milward Terrace, Meath Rd, Bray, Co. Wicklow, and the late Lt. Col. George Edward Brooksby Elmitt. Grave or Memorial Reference: He has no known grave but is listed on Panel 138 to 140 and 162 to 162A and 163A. on the Tyne Cot Memorial in Belgium. He is also listed on the Bray Memorial.

ENGLISH, Michael: Rank: Able Seaman. Regiment or Service: Mercantile Marine. Unit: S.S. *Solway Queen* (Aberdeen).

Age at death: 38. Date of death: 2 April 1918.

Supplementary information: Son of Michael and Anne English. Husband of Catherine English (*née* Byrne), of 26 Weadick Opening, Lower Main Street, Arklow. Born at Arklow. Grave or Memorial Reference: He has no known grave but is listed on the Tower Hill Memorial, UK.

ENNIS, Edward: Rank: Private. Regiment or Service: Canadian Militia. Unit: 103ʳᵈ Regt. Date of death: 13 July 1917. Age at death: 65. Service No: 222.

Supplementary information: Son of William Ennis, of Dunlaven, Co. Wicklow. Husband of Ann Ennis. Grave or Memorial Reference: L.84. B.9.S.P. Cemetery: Calgary Union Cemetery Canada.

ENNIS, John Joseph: Rank: Able Seaman. Regiment or Service: Merchant Navy. Unit: S.S. *Empire Mahseer* (London). Age at death: 29. Date of death: 3 March 1943.

Supplementary information: Son of John and Annie Ennis, of Arklow, Co. Wicklow. Grave or Memorial Reference: He has no known grave but is listed on Panel 43 on the Tower Hill Memorial, UK.

The gravestone of Frederick Henry Erdwin.

ERDWIN, Frederick Henry:
Rank: Sergeant (W. Op./Air Gnr).
Regiment or Service: Royal Air
Force. He was one of the four
crewmen from fifty Squadron
based in Waddington that lost their
way returning from a cancelled raid
(Convoy AD730) on Berlin. They
flew a Hampden Bomber. Date
of death: 17 April 1941. Service
No: 55389. Grave or Memorial
Reference: North-east corner.
Cemetery: Blessington (St Mary)
Church of Ireland Churchyard,
Co. Wicklow.

ERRITY, David: Rank: Gunner.
Regiment or Service: Royal Horse
Artillery and Royal Field Artillery.
Unit, 16th Bn, 41st Brigade. Date
of death: 1 June 1918. Service No:
34393. Born in Arklow. Enlisted in
Wicklow. Died of wounds at Arras.
Entitled to the Mons Star. Grave
or Memorial Reference: II.B.5.
Cemetery: Faubourg D'Amiens
Cemetery, Arras in France.

ERRITY/ERRETY, Thomas:
Rank: Private. Regiment or
Service: Royal Dublin Fusiliers.
Unit: 1st Bn. Date of death: 26
April 1915. Age at death: 20.
Service No: 11313. Occupation on
enlistment: farm labourer. Born in
Newtownmountkennedy. Enlisted
in Maryborough while living in
Dublin. Killed in action.

Supplementary information: Son
of James and Mary Erretty, of 49
Ardleigh Road, Dublin. Native of
Co. Wicklow. Grave or Memorial
Reference: He has no known grave
but is listed on Special Memorial
A.54. in V Beach Cemetery in
Turkey.

EUSTACE, Robert: Rank:
Private. Regiment or Service: Irish
Guards. Unit: 2nd Bn. Date of death:
14 September 1916. Service No:
8608. Born in Avoca, Co. Wicklow.
Enlisted in Wicklow. Killed
in action. Grave or Memorial
Reference: He has no known
grave but is listed on Pier and Face
7D C on the Thiepval Memorial
in France.

EVANS, Samuel: Rank: Private.
Regiment or Service: Leinster
Regiment. Unit: 1st Bn. He was
previously with the Royal Dublin
Fusiliers where his number was
10958. Date of death: 4 May 1915.
Age at death: 24. Service No: 9724.
Born in Wicklow. Enlisted in Naas,
Co. Kildare. Died of wounds.
Supplementary information: Son
of Ernest and Margaret Evans, of
Colley Street, Wicklow. Came from
India to enlist. Grave or Memorial
Reference: He has no known
grave but is listed on Panel 44 on
the Ypres (Menin Gate) Memorial
in Belgium.

EVANS, William Moore: Rank: Lance Corporal. Regiment or Service: Royal Inniskilling Fusiliers. Unit: 9th Bn. Date of death: 16 August 1917. Age at death: 28. Service No: 22681. Born in Greystones, Co. Wicklow. Enlisted in Dublin while living in Greystones. Killed in action.

Supplementary information: Son of Mary J. Evans, of 1 Malvern, Greystones, Co. Wicklow. Grave or Memorial Reference: He has no known grave but is listed on Panel 70 to 72 on the Tyne Cot Memorial in Belgium.

F

FARR, Edward Henry: Rank: Pte. Regiment or Service: New Zealand Training Unit. Section 3. Date of death: 11 August 1916. Service No.: 28867.

Supplementary information: Son of Mrs Farr, of Vale of Avoca, Co. Wicklow. Grave or Memorial Reference: I.1.(S). Cemetery: Wellington (Karori) Cemetery, New Zealand.

FARRELL, Andrew: Rank: Private. Regiment or Service: Machine Gun Corps. Unit: 121st Company. He was previously with the Connaught Rangers where his number was 5821. Date of death: 23 July 1916. Age at death: 21. Service No: 28996. Born in Kilbride, Co. Wicklow. Enlisted in Falkirk. Killed in action. Grave or Memorial Reference: I. F. 30. Cemetery: Maroc British Cemetery, Grenay in France.

FARRELL, James: Rank: Private. Regiment or Service: Royal Dublin Fusiliers. Unit: 2nd Bn. Date of death: 30 November 1916. Service No: 20247. Born in Kilquade, Co. Wicklow. Enlisted in Bray. Killed in action. Grave or Memorial Reference: N. 32. Cemetery: Kemmel Chateau Military Cemetery in Belgium.

FEHILY, Thomas Joseph: Rank: Stoker 2nd Class. Regiment or Service: Royal Navy. Unit: HMS *Courageous*. Age at death: 21. Date of death: 17 September 1939. Service No: D-KX 96612.

Supplementary information: Son of Patrick Joseph and Thomasina Mary Fehily, of Bray, Co. Wicklow. Grave or Memorial Reference: He has no known grave but is listed on Panel 34, Column 3 on the Plymouth Naval Memorial, UK.

FIGGIS, Neville Johnstone: Rank: Lieutenant (T/P). Regiment or Service: Leinster Regiment. Unit: 6th Bn. Date of death: 10 August 1915. Age at death: 23. Killed in action.

Supplementary information: Son of Charles E. and Augusta M. Figgis, of Ingle Field, Greystones, Co. Wicklow. Grave or Memorial Reference: He has no known

The gravestone of Neville Johnstone Figgis.

grave but is listed on Sp. Mem. B. 59. in Embarkation Pier Cemetery, Turkey. He is also commemorated on a marble plaque on the walls of the reading room in Trinity College, Dublin.

FINN, Denis: Rank: Saddler. Regiment or Service: Royal Garrison Artillery. Unit: 196th Heavy Bty. Date of death: 22 November 1918. Age at death: 32. Service No: 225300.

Supplementary information: Son of William and Julia Finn, of Co. Wicklow. Husband of Bridget Finn, of 10 Springfield Cottages, Mullingar, Co. Westmeath. Grave or Memorial Reference: 1685. Cemetery: Mikra British Cemetery, Kalamaria in Greece.

FISHER, Michael: Rank: Private. Regiment or Service: Royal Dublin Fusiliers. Unit: 6th Bn. Date of death: 9 August 1915. Service No: 13012. Born in Kilmacanogue, Co. Wicklow. Enlisted in St Helen's while living in Kilmacanogue. Killed in action. Grave or Memorial Reference: He has no known grave but is listed on Panel 190 to 196 on the Helles Memorial in Turkey.

FITZGERALD, Michael John: Rank: Lance Corporal.

Regiment or Service: Royal Dublin Fusiliers. Unit: 10th Bn. Date of death: 13 November 1916. Service No: 25566. Born in Bray, Co. Wicklow. Enlisted in Dublin. Killed in action. Grave or Memorial Reference: He has no known grave but is listed on Pier and Face 16C on the Thiepval Memorial in France.

FITZGIBBON, Richard John: Rank: Lieutenant. Indian Army. Regiment or Service: 128th Indian Pioneers. Date of death: 4 February 1915. Age at death: 25. Awards: Mentioned in Despatches.

Supplementary information: From De Ruvigny's Roll of Honour: son of Harry Macauley Fitzgibbon of Greystones, Co. Wicklow, Barrister at law, formerly Capt, and Instructor of Musketry in the 4th (Late 5th) Battalion, Connaught Rangers, and now serving on the Musketry staff as Capt, and Brigade Musketry Officer, by his wife, Helen Rebecca, daughter of John Kellock Barton, surgeon. Born in Dublin, 5 July 1889. Educated in Strangeways School, Dublin and Lickey Hills Preparatory School, Barnt Green and Radley College, from which latter he entered Christ Church Oxford, taking his B.A. degree in 1911.

On 6 January 1912 he was appointed to the unattached

Richard Apjohn Fitzgibbon.

list for the Indian Army, and after serving for a year with the 3rd Battalion of the Royal Fusiliers in India he was appointed a double Company Officer in the 128th Pioneers, 5 January 1913 and later went through a course of engineering with the Sappers and Miners at Rurkee, India, becoming Lieutenant 17 April 1913. He was in charge of the escort to the Artillery regiment, near Tussoum on the Suez Canal. His men sank the first pontoon boat, but the second got across. Though wounded quite early in the fight, after a short retirement to the rear to bind up his wound he returned and continued to direct his men. Some two hours or so later it became necessary to transmit an important message to the commander of the artillery. Lieut. Fitzgibbon undertook to take it himself, and crossing an open space of about a quarter of a mile, all the while exposed to heavy fire, he delivered the message. Not until then did he mention that he was wounded. His wound was found to be serious and he was removed to the Signal House at Tussoum Ferry where after being bright and cheerful, he succumbed early next morning, 4 February 1915. He was buried with full military honours in the Ismalia Cemetery, the New Zealanders furnishing the firing party (as his own regiment was at Serapeum). He was especially mentioned in general Sir Maxwell's despatch dated 16 February 1915 (*London Gazette* 21 June 1916), as follows '128th Pioneers, Lieut. R.A. Fitzgibbon behaved with conspicuous gallantry. When severely wounded he ran a considerable distance under fire with a message to the 5th Egyptian Battery. He has died of his wounds.' He was also mentioned in the second list of recommendations, dated 19 August 1915. Lieut. Fitzgibbon was a keen sportsman, and twice coxed the Radley boat at Henley

Regatta. He was also for a time cox of Christ Church, Oxford, and subsequently stroke of their second eight. He was a member of the Leander Rowing Club. rave or Memorial Reference: B.40. Cemetery: Ismalia War Memorial in Egypt. He featured in the Channel 4 programme *Lost Generation*.

FITZPATRICK, James: Rank: Corporal. Regiment or Service: Royal Dublin Fusiliers. Unit: 2nd Bn. Date of death: 21 March 1918. Age at death: 40. Service No: 20184. Born in Dublin. Enlisted in Bray. Killed in action.

Supplementary information: Son of James and Catherine Fitzpatrick. Husband of Anne Fitzpatrick, of 4 Hudson's Terrace, Bray, Co. Wicklow. Grave or Memorial Reference: He has no known grave but is listed in Panels 79 to 80 on the Pozieres Memorial in France.

FITZPATRICK, Patrick: Rank: Gunner. Regiment or Service: Royal Field Artillery Unit: 'A' Bty. 62nd Bde. Date of death: 9 July 1917. Age at death: 19. Service No: 77557. Born in Askamore in Wicklow. Enlisted in Bray. Killed in action.

Supplementary information: Son of Jeremiah and Kate Fitzpatrick, of Ballinaclea, Co. Wicklow. Grave or Memorial Reference: I.J.3. Cemetery: Tilloy British Cemetery, Tilloy-Les-Mofflaines in France.

FITZPATRICK, William: Rank: Private. Regiment or Service: Royal Dublin Fusiliers. Unit: 2nd Bn. Date of death: 24 May 1915. Service No: 8424. Born in Bray, Co. Wicklow. Enlisted in Dublin while living in Bray. Died of wounds. Grave or Memorial Reference: I.F.55. Cemetery: Bailleul Communal Cemetery Extension (Nord) in France.

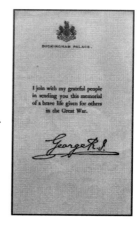

Letter of commiseration from the King.

FLANAGAN, Patrick: Rank: Rifleman. Regiment or Service: Royal Irish Rifles. Unit: 1st Bn. Date of death: 18 August 1916. Service No: 1589. Born in Bray, Co. Wicklow. Enlisted in Dublin. Died of wounds. Grave or Memorial Reference: I.J.74. Cemetery: Chocques Military Cemetery in France.

FLOOD, Thomas: Rank: Lance Corporal. Regiment or Service: Irish Guards. Unit: 2nd Date of death: 31 July 1917. Service No: 10901. Born in Rathvilly, Co. Carlow. Enlisted in Naas while living in Ticknock, Co. Wicklow. Killed in action. He has no known grave but is listed on Panel 11 on the Ypres (Menin Gate) Memorial in Belgium.

FLUSK, Michael: Rank: Able Seaman. Regiment or Service: Merchant Navy. Unit: SS *Ocean Voyager* (Liverpool). Date of death: 29 January 1946.
Supplementary information: Son of Michael and Alice Flusk, of Arklow, Co. Wicklow. Grave or Memorial Reference: Sec. 19.R.C. Grave 932. Cemetery: Liverpool (Allerton) Cemetery, Liverpool, UK.

FLYNN, William: Rank: Private. Regiment or Service: Canadian Infantry (Manitoba Regiment). Unit: 78th Bn. Date of death: 3 January 1917. Age at death: 35. Service No: 148711. Born 21 August 1881 in Knockenargen, Co. Wicklow. Enlisted on 2 February 1916 in Winnipeg while living at 404 Bannatyne Ave, Winnipeg. Occupation on enlistment: glazier. Height: 5'11". Complexion: fresh. Eyes: hazel. Hair: brown. Religion: Church of Ireland. Next of kin listed as William Flynn (Father).
Supplementary information: Son of William Flynn, of Moorspark, Donard, Co. Wicklow. Grave or Memorial Reference: II.D.16. Cemetery: Cabaret-Rouge British Cemetery, Souchez in France.

FOLEY, Peter: Rank: Able Seaman. Regiment or Service: Royal Navy. Unit: HMS *Indefatigable*. Date of death: 31 May 1916. Age at death: 31. Service No: 197672. During the Battle of Jutland the German Battlecruiser Von Der Tann fired 11 inch shells at the Indefatigable. The first two entered 'X' magazine area and blew out the bottom of the ship and she began sinking by the stern. More 11 inch shells from the Van Der Tann destroyed 'A' turret and also blew up the forward magazine and she then sank. There were only two survivors of her crew of 1017 men. The Van Der Tann was scuttled in Scapa flow in June 1919.

Supplementary information: Son of Mary Foley, of 1 King's Terrace, Ferrybank, Arklow, Co. Wicklow, and the late Michael Foley (Pensioner, R.N.). Native of Skibbereen, Co. Cork. He has no known grave but is listed on Plymouth Naval Memorial, UK.

FORTUNE, Edward John: Rank:Private. Regiment or Service: Royal Army Ordnance Corps. Unit: 51 Mobile Laundry Unit. Age at death: 40. Date of death: 6 May 1946. Service No: 13039941.

Supplementary information: Son of Michael and Jane Fortune, of Bray. Husband of Martha Fortune, of Bray. Grave P. 89. Cemetery: Little Bray (St Peters) Catholic Cemetery, Wicklow.

FOX, William, H.: Rank: Private. Regiment or Service: Royal Inniskilling Fusiliers. Unit: 9th Bn. Date of death: 1 July 1916, first day of the Battle of the Somme. Service No: 23771. Born in Delgany, Co. Wicklow. Enlisted in Dublin. Killed in action. He has no known grave but is listed on Pier and Face 4D and 5B on the Thiepval Memorial in France.

FURLONG, Peter: Rank: Sergeant (Flt. Engr.). Regiment or Service: Royal Air. Force Volunteer Reserve. Unit: 425 (R.C.A.F.) Sqdn. Age at death: 23. Date of death: 31 March 1944. Service No: 2214118.

Supplementary information: Son of Thomas Furlong and of Mary Furlong (*née* Brown), of Killincarrig, Co. Wicklow. Grave or Memorial Reference: Coll. grave 11.F. 13–16. Cemetery: Durnbach War Cemetery in Germany.

G

GAGE, John Munro: Rank: Captain. Regiment or Service: Royal Army Medical Corps, Secondary Unit, Royal Field Artillery and attached to the 57ᵗʰ Brigade. Date of death: 29 November 1918.Age at death: 31. Born in Newtownmountkennedy. Died of malaria and pneumonia in Salonika.

Supplementary information: Son of Robert C. and Georgina E. Gage, of Craiglands, Dalkey, Co. Dublin. Entitled to the 1914-medal. Grave or Memorial Reference: 516. Cemetery, Kirechkoi-Hortakoi Military Cemetery in Greece.

GALBRAITH, Alexander Norman: Rank: Captain. Regiment or Service: Ceylon Planters Rifle Corps. Date of death: 16 February 1915. Grave or Memorial Reference: D.39. Cemetery: Powerscourt (St Patrick) Church of Ireland Churchyard, Co. Wicklow.

GALLAGHER, Maurice Patrick: Rank: Sergeant. Regiment or Service: Royal Air Force. Unit: 50 Sqdn. Age at death: 20. Date of death: 17 August 1942. Service No: 574930.

Supplementary information: Son of John Edwin Gallagher, and of Helen Patricia Gallagher, of Bray, Co. Wicklow. Flying Lancaster I R5639 VN- during Operation Onsabruk they took off Swinderby. Lost without trace.The crew is also mentioned in 'Bomber Command Losses'.Vol.3.WR. Chorley. Grave or Memorial Reference: He has no known grave but is listed on Panel 83 on the Runnymede Memorial, UK.

GAMMELL, Patrick: Rank: Private. Regiment or Service: Royal Irish Fusiliers. Unit: 1ˢᵗ Bn. Date of death: 18 April 1918.Age at death: 25. Service No: 29418. Born in Kilquade, Co.Wicklow. Enlisted in Dublin while living in Kilcoole, Co.Wicklow.

Supplementary information: Son of James and Ellen Gammell, of Seaview Cottage, Kilcoole. Grave or Memorial Reference: He has no known grave but is listed on Panel 140 to 141 on the Tyne Cot Memorial in Belgium.

The gravestone of Alexander Norman Galbraith.

GANNON, Patrick: Rank: Private. Regiment or Service: Royal Dublin Fusiliers. Unit: 1st Bn. Date of death: 12 July 1915. Age at death: 27 also listed as 36. Service No: 5044. Born in Arklow, Wicklow. Enlisted in Wicklow. Killed in action in Gallipoli.

Supplementary information: Son of B. and Margaret Gannon, of Wexford Road, Arklow, Co. Wicklow. Grave or Memorial Reference: He has no known grave but is listed on Panel 190 to 196 on the Helles Memorial in Turkey.

GARLAND, Edward: Rank: Company Sergeant Major. Regiment or Service: 2nd Canadian Mounted Rifles Battalion. Date of death: 2 February 1919. Service No: 108238.

Supplementary information: Son of George and Margaret Garland, of Main Street, Blessington. Wounded in France and died in Ripon in Yorkshire. Grave or Memorial Reference: In north-east part. Cemetery: Blessington (St Mary) Church of Ireland Churchyard on the Dublin-Baltinglass Road.

The gravestone of Edward Garland.

The gravestone of B.E Geoghean.

GEOGHAN, John: Rank: Lance Serjeant. Regiment or Service: Royal Inniskilling Fusiliers. Unit: 2nd Bn. Age at death: 26. Date of death: 21 April 1945. Service No: 7043715. Awarded the Military Medal and is listed in the *London Gazette*.

Supplementary information: Son of William and Kathleen Geoghan, of Ashford, Co. Wicklow. Grave or Memorial Reference: I.D.1. Cemetery: Argenta Gap Cemetery in Italy.

GEOGHEGAN, B. E.: Rank: Worker. Regiment or Service: Queen Mary's Army Auxiliary Corps. Date of death: 29 November 1918. Service No: 51922.

Supplementary information: Daughter of Mr P. Geoghegan, of Glencree, Enniskerry. Grave or Memorial Reference: Near East boundary. Cemetery: Curtlestown Catholic Cemetery, Co. Wicklow.

GHENT, Richard: Rank: Private. Regiment or Service: Irish Guards. Unit: 2nd Bn. Date of death: 2 September 1917. Age at death: 33. Service No: 10702.

Supplementary information: Son of John and Mary Ghent. Husband of Katherine Ghent, of Blackrath, Colbinstown, Co. Wicklow. Born at Narraghmore, Ballytore, Co. Kildare. Grave or Memorial Reference: N. 174391. Cemetery: Brompton Cemetery, UK.

GILBERT, Charles: Rank: Sapper. Regiment or Service: Royal Engineers. Unit: 130th Field Coy. Date of death: 3 October 1916. Age at death: 26. Service No: 95580. Born in Manchester. Enlisted in Dublin. Killed in action.

Supplementary information: Son of Charles and Mary Gilbert, of Blessington, Co. Wicklow. Grave or Memorial Reference: He has no known grave but is listed on Special Memorial 7 in Blighty Valley Cemetery, Authuile Wood in France.

GILBERT, Robert Cecil: Rank: Sergeant (Air Gnr.). Regiment or Service: Royal Air Force Volunteer Reserve. Unit: 49 Sqdn. Age at death: 22. Date of death: 7 March 1945. Service No: 197.

Supplementary information: Son of George and Mary Gilbert, of Arklow, Co. Wicklow. Flying Lancaster III PB537 EA-X. During Operation Harburg they took off at 1745hrs Fulbeck to bomb oil facilities. Believed to have come down at 2215hrs at Sandbostel, 9km SSW from the centre of Bremervorde. Those who died now rest in Becklingen War Cemetery, having been brought here from Sandbostel. They are also mentioned in 'Bomber Command Losses'. Vol.6. WR. Chorley. Grave or Memorial Reference: 27.D.10. Cemetery: Becklingen War Cemetery in Germany.

GILLIGAN, Thomas: Rank: Private. Regiment or Service: Royal Irish Fusiliers. Unit: 6th Bn. Date of death: 15 August 1915. Service No: 13757. Born in Wicklow. Enlisted in Dublin. Killed in action in Gallipoli. Grave or Memorial Reference: He has no known grave but is listed on Panel 178 to 180 on the Helles Memorial in Turkey.

GILMOUR, John: Rank: Private. Regiment or Service: Leinster Regiment. Unit: 1st Bn. Date of death: 2 January 1915. Service No: 7361. Born in Newtown, Co. Wicklow. Enlisted in Hyde in Cheshire. Killed in action. Grave or Memorial Reference: He has no known grave but is listed on Panel 10 on Ploegsteert Memorial in Belgium.

GILVARY, John Kevin: Rank: Sergeant. Regiment or Service: Royal Air Force Volunteer Reserve. Unit: Sqdn. 419 (R.C.A.F.). Age at death: 20. Date of death: 18 August 1943. Service No: 1512418.
Supplementary information:

Son of Michael T. and Marian I. Gilvary, of Bray, Co. Wicklow. Flying Halifax II JD458 VR-C during Operation Peenemunde they took off at 2140hrs. Crashed in the Baltic. Only two bodies of the crew were recovered Sgt Baker and Sgt Ramm and they were buried at Greifswald. They are also mentioned in 'Bomber Command Losses' Vol. 4. WR. Chorley. Grave or Memorial Reference: He has no known grave but is listed on panel 150 on the Runnymede Memorial, UK.

GLANVILLE, Thomas: Rank: Sergeant. Regiment or Service: Northamptonshire Regiment. Unit: 'C' Company, 1st Bn. Date of death: 1 November 1914. Age at death: 38. Service No: 7253. Born in Newtown, Wicklow. Enlisted in Dublin. Killed in action.
Supplementary information: Son of the late John William and Elizabeth Glanville. Grave or Memorial Reference: He has no known grave but is listed on Panel 43 and 45 on the Ypres (Menin Gate) Memorial in Belgium.

GLYNN, James: Rank: Private. Regiment or Service: Royal Dublin Fusiliers. Unit: 2nd Bn. Date of death: 15 December 1914. Service No: 4901. Born in Baltinglass, Co. Wicklow. Enlisted in Carlow while living in Baltinglass. Killed in action.

Supplementary information: Son of Mrs K. Glynn, of Chapel Hill, Baltinglass. Grave or Memorial Reference: I.C.7. Cemetery: Prowse Point Military Cemetery in Belgium.

GOODMAN, Henry: Rank: Private. Regiment or Service: Seaforth Highlanders. Unit: 7th Bn. Date of death: 9 April 1917. Age at death: 20. Service No: S/9675. Born in Nuns Cross, Wicklow. Enlisted in Fort George, Inverness-Shire. Killed in action.

Supplementary information: Son of the late William and Eva Goodman, of Co. Leitrim. Grave or Memorial Reference: He has no known grave but is listed in Bay 8 on the Arras Memorial in France.

GOODMAN, John: Rank: Private. Regiment or Service: Royal Munster Fusiliers. Unit: 'C' Company, 1st Bn. He was previously with the Leinster Regiment where his number was 2152. Date of death: 30 September 1916. Age at death: 34. Service No: 5962. Born in Wicklow. Enlisted in Cork while living in Cork. Killed in action.

Supplementary information: Son of John and Ellen Goodman, of Castle Street, Wicklow. Husband of Ellen Goodman, of 77 Shandon Street, Cork. Grave or Memorial Reference: He has no known grave but is listed on Pier and Face 16.C. on the Thiepval Memorial in France.

GORE, Gerard Ribton: Rank: Private. Rank: Second Lieutenant. Regiment or Service: Royal Welsh Fusiliers. Unit: 1st Bn attached to the 2nd Bn. Date of death: 20 December 1914. Age at death: 21. Died of wounds.

Supplementary information: Son of Ada Sophia Gore, of Ferney West, Greystones, Co. Wicklow. Gazetted 2nd Lt. 8 December 1914. From De Ruvigny's Roll of Honour: Only son of Lieut-Col Ribton Gore, of Thornfields, Co. Limerick, late 1st Royal Sussex Regimet. Born: 2 May, 1893. Educated: Cheltenham. Gazetted 2nd Lieut, 3rd Royal Welsh Fusilkiers, 14 March 1914. Served with the Expeditionary Force in France and Flanders, attached to the 2nd Battalion, being posted to the 1st battalion, early in December 1914, and died on the 20 December from wounds received in action the previous day. Grave or Memorial Reference: I.K.2. Cemetery: Merville Communal Cemetery in France. He is also listed on the 'Men of Thomond' Memorial in St Marys Cathedral in Limerick.

GORMAN, Frederick Thomas: Rank: Private. Regiment or Service: Hampshire Regiment. Unit: 2ⁿᵈ Bn. Date of death: 13 August 1915. Service No: 17542. Born in Aldershot, Hants. Enlisted in Naas while living in Wicklow. Died at Sea. Grave or Memorial Reference: He has no known grave but is listed on Panel 125–134 or 223, 226, 228, 229 and 328 on the Helles Memorial in Turkey.

GORMAN, Michael: Rank: Private. Regiment or Service: Royal Dublin Fusiliers. Unit: 1ˢᵗ Bn. Date of death: 29 September 1915. Age at death: 26. Service No: 20213. Born in Newtownmountkennedy. Enlisted in Bray. Killed in action. In Gallipoli.

Supplementary information: Son of Matthew and Esther Gorman, of Newtownmountkennedy, Co. Wicklow. Husband of Sarah Gorman, of Cartronwar, Co. Longford. Grave or Memorial Reference: I.E.10. Cemetery: Azmak Cemetery, Suvla in Turkey.

GRAHAM, Douglas: Rank: Private. Regiment or Service: Royal Inniskilling Fusiliers. Unit: 1ˢᵗ Bn. Date of death: 1 July 1916, the first day of the battle of the Somme. Service No: 10477. Born in Tipperary. Enlisted in Swinford while living in Wicklow. Killed in action. Grave or Memorial Reference: He has no known grave but is listed on Pier and Face 4.D. and 5.B. on the Thiepval Memorial in France.

GRANTHAM, Joseph: Rank: Private. Regiment or Service: Cheshire Regiment. Unit: 8ᵗʰ Bn. Age at death: 40. Service No: 10630. Born in Enniskerry, Co. Wicklow. Enlisted in Birkenhead while living in Bray, Co. Wicklow. Died of wounds in Egypt. Also won the South African Medal. Grave or Memorial Reference: F.191. Cemetery: Alexandria (Chatby) Military and War memorial Cemetery in Egypt.

GRAVES, John: Rank: Private. Regiment or Service: Irish Guards. Unit: 1ˢᵗ Bn. Date of death: 15 September 1916. Service No: 5698. Born in Enniskerry, Co. Wicklow. Enlisted in Bray, Co. Wicklow. Killed in action. Grave or Memorial Reference: He has no known grave but is listed on Pier and Face 7.D. on the Thiepval Memorial in France.

GRAYDON, Richard Joseph: Rank: Private. Regiment or Service: Royal Dublin Fusiliers. Unit: 10ᵗʰ Bn. Date of death: 30

November 1917. Service No: 24951. Born in Dublin. Enlisted in Bray while living in Delgany, Co. Wicklow. Killed in action. Grave or Memorial Reference: II.F.18. Cemetery: Croiselles British Cemetery in France.

GREALEY/GREELEY, Thomas Patrick: Rank: Private. Regiment or Service: Royal West Surrey Regiment. Unit: 2nd Bn. Date of death: 16 May 1915. Age at death: 21. Service No: S/6367. Born in Wicklow. Enlisted in Wicklow while living in Woolwich in Kent. Killed in action.

Supplementary information: Son of James Greeley, of 47 Reidhaven Road, Plumstead, London. Grave or Memorial Reference: He has no known grave but is listed on Panels 4 and 5 on the Le Touret Memorial in France.

GREEN, Thomas: Rank: Private. Regiment or Service: Royal Dublin Fusiliers. Unit: 1st Bn. Date of death: 2 May 1915. Age at death: 24. Service No: 10718. Born in Rathdrum, Co. Wicklow. Enlisted in Dublin. Killed in action in Gallipoli.

Supplementary information: Son of John and Ann Green. Grave or Memorial Reference: He has no known grave but is listed on Panel

190 to 196 on the Helles Memorial in Turkey.

GREEN, Walter Albert: Rank: Rifleman. Regiment or Service: Royal Irish Rifles. Unit: 1st Bn. Date of death: 16 August 1917. Service No: 10040. Born in Arklow, Co. Wicklow. Enlisted in Dublin. Killed in action. Grave or Memorial Reference: He has no known grave but is listed on Panel 138 to 140 and 162 to 162A and 163A on the Tyne Cot Memorial in Belgium.

GREENE, Patrick: Rank: Private. Regiment or Service: Royal Dublin Fusiliers. Unit: 2nd Bn. Date of death: 1 July 1916, first day of the battle of the Somme. Service No: 5660. Born in Baltinglass, Co. Wicklow. Enlisted in Carlow while living in Baltinglass. Killed in action. From a Wicklow newspaper article of the time,

During the week the news has been received in Baltinglass of the death in action of Pte P Greene. Royal Dublin Fusiliers, Bolan Street, Baltinglass. Pte Greene who was home on holidays from the front in April, was the youngest of three brothers serving with the famous Dublins. Paddy was only a boy when he joined just two years ago and was a great favourite with everybody in the district.

Grave or Memorial Reference: Special Memorial 4. Cemetery: Sucrerie Military Cemetery, Colincamps in France.

GREENE, William: Rank: Corporal. Regiment or Service: Royal Electrical and Mechanical Engineers. Age at death: 27. Date of death: 10 October 1944. Service No: 6978107.

Supplementary information: Son of James and Annie Greene, of Ballygannon, Co. Wicklow. Grave or Memorial Reference: III.D.4. Cemetery: Mierlo War Cemetery in Holland.

GREER, Edward Michael: Rank: Ptel. Regiment or Service: London Regiment. Unit: 1st/19th Battalion, also listed as 19th (County of London) Battalion (St Pancras). Age at death: 22. Date of death: 29 September 1916. Service No: 5494. Born in Bray. While working in London he enlisted in Whitehall while living in Gower Street, W.C.1. Killed in action.

Supplementary information: Son of Moses (died 20 December 1926) and Catherine Greer. Grave or Memorial Reference: He has no known grave but is listed on Pier and Face 9.D.

9.C. 13.C. and 12.C. on the Thiepval Memorial in France.

GREGAN, John: Rank: Private. Regiment or Service: South Irish Horse. Date of death: 21 June 1917. Age at death: 24. Service No: 1261. Born in Coolboy, Wicklow. Enlisted in Dublin while living in Coalboy. Died of wounds.

Supplementary information: Son of James and Mary Gregan, of Coolboy, Tinahely. Grave or Memorial Reference: II.B.30. Cemetery: Noeux-Les-Mines Communal Cemetery in France.

GREGAN, Patrick: Rank: Private. Regiment or Service: Queens Own Royal West Kent Regiment. Unit: 6th Bn. Date of death: 9 March 1918. Service No: G/30362. Born in Aughrum, Wicklow. Enlisted in Dublin. Killed in action. Grave or Memorial Reference: B.10. Cemetery: Ville-Sur-Ancre Communal Cemetery Extension in France.

GREGORY, Edward: Rank: Private. Rank: Master. Regiment or Service: Mercantile Marine. Unit: S.S. *W.M. Barkley* (one of the Guinness boats). Date of death: 17 October 1917. Guinness archive says the date was 12 October 1917. The ship was carrying a cargo

Above: 1914–15   Star, British War Medal and the Victory Medal.

Right: Pte Edward Michael Greer. *Picture courtesy of Stephen Mooney.*

of Guinness and was sunk at 7pm by a German Submarine just off the Kish lightship. Seven of the twelve man crew survived.

Supplementary information: Age at death: 46. Son of William and Letitia Gregory, of Lower Main Street, Arklow Co. Wicklow. Husband of Catherine Kearon Gregory, of 2 Meadows Lane, Arklow. Grave or Memorial Reference: He has no known grave but is listed on Panel 71 on the Tower Hill Memorial UK.

GREGORY, William Joseph:
Rank: Leading Seaman. Regiment or Service: Royal Naval Reserve. Unit: S.S. *Fern*. Date of death:

22 April 1918. Age at death: 26. Service No: 5718A.

Supplementary information: Son of Thomas and Ellen Gregory, of 6 Coolgreney Road, Arklow, Co. Wicklow. Husband of Margaret Gregory, of Moires Farm, Kulnuney Grieg, Co. Wexford. Steam Ship Fern was sunk by a torpedo from German Submarine 5 miles east by north of the Kish lighthouse, there were no survivors. Grave or Memorial Reference: 29 on the Plymouth Naval Memorial, UK.

GREY, William: Rank: Private. Regiment or Service: Royal Irish Fusiliers. Unit: 1st Bn. Date of death: 9 April 1918. Age at death: 21. Service No: 16166. Born in Ballinasloe, Co. Galway. Enlisted in Dublin while living in Wicklow. Killed in action.

Supplementary information: Son of Thomas and Emily Grey, of Colley St, Wicklow. Grave or Memorial Reference: He has no known grave but is listed on Panel 140 to 141 on the Tyne Cot Memorial in Belgium.

GRIFFIN, Peter Samuel: Rank: Lance Corporal. Regiment or Service: Royal Inniskilling Fusiliers. Unit: 9th Bn. Date of death: 7 May 1918. Age at death: 29. Service No: 27636. Born in Arklow, Co. Wicklow. Enlisted in Enniskillen. Killed in action also listed as died of wounds received accidentally in Equalberg in France.

Supplementary information: Son of John and Sarah Griffin, of Knocknaboley, Hacketstown, Co. Carlow. Husband of Mary Margaret Griffin, of Cappagh, Aughrim, Co. Wicklow. Grave or Memorial Reference: I.C.21. Cemetery: Esquelbeco Military Cemetery in France.

GRIFFIN, Robert Grattan Gurney: Rank: Sergeant (W. Op. Air Gnr.). Regiment or Service: Royal Air Force Volunteer Reserve. Unit: 103 Sqdn. Age at death: 21. Date of death: 5 August 1941.

Service No: 947898.

Supplementary information: Son of H. Gratton and Daphne F.I. Griffin, of Greystones, Co. Wicklow. Flying a Wellington IC W5656 PM. They took off 2245hrs Elsham Wolds during Operation Frankfurt. Reported crashed at Chateau Ledquent, Marquise (Pas-de-Calais) 15km south-west of Calais. He is also listed in 'Bomber Command Losses'. Vol.2. WR. Chorley. Grave or Memorial Reference: 3.D.5. Cemetery: Calais Canadian War Cemetery in France.

GRIFFITH/GRIFFITHS, Henry John: Rank: Lance Serjeant. Regiment or Service: Royal Dublin Fusiliers. Unit: 'C' Coy. 8th Bn. Age at death: 35. Date of death: 7 August 1917. Service No: 18898. Born in Baileboro Co. Cavan and enlisted in Bray, Co. Wicklow. Died of wounds.

Supplementary information: Son of Francis and Margaret Griffiths, of Navan. Husband of Annie Griffiths, of 6 Hudson's Terrace, Bray. Grave or Memorial Reference: IV.A.30. Cemetery: Mendingham Military Cemetery in Belgium.

GRIFFITH, Walter Berry Barclay Harry: Rank: Flight Lieutenant. Regiment or Service: Royal Air Force. Date of death:

24 September 1942. Service No: 40696. Cemetery: Newcastle Church of Ireland Churchyard, Co. Wicklow.

GRIMES, Edward: Rank: Private. Regiment or Service: Royal Dublin Fusiliers. Unit: 1ˢᵗ Bn. Date of death: 10 June 1918. Service No: 19259. Born in Rathdrum, Co. Wicklow. Enlisted in Bray, Co. Wicklow. Died 'by accident' in Egypt. Grave or Memorial Reference: C.14. Cemetery: Ismalia War Memorial in Egypt.

GRIMES, George: Rank: Private. Regiment or Service: Royal Army Medical Corps. Date of death: 28 October 1918. Age at death: 39 also listed as 40. Service No: 83523. Born in Rathdrum, Co. Wicklow. Enlisted in Wicklow while living in Rathdrum. Died of pneumonia in India.
Supplementary information: Son of George Grimes, of Fairgreen, Rathdrum. Grave or Memorial Reference: He has no known grave but is listed on face 11 on the 1914–1918 Memorial in India.

GRIMES, Patrick: Rank: Lance Corporal. Regiment or Service: Royal Dublin Fusiliers. Unit: 1ˢᵗ Bn. Date of death: 29 March 1918. Service No: 19576. Born in Rathdrum, Co. Wicklow. Enlisted in Manchester. Killed in action. Grave or Memorial Reference: He has no known grave but is listed in Panels 79 to 80 on the Pozieres Memorial in France.

GRIMES, Peter: Rank: Private. Rank: Rifleman. Regiment or Service: Royal Irish Rifles Unit: 1ˢᵗ Bn. Age at death: 22. Date of death: 28 March 1918. Killed in action. Service No: 9931. Born in Dublin and enlisted in Dublin.
Supplementary information: Brother of Mrs Rose McCarthy, of Trinity, Ashford, Co. Wicklow. Grave or Memorial Reference: He has no known grave but is listed in Panels 74 to 76 on the Pozieres Memorial in France.

GROGAN, Hubert Lawrence: Rank: Captain. Regiment or Service: Worcestershire Regiment. Unit: 4ᵗʰ Bn. Age at death: 21. Date of death: 5 May 1918. He was awarded the Military Cross and is listed in the *Lonzon Gazette.*
Supplementary information: Son of Captain and Mrs J. Hubert Grogan, of Slaney Park, Baltinglass, Co. Wicklow. Educated at Haileybury College and at R.M.C, Sandhurst. Born: 23 June 1896. Killed in action. Brother R.T. Grogan

Killed in action in the sinking of HMS *Hood* 24 May 1941. Note; R.T. Grogan is not included in this book as he does not show any connection to County Wicklow (Son of Capt. John Hubert Grogan, and of Alice Evelyn Manners Grogan, of Lower Walmer, Kent.) Grave or Memorial Reference: C.8. Cemetery: Cinq Rues British Cemetery, Hazebrouck in France. He is also listed on the Haileybury Memorial, UK.

GROVES, Charles Henry: Rank: Sergeant. Rank: Serjeant. Regiment or Service: Middlesex Regiment. Unit: 4th Bn. Date of death: 20 October 1914. Age at death: 36. Service No: L/6848. Born in Chipping Norton, Oxon, UK. Enlisted in Enniscorthy while living in Wexford. Killed in action.

Supplementary information: Husband of Hannah Mary Groves, of The Cottage, Upper Dargle Road, Bray, Co. Wicklow. Grave or Memorial Reference: He has no known grave but is listed on Panels 31 and 32 on the Le Touret Memorial in France.

GROVES, L.: Rank: Private. Regiment or Service: Leinster Regiment. Unit: 1st Bn. Secondary Regiment: Royal Engineers. Secondary Unit: attd. 181st Field Coy. Date of death: 25 November 1915. Service No: 4897.

Supplementary information: Son of Mrs C. Sutton, of Banen Street, Baltinglass, Co. Wicklow. Grave or Memorial Reference: II.L.8. Cemetery: Estaires Communal Cemetery and Extension in France.

GUNNING, Joseph: Rank: Private. Regiment or Service: Royal Dublin Fusiliers. Unit: 8th Bn. Date of death: 27 April 1916. Age at death: 20. Service No: 23439. Born in Greystones, Co. Wicklow. Enlisted in Glasgow while living in Bridgeton, Glasgow. Killed in action.

Supplementary information: Husband of Mary Gunning, of Grove Cottage, Greystones. Grave or Memorial Reference: He has no known grave but is listed on Panel 127 to 129 on the Loos Memorial in France.

H

HACKMAN, Christopher: Rank: Private. Regiment or Service: Royal Dublin Fusiliers. Unit: 3rd Bn. Date of death: 2 February 1916. Age at death: 30. Service No: 20384. Born in Greystones, Co. Wicklow. Enlisted in Greystones. Died at home.

Supplementary information: Husband of Norah Hackman of Knockrow, Delgany. Alternative Commemoration. Buried in Kilcool Old Graveyard, Co. Wicklow also listed in Panel 8 (Screen Wall) on the Grangegroman Memorial in Dublin.

HACKMAN, Patrick: Rank: Lance Sergeant. Regiment or Service: Royal Dublin Fusiliers. Unit: 9th Bn. Date of death: Service No: 15177. Born in Dublin. Enlisted in Dublin while living in Kilcool, Co. Wicklow. Killed in action. Grave or Memorial Reference: He has no known grave but is listed on Panel 144 to 145 on the Tyne Cot Memorial in Belgium.

HADDEN, Evans: Rank: Acting Corporal. Regiment or Service: Royal Dublin Fusiliers. Unit: 10th Bn. Date of death: 2 May 1917. Age at death: 19. Service No: 25353. Born in Kilcomon, Co. Wicklow. Enlisted in Wicklow. Died of wounds.

Supplementary information: Son of William and Alice Hadden, of Johnstown, Tinahely, Co. Wicklow. Grave or Memorial Reference: II.Q.34. Cemetery: Duisnas British Cemetery, Etrun in France.

HADOKE, Patrick Oswald Fitzgerald: Rank: Private. Regiment or Service: Federated Malay States Volunteer Force. Unit: 2nd (Selangor) Bn. Age at death: 31. Date of death: 26 June 1944. Service No: 13016.

Supplementary information: B. Sc. Forestry (Edin.). Son of Major W.C. Hadoke and Mabel Hadoke, of Greystones, Co. Wicklow. Grave or Memorial Reference: He has no known grave but is listed on Column 392 on the Singapore Memorial in Kranji War Cemetery in Singapore. He is also listed on the Hadoke Memorial in Christ Church in Delgany, Co. Wicklow.

The gravestone of Christopher Hackman.

HAGAN, James: Rank: Able Seaman. Regiment or Service: Mercantile Marine. Unit: SS *Tasman* (London). Age at death: 40. Date of death: 16 September 1918.

Supplementary information: Son of the late James and Anne Hagan. Born at Arklow. Grave or Memorial Reference: He has no known grave but is listed on the Tower Hill Memorial, UK.

HALL, David: Rank: Private. Regiment or Service: Royal Dublin Fusiliers. Unit: 1st Bn. Date of death: 1 July 1916, first day of the Battle of the Somme. Service No: 9209. Born in Wicklow. Enlisted in Wicklow. Killed in action. Was on reserve when war broke out and rejoined immediately and for many months saw active service in France. In September 1915 he was temporarily invalided home with gas poisoning and a few months later was sent to the Mediterranean. Grave or Memorial Reference: He has no known grave but is listed on Pier and Face 16.C. on the Thiepval Memorial in France.

HALL, Edward: Rank: Private. Regiment or Service: Royal Dublin Fusiliers. Unit: 2nd Bn. Date of death: 24 May 1915. Age at death: 20. Service No: 9011. Born in Wicklow. Enlisted in Wicklow. Killed in action.

Supplementary information: Son of Edward and Jane Hall, of Castle Street, Wicklow. Grave or Memorial Reference: He has no known grave but is listed on Panel 44 and 46 on the Ypres (Menin Gate) Memorial in Belgium.

HALLIGAN, Patrick: Rank: Private. Regiment or Service: Irish Guards. Unit: Reserve Bn. Date of death: 10 October 1918. Age at death: 29. Service No: 7938. Born in Kilbride, Co. Wicklow. Enlisted in Dublin. Died at sea.

Supplementary information: Son of John and Mary Halligan, of 70 St Paul Street, Dublin. Grave or Memorial Reference: He has no known grave but is listed on the Hollybrook Memorial in Southampton, UK.

HALLIGAN, Michael: Rank: Private. Regiment or Service: Australian Infantry, A.I.F. Unit: 14th Bn, 2nd Reinforcement. Date of death: 20 August 1915. Age at death: 23. Killed in action in Gallipoli. Service No: 1471. Unit embarked from Melbourne, Victoria, on board HMAT A46 *Clan Macgillivray* on 2 February 1915. Born in Droust (also listed as being born in Blessington) Kilbride, Co. Wicklow. Went to School in Mount Kilbride, Co. Wicklow. Enlisted aged 23 years in

Melbourne. Height: 5'4¼", Hair: brown. Complexion: ruddy., Eyes: blue. Religious Denomination: Roman Catholic. Occupation on enlistment: labourer. Next of kin listed as Mr J Halligan, 54 Parnell Street, Dublin.

Supplementary information: Son of John and Mary Halligan, of 70 St Paul Street, Dublin. Both received a pension on his death of 10 shillings per week effective from 28 February 1918. Native of Manor, Kilbride. Entitled to the 1914–15 Star, British War Medal and the Victory Medal. His identity discs were sent to his mother in May 1916. Grave or Memorial Reference: He has no known grave but is listed on the Lone Pine Memorial in Gallipoli and he is also listed on panel 72 of the Australian War Memorial.

HAMILTON, Douglas: Rank: 2 Lt. Regiment or Service: Royal Irish Rifles. Unit: 1st Bn. Date of Death: 9 May 1915. Killed in action.

Supplementary information: from Jimmy Taylor. Born in 1893 at Enniskerry, Co. Wicklow, and was a clerk. He later lived at Duncairn Terrace, Bray, Co. Wicklow, and moved to Vernon, British Columbia. Returned from Canada and enlisted at Westminster, London, as Guardsman 5084 in 1st Irish Guards 4 September 1914.

Age: 21. Height: 5'11¾". Chest 33½–38½". Weight: 155 pounds. Appointed L/Cpl, 31 December 1914, and went overseas 3 January 1915. Gazetted to a commission in the RIR, 20 March 1915, and joined 1st RIR 26 March 1915. Killed in action 9 May 1915. He was unmarried and both of his parents were deceased. He left no will and the next of kin was his brother, Albert Hamilton, 20 Glebe Place, Chelsea, London. A WO telegram notifying death was sent 18 May. There is also a WO minute on the file which refers to some forms having been returned by a L/Cpl C.R. Hamilton of 23 Carlyle Mansions, Cheyne Walk, Chelsea. This man appears on a later document as 2/ Lt. Charles Robert Hamilton, Irish Guards. There is also reference to an aunt, Mrs Rooke of 2 Clarinda Park East, Kingstown, Co. Dublin. A further scribbled note says 'For A. Hamilton, who is on active service.' Grave or Memorial Reference: He has no known grave but is listed on Panel 9 on Ploegsteert Memorial in Belgium.

HAND, Francis Joseph: Rank: Corporal. Regiment or Service: Royal Dublin Fusiliers. Unit: 1st Bn. Date of death: 24 April 1917. Age at death: 23. Service No: 9026. Born in Bray, Co. Wicklow. Enlisted in Dublin. Killed in action.

Supplementary information: Son of Christopher Hand, of 2 Cuffe Street, Dublin. Grave or Memorial Reference: He has no known grave but is listed in Bay 9 on the Arras Memorial in France.

HANLON, Patrick: Rank: Private. Regiment or Service: Royal Irish Regiment. Unit: 1st Garrison Bn. He was previously with the Royal Munster Fusiliers where his number was 6686 and with the Royal Irish Fusiliers where his number was 26683. Date of death: 4 May 1917. Service No: 5634. Born in Avoca, Co. Wicklow. Enlisted in Wicklow while living in Avoca. Died at Sea.

Supplementary information: Son of John and Sarah Hanlon. Husband of Bessie Hanlon, of Castle Howard, Avoca. Served in the Chitral Campaign (1895). Grave or Memorial Reference: C.II. Cemetery, Savona Town Cemetery in Italy.

HARBOURNE, Michael James: Rank: Private. Regiment or Service: Australian Infantry. AIF. Unit: 39th Bn. Killed in action. Date of death: 10 September 1918 in Peronne in France. Age at death 21. Service No: 2410.

Supplementary information: Born in Baltinglass. Educated in Baltinglass School and by private tutor. Entered Australia aged 16. Enlisted aged 19 in Royal Park, Ballarat, Victoria on 2 October 1916. Address: Windermere PO, Windermere, Victoria. He was previously refused enlistment as he was under size and had weak eyesight. Occupation on enlistment: labourer. Marital status: single. Height: 5'3.75". Weight: 130lbs. Hair: brown. Eyes: grey. Complexion: fair. Next of kin listed as father, Michael James Harbourne, Bridge Hotel, Baltinglass. Son of Michael and Elizabeth Harbourne, The Bridge Hotel, Baltinglass. He also had cousins in Australia who were also killed in the war. Unit embarked from Melbourne, Victoria, on board HMAT A17 *Port Lincoln* on 20 October 1916. War service: Western Front; Embarked Melbourne on HMAT *Port Lincoln*, 20 October 1916. Transferred to HMAT *Borda*, Sierra Leone, 2 December 1916. Disembarked Plymouth, England, 9 January 1917. Marched into 10th Training Bn, 10 January 1917. Admitted to 1st Australian Dermatological Hospital, Bulford, 23 January 1917. Discharged to 10th Training Bn, 4 April 1917. Found guilty at Durrington, 25 June 1917 of: (1) conduct to the prejudice of good order and military discipline in that when he was told be a non-commissioned officer to be careful of what he was doing he made use of obscene language, and (2) conduct to the prejudice of good order on military discipline in that when told to double to his clothes he said that he would sooner do clink first, 25 June 1917: awarded 8 days' Field Punishment No 2. Proceeded to France through Southampton, 10 September 1917. Marched into 3rd Australian Divisional Base Depot, Rouelles, 11 September 1917. Moved into the field, 19 September 1917. Taken on strength of 39th Bn, 22 September 1917. Admitted to 10th Australian Field Ambulance, 19 December 1917 (defective vision). Transferred to 11th Australian Field Ambulance, 20 December 1917. Discharged to duty, 26 December 1917. Rejoined unit from hospital, 27 December 1917. Proceeded on leave to the United Kingdom, 22 January 1918. Rejoined unit from leave, 8 February 1918. Admitted to 10th Australian Field Ambulance, 22 March 1918. Transferred to New Zealand Stationary Hospital, Wisques, 22 March 1918 (tonsilitis). Discharged to duty, 8 April 1918. Rejoined unit from hospital, 13 April 1918. Admitted to 11th Australian Field Ambulance on 14 April 1918 (pyrexia). Discharged to duty, 15 April 1918. Rejoined unit from hospital, 16 April 1918. Admitted to 10th Australian Field Ambulance, 20 June 1918 (pyrexia); admitted to 47th Casualty Clearing Station, 21 June 1918. Discharged to duty, 28 June 1918. Rejoined unit from hospital, 29 June 1918. Killed in action, 10 September 1918. Entitled to the British War Medal and the Victory Medal. He was temporarily buried in Buire British Cemetery near Tincourt, 4½ miles east of peronne and moved to Grave or Memorial Reference: Plot I, Row E, Grave No. 13. Cemetery: Cerisy-Gailly French National Cemetery in France.

HARDING, William James: Rank: Constable. Regiment or Service: Royal Marine Police. Date of death: 21 September 1947. Service No: PO-795.

Supplementary information: Son of Patrick and Elizabeth J. Harding, of Newcastle, Co. Wicklow. Grave or Memorial Reference: New Gd. F.7.7. Cemetery: Haslar Royal Cemetery, UK.

HARMAN, Edward: Rank: Lance Corporal. Regiment or Service: Royal Inniskilling Fusiliers. Unit: 8th Bn. He was previously with the Royal Dublin Fusiliers where his number was 23383. Date of death: 29 April 1916. Service No: 26566. Born in Dunlavin, Co. Wicklow. Enlisted in Dublin. Died of wounds. Grave or Memorial Reference: He has no known grave but is listed on Panel 60 on the Loos Memorial in France.

HARNEY, Martin: Rank: Private. Regiment or Service: Royal Dublin Rifles. Unit: 1st Bn. Date of death: 9 May 1915. Age at death: 25. Service No: 10036. Born in Arklow, Co. Wicklow. Enlisted in Dublin. Killed in action.

Supplementary information: Brother of Mrs S.M. Dennerly, of 60 Preston Road, Chorley, Lancs. Grave or Memorial Reference: He has no known grave but is listed on Panel 5 on Ploegsteert Memorial in Belgium.

HART, Thomas: Rank: Able Seaman. Regiment or Service: Royal Navy. Unit: HMS *Gloucester*. Age at death: 23. Date of death: 22 May 1941. Service No: D-SSX 24894.

Supplementary information: Son of James Hart, and of Esther Hart, of Arklow, Co. Wicklow. Grave or Memorial Reference: He has no known grave but is listed on Panel 47, Column 2 on the Portsmouth Memorial, UK.

HARTE, Andrew: Rank: Private. Regiment or Service: Royal Dublin Fusiliers. Unit: D Company 8th Bn. Date of death: 29 April 1916. Service No: 16238. Born in Barraniskey, Co. Wicklow. Enlisted in Dublin while living in Hanley, Staffs. Killed in action.

Supplementary information: Son of Mrs Mary Harte. Husband of Annie Stanley (formerly Harte), of 27 Victor Street, Hanley, Stoke-on-Trent. Grave or Memorial Reference: He has no known grave but is listed on Panel 127 to 129 on the Loos Memorial in France.

HAYDEN, Thomas: Rank: Private. Regiment or Service: Royal Welsh Fusiliers. Unit: 2nd Bn. He was previously with the Welsh Regiment where his number was 12738. Date of death: 19 August 1916. Service No: 38565. Born in Kilbride, Co. Wicklow. Enlisted in Neath. Killed in action. Grave or Memorial Reference: He has no known grave but is listed on Pier and Face 4.A. on the Thiepval Memorial in France.

HAYES, James: Rank: Private. Regiment or Service: Royal Dublin Fusiliers. Unit: 2nd Bn. Date of death: 23 October 1916. Service No: 20368. Born in Ballinatone, Co. Wicklow. Enlisted in Wicklow. Killed in action. He has no known grave but is listed on Pier and Face 16 C on the Thiepval Memorial in France.

HEALY, Michael Darnien: Rank: Lieutenant. Regiment or Service: Australian Infantry, A.I.F. Unit: 25th Bn. Date of death:

20 September 1917. Age at death: 27. Killed in action in Polygon Woods.

Supplementary information: Son of William Francis Healy, of 55 Washington Avenue, Brooklyn, Wellington, New Zealand, and Annie Mary Delahunty (his wife). Native of New Zealand. Born in Blessington. Grave or Memorial Reference: He has no known grave but is listed on Panel 7.17.23.25.27.29.31. on the Ypres (Menin Gate) Memorial in Belgium.

HEANEY, Daniel: Rank: Seaman. Regiment or Service: Royal Naval Reserve. Unit: HMS *Laurentic.* See **HEANEY, John**. Age at death: 26. Date of death: 25 January 1917. Service No: 4995A.

Supplementary information: Son of Michael and Rosanna Heaney, of 36 Probys Row, Arklow, Co. Wicklow. The vessel sank in 1917 with the loss of 354 of its crew when it hit a mine at Fanad Head *en route* to Halifax, Nova Scotia. Some 121 crew members survived. The Laurentic was carrying the 1917 equivalent of £5million in gold and a reported £3million in silver coins to pay for arms for the British war effort. Grave or Memorial Reference: 23. Memorial: Plymouth Naval Memorial, UK.

HEANEY, John: Rank: Seaman. Regiment or Service: Royal Naval Reserve. Unit: HMS *Laurentic.* Age at death: 26. Date of death: 25 January 1917. Service No: 4997A(Dev). Grave or Memorial Reference: Upper Fahan (St Mura's) Church of Ireland Cemetery, County Donegal.

HEARN, Henry: Rank: Private. Regiment or Service: Kings Liverpool Regiment. Unit: 1st Bn. Date of death: 20 September 1914. Age at death: 24. Service No: 11552. Born in Drogheda. Enlisted in Dublin while living in Ashford, Co. Wicklow. Killed in action.

Supplementary information: Son of William Hearn Ellen Smith (formerly Hearn), of Woodbine Cottage, Ballycullen, Ashford. He has no known grave but is listed on the La-Ferte-Sous-Jouarre Memorial in France.

HEATH, William Aitken: Rank: Chief Engine Room Artificer. Regiment or Service: Royal Navy. Unit: HMS *Hecla.* Age at death: 52. Date of death: 12 November 1942. Service No: C-M 12519.

Supplementary information: Son of Robert and Francis Heath. Husband of Victoria May Heath, of Woodenbridge, Co. Wicklow. HMS *Hecla* was a Destroyer Depot Ship. She hit a mine in April 1942 but stayed afloat long enough to be repaired however while on a voyage off Cape Vincent/ Casablanca on 12 November 1942 she was struck by 5 torpedoes from German Submarine U515 and sunk. 279 men died and 568 men survived. U515 was damaged and submerged in 1944 by rockets fired from two Aircraft and when then it was depth charged by 4 American Destroyers. Sixteen of her crew died. Grave or Memorial Reference: 60.1. He has no known grave but is listed on the Chatham Naval Memorial, UK.

HEMPENSTALL, Charles: Rank: Seaman. Regiment or Service: Mercantile Marine. Unit: SS *Belgian Prince* (Newcastle). Age at death: 26. Date of death: 31 July 1917.

Supplementary information: Son of John Hempenstall, of Wexford Road, Arklow. Born at Arklow. He has no known grave but is listed on the Tower Hill Memorial, UK.

HENNESSY, James: Rank: Private. Regiment or Service: Irish Guards. Unit: 1st Bn. Date of death: 8 August 1915. Age at death: 25. Service No: 5054. Born in Baltinglass, Co. Wicklow. Enlisted in Tamworth, Staffs while living in Baltinglass. Died of wounds.

Supplementary information: Son of William and Kate Hennessey, of Chapel Hill, Baltinglass. Grave or Memorial Reference: I.A.14. Cemetery; Guards Cemetery, Windy Corner, Cuinchy in France.

HENNESSY, William: Rank: Private. Regiment or Service: Royal Inniskilling Fusiliers. Unit: 11th Bn. Date of death: 1 July 16, first day of the Battle of the Somme. Age at death: 22. Service No: 15185. Born in Kilcoman, Co. Wicklow. Enlisted in Mullingar while living in Tinahely. Killed in action.

Supplementary information: Son of Thomas Hennessy, of River View, Tinahely, Co. Wicklow. He has no known grave but is listed on Pier and Face 4.D. and 5.B. on the Thiepval Memorial in France.

HEUSTON, Francis Robert: Rank: Lieutenant. Regiment or Service: Canadian Infantry (Quebec Regiment). Unit: 14th Bn. Date of death: 7 April 1916. Age at death: 22. Born 17 June 1893 in Dublin. Enlisted on 21 September 1914 in Valcartier. Occupation on enlistment: gentleman. Previous Miltary experience: attached to the Royal Dublin Fusiliers for one year (1913) as a Second Lieutenant. Height: 5'6". Complexion: fair. Eyes: blue. Hair: dark. Religion:

Church of Ireland. Next of kin listed father as F.T. Heuston MD of 15 St Stephen's Green, Dublin.

Supplementary information: Son of Mrs Frances T Heuston, of St David's, Greystones, Co. Wicklow. Grave or Memorial Reference: V.A.16. Cemetery: Lijssenthoek Military Cemetery in Belgium.

HICKEY, Christopher: Rank: Stoker 1st Class. Regiment or Service: HMS *Pembroke*. Date of death: 20 March 1917. Service No: K/28793. Died of wounds in the Royal Naval Hospital in Chatham. Age at death: 26. Born in Wicklow. Grave or Memorial Reference: Naval RC 7 331. Cemetery: Gillingham (Woodlands) Cemetery in Kent.

HICKEY, James: Rank: Lance Corporal. Regiment or Service: Royal Dublin Fusiliers. Unit: 1st Bn. Date of death: 30 April 1915. Service No: 10168. Born in Rathdrum, Co. Wicklow. Enlisted in Naas while living in Rathdrum. Killed in action in Gallipoli. Grave or Memorial Reference: He has no known grave but is listed on Panel 190 to 196 on the Helles Memorial in Turkey.

HICKEY, Patrick: Rank: Private. Regiment or Service: Royal Irish

Regiment. Unit: 2nd Bn. Date of death: 27 September 1918. Service No: 5017. Born in Arklow, Co. Wicklow. Enlisted in Clonmel, Co. Tipperary. Killed in action. Grave or Memorial Reference: A.54. Cemetery: Sucrerie British Cemetery, Graincourt Les Havrincourt in France.

HIGGINS, Peter Joseph: Rank: Private. Regiment or Service: Durham Light Infantry. Unit: 1/7th Bn. Date of death: 6 November 1917. Service No: 277175. Born in Arklow. Enlisted in Basingstoke while living in Tunworth. Killed in action. Grave or Memorial Reference: VIII. C. 29. Cemetery: Cement House Cemetery in Belgium.

HILL, John Kenneth: Rank: Pilot Officer (Pilot). Regiment or Service: Royal Air Force Volunteer Reserve. He was one of the four crewmen from fifty Squadron based in Waddington that lost their way returning from a cancelled raid (Convoy AD730) on Berlin. They flew a Hampden Bomber. Age at death: 23. Date of death: 17 April 1941 Service No: 83253.

Supplementary information:: Son of John Henry James and Maud Hill, of East Croydon, Surrey. Grave or Memorial Reference:

north-east Corner. Cemetery: Blessington (St Mary) Church of Ireland Churchyard, Co. Wicklow.

HILL, William: Rank: Private. Regiment or Service: Irish Guards. Unit: 'C' Company 2nd Bn. Date of death: 7 October 1915. Age at death: 22. Service No: 6900. Enlisted in Dublin while living in Cappagh, Co. Wicklow. Killed in action.

Supplementary information: Son of Joseph and Elizabeth Hill, of Cappagh, Aughrim, Co. Wicklow. Grave or Memorial Reference: XIV. B.9. Cemetery: Vermelles British Cemetery in France.

HOFFE, Thomas Mitchell: Rank: Captain. Regiment or Service: Cape Corps, S.A. Forces. Unit: Adjt. Age at death: 36. Date of death: 23 September 1917.

Supplementary information: Husband of Phyllis Maitland Ruxton (formerly Hoffe), of The Outspan, Lee-on-the-Solent, England. From De Ruvigny's Roll of Honour: third son of the Revd John Hoffe, Rector of Kilbride, Arklow, by his wife, Susan Aitken (Merton, Arklow), daughter, of Richard Couby. Born: Kilbride Rectory, 9 December 1880. Educated: Intermediate Schools, Kilbride. He went to South Africa in 1901 and joined Baden-Powells Police Force in January, 1901, with which force he served seven years. Volunteered for service, and joined the Special Service Squadron of the Natal Carabiners as a Trooper in 1914, under Col, (then Major) George Morris. Was given a commission as Lieut, in the Natal Carabiners; served throughout the rebellions of 1914 as Adjutant of the Special Service Carabiners; proceeded to German West Africa in 1915, and to German East Africa in January 1917, and died in the Military Field Hospital at Dodoma, 23 September 1218 from pneumonia, contracted while on active service. Buried there. Capt, Hoffe was awarded the King's Medal and Gallantry Badge for conspicuous bravery while serving with the South African Constabulary. He married at Johannesburg, 21 June 1913 to Phyllis Maitland, daughter, of (-) Wood, and had a daughter, Nora Kathleen, born 29 May 1916. Grave or Memorial Reference: I.C.3. Cemetery: Dodoma Cemetery in Tanzania.

HOLLINSHEAD, Alfred Lea: Rank: Lieutenant. Regiment or Service: Black Watch (Royal Highlanders). Unit: 6th Bn. Age at death: 24. Date of death: 12 April 1943. Service No: 132428.

Supplementary information: Born in Cheshire. Son of Alfred and Lily Hollinshead, of Bray, Co. Wicklow. Grave or Memorial Reference:

The gravestone of John Kenneth Hill.

III.E.8. Cemetery: Massicault War Cemetery in Tunisia.

HOLLINSHEAD, John Geoffrey: Rank: Sub-Lieutenant. Regiment or Service: Royal Naval Reserve. Unit: HMS *Dunedin*. Age at death: 23. Date of death: 24 November 1941.

Supplementary information: Son of Alfred and Lily Hollinshead, of Bray, Co. Wicklow. HMS *Dunedin* was torpedoed in the South Atlantic. 419 men died when the ship went down. Grave or Memorial Reference: Panel 60, Column 1. Grave or Memorial Reference: He has no known grave but is listed on the Portsmouth Naval Memorial, UK.

HOLOHAN, James: Rank: Private. Regiment or Service: Royal Dublin Fusiliers. Unit: 2nd Bn. Date of death: 26 April 1915. Service No: 13339. Born in Arklow, Co. Wicklow. Enlisted in Naas while living in Athy. Killed in action. Grave or Memorial Reference: He has no known grave but is listed on Panel 44 and 46 on the Ypres (Menin Gate) Memorial in Belgium.

HOOD, James: Rank: Private. Regiment or Service: Irish Guards. Unit: 1st Bn. Date of death: 12 November 1916. Age at death: 21. Service No: 9352. Born in Ballymurray, Co. Roscommon. Enlisted in Liverpool in Lancashire while living in Tumhawick, Co. Wicklow. Killed in action.

Supplementary information: Son of James and Margaret Hood, of Tinnahinch, Avoca, Co. Wicklow. Grave or Memorial Reference: He has no known grave but is listed on Pier and Face 16.C. on the Thiepval Memorial in France.

HUMPHREYS, Thomas Tector: Rank: Private. Regiment or Service: Irish Guards. Unit: 1st Bn. Age at death: 21. Date of Death, 8 November 1914. Service No: 3311. Born in Kilnamanagh, Co. Wexford and enlisted in Enniscorthy. Died of wounds.

Supplementary information: Son of Richard and Amelia Humphreys, of Ballinahoun Wells, Gorey, Co. Wexford. Grave or Memorial Reference: A.7. Cemetery: Halluin Communal Cemetery, Nord in France.

HUNTER, George: Rank: Private. Regiment or Service: South African Infantry, Irish Platoon. Unit: 3rd Regt. Date of death: between 15 July 1916 and 20 July 1916. Killed in action in Delville wood. Age at death: 37. Service No: 2281.

Supplementary information: Son of Robert and Elizabeth Hunter, of The Newrath Bridge Hotel, Rathnew, Co. Wicklow. Decorations, South African Ribbon and German West Africa Medal. Grave or Memorial Reference: He has no known grave but is listed on Pier and Face 4.C. on the Thiepval Memorial in France.

I

IRELAND, Henry: Rank: Private. Regiment or Service: Irish Guards. Unit: 1st Bn. Date of death: 18 May 1915. Age at death: 22. Service No: 4803. Born in Shillelagh, Co. Wicklow. Enlisted in Carlow, Co. Carlow. Killed in action.

Supplementary information: Son of Henry and Sarah Ireland, of Whaley Abbey, Rathdrum, Co. Wicklow. Grave or Memorial Reference: He has no known grave but is listed on Panels 31 and 32 on the Le Touret Memorial in France.

J

JACKSON, Walter Thomas:
Rank: Warrant Officer. Regiment
or Service: Royal Air Force Age
at death: 28 Date of death: 19
July 1947 Service No: 545756.
Additional information: Son of
William and Annie Sarah Jackson,
of Hacketstown, Co. Carlow.
Cemetery: Kiltegan (St Peter)
Church of Ireland Cemetery, Co.
Wicklow.

JAMESON, A.: Rank: Driver.
Regiment or Service: Royal Field
Artillery. Unit: 49th Res. Bty. Age at
death: 25. Date of death: 27 May
1917. Service No: 6048.

Supplementary information: Son
of Mrs Ellen Jameson, of Rathnew.
Grave or Memorial Reference:
R.C. ground 4.H.1123. Cemetery:
Rathnew Cemetery, Co. Wicklow.

JAMESON, M.: Rank: Private.
Regiment or Service: Royal
Dublin Fusiliers. Unit: 3rd Bn.
Age at death: 46. Date of death: 5
January 1917. Service No: 20188.

Supplementary information:
Husband of Ellen Jameson, of
Rathnew. Grave or Memorial

Reference: R.C. ground 4.H.1128.
Cemetery: Rathnew Cemetery,
Co. Wicklow.

JOCEYLINN, Patrick: Rank:
Private. Regiment or Service:
Royal Dublin Fusiliers. Unit: 1st
Bn. Date of death: 9 May 1918.
He won the Military Medal and
is listed in the London Gazette.
Service No: 11156. Born in
Kilmacanogue, Bray, Co. Wicklow.
Enlisted in Bray while living in
Wicklow. Died of wounds.

Supplementary information: Son of
Mr W. Joceylinn, of Glencormack,
Bray. He has two listings in Ireland's
Memorial Records where his
name is also spelled Josylinn. Grave
or Memorial Reference: I.E.34.
Cemetery: Ebblinghem Military
Cemetery in France.

JOHNSTONE, Robert: Rank:
Private. Regiment or Service: Royal
Air Force. Date of death: 12 November
1918 Service No: 309080.
Grave or Memorial Reference: West
of main path. Cemetery: Delgany
(Christ Church) Church of Ireland
Churchyard, Co. Wicklow.

The gravestone of A. Jameson.

The gravestone of M. Jameson.

The gravestone of Robert Johnstone.

JONES, Andrew: Rank: Private. Regiment or Service: Royal Dublin Fusiliers. Unit: 1st Bn. Date of death: 1 July 1916, first day of the battle of the Somme. Age at death: 39. Service No: 20339. Born in Baltinglass, Co. Wicklow. Enlisted in Baltinglass. Killed in action.

Supplementary information: Son of the late William and Essie Jones. Grave or Memorial Reference: He has no known grave but is listed on Pier and Face 16 C on the Thiepval Memorial in France. See page 150.

JONES, John: Rank: Private. Regiment or Service: Royal Irish Fusiliers. Unit: 6th Bn. Date of death: 7 August 1915. Service No: 17620. Born in Portinas, Co. Wicklow. Enlisted in Coatbridge, Lanarks while living in Glenboig, Lanarks. Killed in action in Gallipoli. Grave or Memorial Reference: He has no known grave but is listed on Panel 178 to 180 on the Helles Memorial in Turkey.

JONES, Richard: Rank: Corporal. Regiment or Service: Royal Horse Artillery and Royal Field Artillery. Unit, S Battery. Date of death: 8 March 1916. Age at death: 29. Service No: 50067. Born in Wicklow. Enlisted in Dublin. Killed in action in Mesopotamia.

Supplementary information: Son of the late Griffith and Alicia Jones.

Grave or Memorial Reference: He has no known grave but is listed on Panel 3 and 60 on the Basra Memorial in Iraq.

JONES, Thomas: Rank: Gunner. Regiment or Service: Royal Horse Artillery and Royal Field Artillery. Unit: 29th Div Ammunition Park. Date of death: 21 December 1915. Service No: 26476. Born in Wicklow. Enlisted in Dublin. Grave or Memorial Reference: J.14. Cemetery: Lancashire Landing Cemetery Extension in Turkey.

JORDAN, Edward: Rank: Corporal. Regiment or Service: Rifle Brigade. Unit: 7th Bn. He was previously with the K.E.H. where his number was 1156. Date of death: 22 February 1917. Age at death: 27. Service No: B/200715. Born in Wicklow. Enlisted in Hounslow in Middlesex while living in Holloway in Middlesex.

Supplementary information: Son of Mr and Mrs Jordan, of Co. Carlow. Husband of Edith Jordan, of 16 Scholefield Road, Upper Holloway, London. Grave or Memorial Reference: I.D.9. Cemetery: Mount Huon Military Cemetery, Le-Treport in France.

JORDAN, Thomas: Rank: Private. Regiment or Service:

Andrew Jones.

Royal Dublin Fusiliers. Unit: 9th Bn. Date of death: 9 September 1916. Service No: 24597. Born in Rathnew, Co. Wicklow. Enlisted in Wicklow while living in Clonakilty. Killed in action. Grave or Memorial Reference: He has no known grave but is listed on Pier and Face 16.C. on the Thiepval Memorial in France.

JOYCE, Thomas William: Rank: Private. Regiment or Service: Royal Dublin Fusiliers. Unit: 1st Bn. Date of death: 25 April 1915. Service No: 9789. Born in Glenealy, Co. Wicklow. Enlisted in Naas. Killed in action in Gallipoli. Grave or Memorial Reference: He has no known grave but is listed on Special Memorial B. 7 in V Beach Cemetery in Turkey.

K

KANE, Michael: Rank: Driver. Regiment or Service: Royal Field Artillery and Royal Horse Artillery. Unit: 56ᵗʰ Brigade Ammuniton Column. He was previously with the Royal Army Service Corps where his number was R/4/089438. Date of death: 21 October 1917. Service No: 215553. Enlisted in Dublin while living in Baltinglass, Co. Wicklow. Killed in action. Grave or Memorial Reference: I.C.10. Cemetery: Welsh Cemetery (Caesars Nose) in Belgium.

KANE, Patrick: Rank: Private. Regiment or Service: Royal Dublin Fusiliers. Unit: 2ⁿᵈ Bn. Date of death: 1 July 1916, first day of the battle of the Somme. Service No: 5639. Born in Baltinglass, Co. Wicklow. Enlisted in Naas while living in Baltinglass. Killed in action. Next of kin: mother, Mrs Kane, Holdenstown, Baltinglass. No burial details available.

KAVANAGH, Annesley Richard: Rank: Aircraftman 2ⁿᵈ Class. Regiment or Service: Royal Air Force Volunteer Reserve. Age at death: 29. Date of death: 25 January 1944. Service No: 1795814.

Supplementary information: Son of Charles and Sarah Jane Kavanagh, of Rathnew. Grave or Memorial Reference: Grave 261. Cemetery: Rathnew Cemetery, Co. Wicklow.

KAVANAGH, Edward: Rank: Able Seaman. Regiment or Service: Merchant Navy. Unit: SS *Eastlea* (Newcastle-on-Tyne). Age at death: 29. Date of death: 30 March 1941.

Supplementary information: Son of Denis and Julia Kavanagh, of Arklow, Co. Wicklow. SS *Eastlea* was sunk by Submarine U48 carrying a cargo of cotton seed. This Submarine was Commanded by U-Boat Ace *Herbert Schultze.* Grave or Memorial Reference: He has no known grave but is listed on panel 36 on the Tower Hill Memorial, UK.

KAVANAGH, Edward: Rank: Able Seaman. Regiment or Service: Merchant Navy. Unit: M.V. *Shelbrit I.* (Swansea). Age at death: 58. Date of death: 19 September 1940.

Supplementary information: Husband of Anne Kavanagh, of Arklow, Co. Wicklow. The coastal tanker *Shelbrit I*, on a voyage from Grangemouth to Inverness in ballast, blew up, caught fire and sank on 19 September 1940, in the Moray Firth. All her crew of twenty and the gunner were lost. Edward has no known grave but is listed on panel 96 on the Tower Hill Memorial, UK.

KAVANAGH, James: Rank: Private. Regiment or Service: Royal Irish Fusiliers. Unit: 1st Bn. Date of death: 21 March 1918. Service No: 20000. Born in Ballybrack, Co. Dublin. Enlisted in Bray while living in Enniskerry. Killed in action. Grave or Memorial Reference: He has no known grave but is listed in Panels 76 to 77 on the Pozieres Memorial in France.

KAVANAGH, John: Rank: Private. Regiment or Service: Royal Inniskilling Fusiliers. Unit: 1st Bn. He was previously with the Royal Irish Regiment where his number was 3604. Date of death: 1 March 1917. Age at death: 25. Service No: 25292 also listed as 8/25292. Born in Bray, Co. Wicklow. Enlisted in Bray. Died at home. *Supplementary information:* (Served as **ASHFORD, P.**). Son of William and Annie Kavanagh, of 6 Back Street, Little Bray. Grave or Memorial Reference: old side of ruin. Cemetery: Old Connaught Cemetery, Dublin.

KAVANAGH, Peter: Rank: Driver. Regiment or Service: Royal Horse Artillery and Royal Field Artillery. Date of death: 1 November 1914. Age at death: 23. Service No: 57943. Born in Wicklow. Enlisted in Dundalk. Killed in action. *Supplementary information:* Brother of Mrs Catherine Fitzpatrick, of Johnstown, Sea Road, Arklow, Co. Wicklow. Grave or Memorial Reference: He has no known grave but is listed on Panel 5 and 9 on the Ypres (Menin Gate) Memorial in Belgium.

KAVANAGH, Patrick: Rank: Gunner. Regiment or Service: Royal Garrison Artillery. Unit: 8th Mountain Battery. Date of death: 28 June 1915. Service No: 14715. Born in Wicklow. Enlisted in Wicklow. Died in India. *Supplementary information:* (Buried Peshawar (Right) B.C.XXI.283). Grave or Memorial Reference: He has no known grave but is listed on face of the Delhi Memorial in India.

Left: Herbert Schultze. Captain of the U-Boat that sank the Steamship, Eastlea.

Right: The Military Medal.

KAVANAGH, Patrick: Rank: Private. Regiment or Service: Royal Inniskilling Fusiliers. Formerly he was with the Royal Irish Regiment where his number was 3604. Unit: Depot. Date of death: 1 March 1917. Service No: 25292. Born in Little Bray, Co. Wicklow. Enlisted in Bray. Died at home. Grave or Memorial Reference: I.F.21. Cemetery, Brown's Copse Cemetery, Roeux in France.

KAVANAGH, Thomas: Rank: Private. Regiment or Service: Irish Guards. Unit: 1st Bn. Date of death: 26 February 1917. Age at death: 25. Service No: 7325. Born in Aughrim, Co. Wicklow. Enlisted in Dublin. Killed in action.

Supplementary information: Nephew of Michael Kavanagh, of Cronesallagh, Aughrim. Grave or Memorial Reference: II.C.21. Cemetery: Combles Communal Cemetery Extension in France.

KAVANAGH, Thomas: Rank: Able Seaman. Regiment or Service: Mercantile Marine. Unit: SS *Lodes* (Middlesbrough). Age at death: 41. Date of death: 5 May 1917.

Supplementary information: Son of Patrick and Mary Kavanagh. Husband of Elizabeth Kavanagh (*née* Neil), of 10 Tyndall's Lane, Arklow, Co. Wicklow. Born at Arklow. The Ballycotton lifeboat went to the ships rescue and saved two of her crew after she was mined and sunk 4 miles east of Ballycotton. The Captain and six of her crew died. Grave or Memorial Reference: He has no known grave but is listed on the Tower Hill Memorial UK.

KAVANAGH, William: Rank: Private. Regiment or Service: Irish Guards. Unit: 1st Bn. Date of death: 1 November 1914. Service No: 1258. Born in Castetown, Co. Wexford. Enlisted in Liverpool, Lancashire while living in Cloneraney, Co. Wicklow. Killed in action. Grave or Memorial Reference: He has no known grave but is listed on Panel 44 and 11 on the Ypres (Menin Gate) Memorial in Belgium.

KEANE, William: Rank: Private. Regiment or Service: Irish Guards. Unit: 1st Bn. Date of death: 1 November 1914. Service No: 2545. Born in Kilquade, Co. Wicklow. Enlisted in Dublin while living in Downs, Co. Wicklow. Killed in action. Grave or Memorial Reference: He has no known grave but is listed on Panel 44 and 11 on the Ypres (Menin Gate) Memorial in Belgium.

KEARNEY, Andrew: Rank: Private. Regiment or Service: Royal Dublin Fusiliers Unit: 1st Bn. Date of death: 7 August 1915. Killed in action in Gallipoli. Age at death: 18. Service No: 19446. Born in Rathdrum and enlisted in Bray.

Supplementary information: Son of Norah Kearney, of Brewery Cottage, Rathdrum, Co. Wicklow. Grave or Memorial Reference: VII.F.4. Cemetery: Twelve Tree Copse Cemetery in Turkey.

KEARNEY, James: Rank: Private. Regiment or Service: Irish Guards. Unit: 1st Bn. Date of death: 15 March 1917. Service No: 9875. Born in Linlithgow. Enlisted in Dublin while living in Rathallen, Co. Wicklow. Killed in action. Grave or Memorial Reference: IV.E.5. Cemetery: Sailly-Sur-La-Lys-Canadian Cemetery in France.

KEARON, Anna Marjorie: Rank: Sister. Regiment or Service: Queen Alexandra's Imperial Military Nursing Service. Date of death: 12 September 1943. Service No: 221059. Grave or Memorial Reference: Grave 70. W. on Border N. Cemetery: Arklow Cemetery, Co. Wicklow.

KEARON, Edward Victor: Rank: Mate. Regiment or Service: Mercantile Marine. Unit: SS *Lapwing* (Arbroath). Age at death: 19. Date of death: 10 November 1917.

Supplementary information: Son of Joseph and Frances Kearon, of Kylemore Arklow, Co. Wicklow. Born at Arklow. The 1192 gross-ton steamship *Lapwing* was built in 1911 and was mined and sunk by the

German Submarine UC4 in the North Sea 9 miles south-east from Southwold on 11 of November 1917. She was carrying a general cargo from Rotterdam to London. It was reported that all the crew and the Captain were saved. Note that Edward is listed as having died the day before the sinking. Grave or Memorial Reference: He has no known grave but is listed on the Tower Hill Memorial UK.

KEARON, George Roberts: Rank: Ordinary Seaman. Regiment or Service: Mercantile Marine. Unit: SS *Lapwing* (Arbroath). Age at death: 17. Date of death: 10 November 1917.

Supplementary information: Son of Joseph and Frances Kearon, of Kylemore, Arklow, Co. Wicklow. The 1192 gross-ton steamship *Lapwing* was built in 1911 and was mined and sunk by the German Submarine UC4 in the North Sea 9 miles south east from Southwold on 11 of November 1917. She was carrying a general cargo from Rotterdam to London. It was reported that all the crew and the Captain were saved. Note that George Roberts is listed as having died the day before the sinking. Grave or Memorial Reference: He has no known grave but is listed on the Tower Hill Memorial.

KEARON, John: Rank: Mate. Regiment or Service: Mercantile Marine. Unit: SS *Lodes* (Middlesbrough). Date of death: 5 May 1917. Age at death: 53.

Supplementary information: Son of the late Michael and Kate Kearon. Husband of Kate Kearon (*née* Woolatan), of 57 Lower Main Street, Arklow, Co. Wicklow. Born at Arklow. The Ballycotton life-boat went to the ships rescue and saved two of her crew after she was mined and sunk 4 miles East of Ballycotton. The Captain and six of her crew died. Grave or Memorial Reference: He has no known grave but is listed on the Tower Hill Memorial UK.

KEARON, Joseph: Rank: Master. Regiment or Service: Mercantile Marine. Unit: SS *Lapwing* (Arbroath). Age at death: 65. Date of death: 10 November 1917.

Supplementary information: Son of the late Edward and Catherine Kearon, of Meadows Lane, Arklow. Husband of Frances Kearon, of Kylemore, Arklow, Co. Wicklow. The 1192 gross-tons steamship *Lapwing* was built in 1911 and was mined and sunk by the German Submarine UC4 in the North Sea 9 miles south-east from Southwold on 11 of November 1917. She was carrying a general cargo from Rotterdam to London. It was reported that all the crew and the

Captain were saved. Note that Joseph is listed as having died the day before the sinking. Grave or Memorial Reference: He has no known grave but is listed on the Tower Hill Memorial UK.

KEARON, Patrick: Rank: Sergeant. Regiment or Service: Lancashire Fusiliers. Unit: 2nd/7th Battalion. Number: 280802. Enlisted in Salford in Lancashire. Age at death: 38. Date of death: 10 October 1917. Killed in action.

Supplementary information: Son of John Joseph and Ellen Kearon. Husband of Elizabeth Barry (formerly Kearon), of 25 St. James' Street, Salford, Manchester. From De Ruvigny's Roll of Honour: third son of John Joseph Kearon, of Arklow, Co. Wicklow, by his wife, Ellen, daughter, of Thomas Brien. Born: Dublin, 16 November, 1878; enlisted in the 4th Battalion, The King's Own (Royal Lancaster Regiment) 31 May, 1897. Served in the South African War 1900–1902 (Queen's Medal with five clasps). He was subsequently employed by the Manchester Ship Canal. Soon after the outbreak of war he rejoined the Army as a private in the Lancashire Fusiliers 14 December 1914 and was made a sergeant in April 1915. He served with the Expeditionary Force in France from Febuary, 1917, and was killed in action during the fighting at the Passchendaele Ridge on about 10 October following. Captain Turner, Commanding Officer of his Company, wrote; 'He was magnificent and died a noble death. I miss him very much, and so do all the company…He was a gallant soldier, and as such he died, leading his men in a great and glorious battle an serving his country.' He married on 12 May 1903 to Elizabeth (25 St. Jame's Street, Trafford Road, Salford), daughter of Joseph Jones, and had six children; Joseph Patrick, born: 10 August 1909. Elizabeth, born: 2 June 1905. Kathleen, born: 24 January 1908. Ellen, born 2 June 1911. Mary, born: 31 May 1913, and Amy, born 21 October 1915. Grave or Memorial Reference: XXIV. B.5. Cemetery, Tyne Cot Cemetery in Belgium.

KEARON, Robert Valentine: Rank: Master. Regiment or Service: Mercantile Marine. Unit: SS *Jane Williamson*. Age at death: 40. Date of death: 12 September 1917.

Supplementary information: Son of Robert and Anne Kearon, of Beulah, Ferrybank, Arklow. Grave or Memorial Reference: Old Ground. 30. Cemetery: Kilbride Church of Ireland Churchyard, two miles from Arklow on the Avoca Road, Co. Wicklow. See page 158.

KEARON, Thomas Randolph: (Also listed as Thomas Rudolph on the 1901 census) Rank: Second Mate. Regiment or Service: Mercantile Marine. Unit: SS *Solway Queen* (Aberdeen). Age at death: 19. Date of death: 2 April 1918.

Supplementary information: Son of Richard and Margaret Kearon, of Salem House, Arklow, Co. Wicklow. Born at Arklow. The Steamship *Solway Queen* was sunk by a German submarine 7 miles west of Black Head, Wigtownshire carrying a cargo of coal. The Captain and ten of her crew died. The Submarine U-101 was commanded by Carl Siegfried Ritter Von Georg. Ten days after the war ended the Submarine surrendered and was broken up in Morcombe in 1920. Thomas had a brother, Robert Edward Kearon who was a sailor and emigrated to Australia. Robert Edward served in the Australian Infantry AIF as a Private, No 2436 in the 5th Bn 5th Reinforcement. He had joined up on the first day of the battle of the Somme and survived the war. Grave or Memorial Reference: He has no known grave but is listed on the Tower Hill Memorial, UK.

KEARON, William Thomas Fiddler: Rank: Master. Regiment or Service: Merchant Navy. Unit: SS *Moortoft* (Middlesbrough). Age at death: 40. Date of death: 3 December 1939.

Supplementary information: Son of Joseph and Frances Kearon; husband of Margaret Kearon, of Arklow, Co. Wicklow. Steamship *Moortoft* was lost by an unknown cause in the North Sea after leaving the Humber for Calais. All thirteen of her crew died. In Avoca Graveyard in the Kearon section there is a reference to Captain William T. F. Kearon its says that he was 'lost at sea in SS *Moortoft* due to enemy action on Dec 3-1939'. Grave or Memorial Reference: He has no known grave but is listed on panel 71 on the Tower Hill Memorial, UK.

KEARNS, Thomas: Rank: Private. Regiment or Service: Royal Dublin Fusiliers. Unit: 1st Bn. Date of death: 25 April 1915. Service No: 9913. Born in Bray, Co. Wicklow. Enlisted in Dublin. Killed in action in Gallipoli. Grave or Memorial Reference: He has no known grave but is listed on Panel 190 to 196 on the Helles Memorial in Turkey.

KEARNS, William: Rank: Private. Regiment or Service: Royal Irish Fusiliers. Unit: 7th Bn. He was previously with the Royal Dublin Fusiliers where his number was 22546. Date of death: 8 September 1916. Age at death:

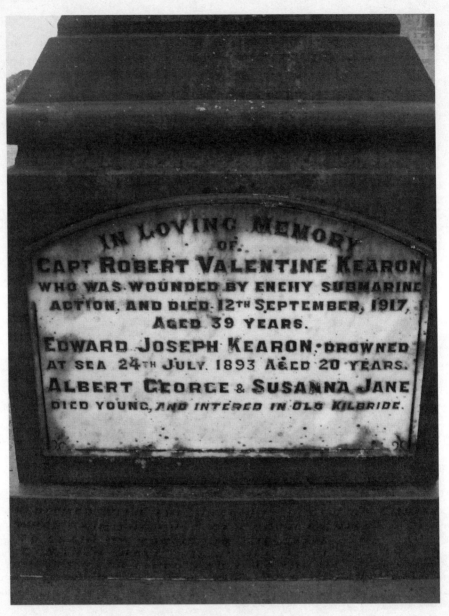

IN LOVING MEMORY
OF
CAPT ROBERT VALENTINE KEARON
WHO WAS WOUNDED BY ENEMY SUBMARINE
ACTION, AND DIED 12TH SEPTEMBER, 1917,
AGED 39 YEARS.

EDWARD JOSEPH KEARON, DROWNED
AT SEA 24TH JULY, 1893 AGED 20 YEARS.

ALBERT GEORGE & SUSANNA JANE
DIED YOUNG, AND INTERED IN OLD KILBRIDE.

Gravestone of Robert Valentine Kearon.

16. Service No: 22915. Born in Bray, Co. Wicklow. Enlisted in Dublin while living in Bray. Died of wounds.

Supplementary information: Son of James and Maria Kearns, of Bray, Co. Wicklow. Grave or Memorial Reference: II.C.35. Cemetery: La Neuville British Cemetery, Corbie in France.

KEATING, Joseph: Rank: Lance Corporal. Regiment or Service: Irish Guards. Unit: 1st Bn. Date of death: 5 December 1917. Service No: 6505. Born in Usk, Co. Wicklow. Enlisted in Curragh while living in Usk. Killed in action. Grave or Memorial Reference: He has no known grave but is listed on Panel 2 and 3 on the Cambrai Memorial in Louveral, France.

KEEGAN, Christopher: Rank: Private. Regiment or Service: East Lancashire Regiment. Unit: 2nd Bn. Date of death: 5 May 1915. Service No: 9374. Born in St Thomas, in Dublin. Enlisted in Dublin. Died of wounds. Grave or Memorial Reference: III.D26. Cemetery, Boulogne Eastern Cemetery in France.

KEEGAN, George: Rank: Driver. Regiment or Service: Royal Army Service Corps. Date of death: 20 November 1914. Service No: T/26151. Born in Wicklow. Enlisted in Dublin while living in Dublin. Died at home. Son of Mr J. Keegan, of 33 Merchant's Quay, Dublin. Grave or Memorial Reference: CE. 576. Cemetery, Grangegorman Military cemetery in Dublin.

KEEGAN, Michael John: Rank: Private. Regiment or Service: Canadian Infantry (Central Ontario Regiment). Unit: 4th Bn. Date of death: 1 October 1918. Age at death: 32. Service No: 1027447. Born 17 April 1889 in Wicklow, Ireland. Enlisted on 6 November 1916 in Belleville while living in Belleville. Occupation on enlistment: waiter. Height: 6'. Complexion: fair. Eye: light blue. Hair: black. Religion: Roman Catholic. Next of kin listed as Mary Keegan (Mother) of 3 St Catherine's House, Chord Road, Drogheda.

Supplementary information: Son of Patrick and Mary Keegan, of 3 St Catherine's Terrace, Chord Road, Drogheda. Grave or Memorial Reference: I.D.36. Cemetery: Sancourt British Cemetery in France.

KEEGAN, Richard: Rank: Fireman and Trimmer. Regiment or Service: Mercantile Marine.

The gravestone of Thomas Kearns.

Unit: SS *Snowdon Range* (Liverpool). Date of death: 28 March 1917. Age at death: 29. *Supplementary information:* (Served as **HENDERSON**). Son of John and Martha Keegan, of 2 Essex Quay, Dublin. Born at Carnew, Co. Wicklow. Steamship *Snowdon Range* was sunk by a German submarine off the coast of Waterford. Grave or Memorial Reference: He has no known grave but is listed on the Tower Hill Memorial UK.

KEEGAN, William Francis: Rank: Guardsman. Regiment or Service: Irish Guards. Unit: 2ⁿᵈ Bn. Date of death: 27 January 1943. Age at death: 32. Service No: 2721883.

Supplementary information: Son of William Thomas and Emily Alice Keegan, of Kilmonogue, Co. Cork. Cemetery: Glenealy Church of Ireland Churchyard in Wicklow.

KEENAN, Michael: Rank: Private. Regiment or Service: Leinster Regiment. Unit: 2ⁿᵈ Bn. Date of death: 4 September 1918. Service No: 3366. Born in Granford, Co. Wexford. Enlisted in Dublin while living in Arklow, Co. Wicklow. Killed in action. From an article in the *Enniscorthy Guardian* in 1916,

Private Michael Keenan,

Castletown, Wounded. Your readers will perhaps remember some months ago extracts from Private Keenan's very interesting letters from France to his friend, Mrs Andrew Leonard, Kilmichael. He is now lying wounded, poor fellow, in the War Hospital, Whitechurch, Cardiff. He received his wounds in an action near Loos in June last. He is making satisfactory progress towards recovery. Private Keenan is and adept with the brush and pencil and, as I think I told your readers before, there is many a souvenir of his art amongst his friends and neighbours around Castletown. The greater number of these are pencil and pen and ink sketches dashed off in a few minutes and are marvellous and lifelike likenesses of these friends. He painted a small seascape in water colours a few weeks ago in the hosipital. From a bundle of sketches of his which I had the privilege of seeing a few years ago I often thought it was a pity that he was not on some of our few (too few indeed) illustrated Irish Papers. His work in my opinion, and my opinion is founded on 30 years observation of Irish art, for what passes as Irish art, as interpreted in our picture papers-is far above the average of our small number of black and white artists. The accompanying photo of Private

Keenan in Whitechurch War Hospital.

A correspondant.

Grave or Memorial Reference: Bristol. Castle Cem Mem 2. Messines Ridge British Cemetery in Belgium.

KEHOE, James: Rank: Private. Regiment or Service: Connaught Rangers. Unit: 5th Bn. He was previously with the Royal Irish Fusiliers where his number was 1226. Date of death: 8 October 1915. Age at death: 27. Service No: 4931. Born in Davidstown, Co. Wicklow. Enlisted in Naas while living in Stratford-on-Slaney, Co. Wicklow. Died in Salonika.
Supplementary information: Son of James and Bridget Kehoe, of Eadstown Hill, Stratford-on-Slaney. Grave or Memorial Reference: III.A.30. Cemetery: East Mudros Military Cemetery in Greece.

KEHOE, Joseph: Rank: Sapper. Regiment or Service: Royal Engineers. Unit: 940 (I.W.T.) Coy. Age at death: 23. Date of death: 8 August 1945. Service No: 4350813.
Supplementary information: Son of James and Elizabeth Kehoe, of Baltinglass, Co. Wicklow. Husband of Margaret Kehoe. Grave or Memorial Reference: 3. E. 21.

Cemetery: Munster Heath War Cemetery in Germany.

KEHOE, Michael: Rank: Sapper. Regiment or Service: Royal Engineers. Unit: Formerly he was with the Irish Guards 170th Tunnelling Company where his number was 5328. Date of death: 3 July 1915. Age at death: 25. Service No: 86131. Born in Carlisle in Cumberland. Enlisted in Glasgow while living in Avoca.
Supplementary information: Son of Annie Byrne (formerly Kehoe), of Shraughmore, Avoca, and Charles Kehoe. Grave or Memorial Reference: A.17. Cambrin Military Cemetery in France.

KEHOE, Patrick Joseph: Rank: C.S.M. Regiment or Service: East Yorkshire Regiment. Unit: 2nd Bn. Date of death: 13 May 1915. Service No: 5603. Born in Baltinglass, Wicklow. Enlisted in Dublin while living in Baltinglass. Died of wounds. Grave or Memorial Reference: I.A.112. Cemetery: Bailleul Communal Cemetery Extension (Nord) in France.

KEHOE/KEOGH, William Patrick: Rank: Private. Regiment or Service: Australian Infantry, A. I. F. Service No: 1390. Unit: 4th Battalion, 2nd reinforcements

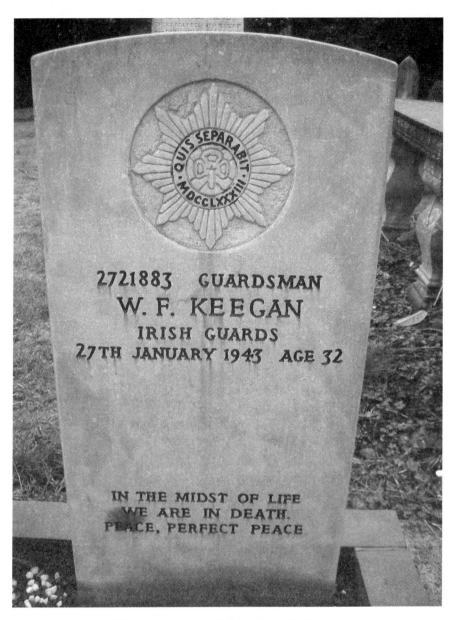

The gravestone of William Francis Keegan.

embarked from Sydney, New South Wales, on board HMAT A48 Seang Bee on 11 February 1915. Born in Wicklow. Enlisted in Liverpool, New South Wales on 20 November 1914 aged 23. Weight: 13st 6lbs, Height: 6'. Complexion: dark. Hair: dark brown. Eyes: blue. Religious denomination: Roman Catholic. Occupation on enlistment: policeman. Next of Kin: Father, John Kehoe, Dunbar, County Wicklow. Date of death: 5 November 1916. Age at death: 25. Wounded in Alexandria, 1 May 1915 by a shell to the thigh and treated in Adelaide hospital. Returned to duty five weeks later. Trained in Salisbury plain, Malta and also in the famous Bull Ring in Etaples in France. Served in Gallipoli from 5 January 1915 in camp Mustapha and afterwards in France. Suffered from Pyrexia in Anzac in Gallipoli and treated in Anzac Hospital. Wounded in action again on 3 November 1916 in France. Removed from the line by 35th Casualty Clearing Station to 27th Ambulance train for treatment. Died of wounds received in action at No 3 Stationary Hospital, Rouen in France. Wounds were gunshot wounds to the right arm, right wrist and right thigh. William's estate was entitled to two pensions one Australian and one French. The French one was awarded to him on 2 November 1917 by the French Government. The death plaque and his medals were sent to his Father. Grave or Memorial Reference: O.I.F.1. Cemetery: St Sever Cemetery Extension, Rouen in France.

KELLY, Alfred: Rank: Private. Regiment or Service: Royal Dublin Fusiliers. Unit: 8th Bn. Date of death: 27 April 1916. Service No: 14266. Born in Bray, Co. Wicklow. Enlisted in Bray. Killed in action. Grave or Memorial Reference: He has no known grave but is listed on Panel 127 to 129 on the Loos Memorial in France.

KELLY, Alfred: Rank: Private. Regiment or Service: Royal Irish Fusiliers. Unit: 1st Bn. Date of death: 26 October 1914. Service No: 7617. Born in Newtownmountkennedy, Co. Wicklow. Enlisted in Wicklow while living in Newtownmountkennedy. Died of wounds. Grave or Memorial Reference: IX.A.42. Cemetery: Cite Bonjean Military Cemetery, Armentieres in France.

KELLY, Edward: Rank: Sergeant. Regiment or Service: North Lancashire Regiment. Unit: 6th Bn. Date of death: 28 May 1916. Service No: 11191. Born in Wicklow. Enlisted in Bolton while living in Wicklow. Died in

Mesopotamia. Grave or Memorial Reference: VII.F.11. Cemetery: Amara War Cemetery in Iraq.

KELLY, James: Rank: Private. Regiment or Service: Royal Dublin Fusiliers. Unit:'D' Company, 9th Bn. Date of death: 9 September 1916. Age at death: 34. Service No: 15132. Born in Newtown, Co. Wicklow. Enlisted in Dublin while living in Kildrain, Co. Wicklow. Died of wounds. Grave or Memorial Reference: Plot 2. Row C. Grave 57. Cemetery: Corbie Communal Cemetery Extension in France.

KELLY, John: Rank: Private. Regiment or Service: Royal Dublin Fusiliers. Unit: 1st Bn. Date of death: 3 September 1916. Age at death: 19. Service No: 5809. Born in Ballyconnell, Co. Wicklow. Enlisted in Naas while living in Tullow, Co. Carlow. Killed in action.
Supplementary information: Son of Daniel and Mary Kelly, of Ballygalduff, Tobinstown, Tullow, Co. Carlow. Grave or Memorial Reference: He has no known grave but is listed on Pier and Face 15A on the Thiepval Memorial in France.

KELLY, John: Rank: Private. Regiment or Service: Irish Guards.

Unit: 1st Bn. Date of death: 13 December 1916. Service No: 8779. Born in Killaveney, Co. Wicklow. Enlisted in Dublin while living in Mangans, Co. Wicklow. Killed in action. Grave or Memorial Reference: VI.J.7. Cemetery: Sailly Saillisel British Cemetery in France.

KELLY, John: Rank: Gunner. Regiment or Service: Royal Garrison Artillery. Unit: 61st Trench Mortar Battery. Date of death: 25 September 1915. Service No: 13141. Born in Bray, Co. Wicklow. Enlisted in Cork. Died of wounds. Grave or Memorial Reference: IV.E.3. Cemetery: Merville Communal Cemetery in France.

KELLY, Kerin Thomas: Rank: Private. Regiment or Service: Royal Dublin Fusiliers. Unit: 9th Bn. Date of death: 7 July 1916 also listed as 5 July 1916. Service No: 24476. Born in Dublin and also listed as born in Blessington. Killed in action in the Battle of the Somme.
Supplementary information: Husband of Mary Mahoney (formerly Kelly), of 9 Camack Villas, Blue Bell, Inchicore, Dublin. Grave or Memorial Reference: F. 2. Cemetery: Bois-Carre Military Cemetery in France.

KELLY, Lawrence Kevin: Rank: Able Seaman. Regiment or Service: Merchant Navy. Unit: SS *Bayano* (Glasgow). Age at death: 22. Date of death: 8 May 1944.

Supplementary information: Son of Patrick and Mary Kelly, of Wicklow. Grave or Memorial Reference: Grave 610. Cemetery: Rathnew Cemetery, Co. Wicklow.

KELLY, Michael: Rank: Private. Regiment or Service: Royal Irish Regiment. Unit: 6th Bn. Date of death: 16 August 1917. Age at death: 32. Service No: 1198. Born in St Mary's, Enniscorthy, Co. Wexford. Enlisted in Enniscorthy while living in Bray, Co. Wicklow. Died of wounds.

Supplementary information: Son of Steven and Margaret Kelly. Grave or Memorial Reference: II.B.14. Cemetery: Brandhoek Military Cemetery in Belgium.

KELLY, Patrick: Rank: Private. Regiment or Service: Royal Irish Fusiliers. Unit: 1st Bn. Date of death: 9 November 1914. Service No: 6303. Born in Bray, Co. Wicklow. Enlisted in Monkstown, Co. Dublin. Killed in action. Grave or Memorial Reference: I.X.N.7. Cemetery: Strand Military Cemetery in Belgium.

KELLY, Patrick: Rank: Private. Regiment or Service: Royal Irish Regiment. Unit: 6th Bn. Date of death: 29 January 1917. Age at death: 23. Service No: 10203. Born in Arklow, Co. Wicklow. Enlisted in Dublin. Killed in action.

Supplementary information: Son of Thomas and Norah Kelly, of 8 Gerald Street, Barrow Street, Dublin. Grave or Memorial Reference: G. 15. Cemetery: Pond Farm Cemetery in Belgium.

KELLY, Patrick: Rank: Private. Regiment or Service: Royal Dublin Fusiliers. Unit: 1st Bn. Date of death: 30 April 1915. Age at death: 22. Service No: 11056. Born in Barndarrig, Co. Wicklow. Enlisted in Dublin while living in Barndarrig. Killed in action.

Supplementary information: Son of Peter and Bridget Kelly, of Kilmurry, Kilbride, Co. Wicklow. Grave or Memorial Reference: He has no known grave but is listed on Panel 190 to 196 on the Helles Memorial in Turkey.

KELLY, Timothy: Rank: Lance Corporal. Regiment or Service: Leinster Regiment. Unit: 6th Bn. He was previously with the Royal Field Artillery where his number was 2926. Date of death: 13 July 1916. Age at death: 40. Service No: 4581. Born in Wicklow. Died in

Salonika.

Supplementary information: Husband of Elizabeth Kelly, of Upper Monkton, Bow, Wicklow. Grave or Memorial Reference: 241. Cemetery: Salonika (Lambet Road) Military Cemetery in Greece.

KELLY, William: Rank: Private. Regiment or Service: Irish Guards. Unit: 1st Bn. Date of death: 3 August 1917. Service No: 11446. Born in Kiltegan, Co. Wicklow. Enlisted in Naas, Co. Kildare while living in Baltinglass, Co. Wicklow. Killed in action. Grave or Memorial Reference: He has no known grave but is listed on Panel 11 and 11 on the Ypres (Menin Gate) Memorial in Belgium.

KELLY, William: Rank: Private. Regiment or Service: Irish Guards. Unit: 1st Bn. Date of death: 15 September 1916. Age at death: 22. Service No: 7306. Born in Bray, Co. Wicklow. Enlisted in Dublin while living in Bray, Co. Wicklow. Killed in action.

Supplementary information: Son of Joseph and Elizabeth Kelly, of 5 Elmgrove Terrace, Duncairn Avenue, Bray. Grave or Memorial Reference: He has no known grave but is listed on Pier and Face 7.D. on the Thiepval Memorial in France.

KENNA, Patrick: Rank: Private. Regiment or Service: Royal Irish Fusiliers. Unit: 8th Bn. Date of death: 9 May 1916. Age at death: 22. Service No: 19997. Born in Bray, Co. Wicklow. Enlisted in Bray. Died of wounds.

Supplementary information: Son of Mrs Mary Kenna, of 3 Casey Cottages, Little Bray. Grave or Memorial Reference: V.C.91. Cemetery: Bethune Town Cemetery in France.

KENNEDY, Charles: Rank: Private. Regiment or Service: Irish Guards. Unit: 1st Bn. Date of death: 28 June 1916. Service No: 7382. Born in Wicklow. Enlisted in Dublin while living in Wicklow. Killed in action. Grave or Memorial Reference: I.Q.10. Cemetery: Essex Farm Cemetery in Belgium.

KENNEDY, Michael: Rank: Private. Regiment or Service: Royal Irish Fusiliers. Unit: 2nd Bn. Date of death: 23 October 1916. Age at death: 20. Service No: 20251. Born in Rathnew, Co. Wicklow. Enlisted in Wicklow while living in Rathnew. Killed in action.

Supplementary information: Son of Mrs Mary Kennedy, of Rathnew. He has no known grave but is listed on Pier and face 16.C. on the Thiepval Memorial in France.

KENNEDY, Patrick: Rank: Gunner. Regiment or Service: Royal Garrison Artillery. Unit, 8th Siege Battery. Date of death: 16 May 1917. Service No: 16886. Born in White Rock, Co. Wicklow. Enlisted in Dublin. Killed in action. Grave or Memorial Reference: II.E.12. Cemetery: Feuchy British Cemetery in France.

KENNY, John: Rank: Seaman. Regiment or Service: Royal Naval Reserve. Unit: HMS *Laurentic*. Age at death: 22. Date of death: 25 January 1917. Service No: 4996A.

Supplementary information: Son of James Kenny, of 32 Fair Green, Arklow. The vessel sank in 1917 with the loss of 354 of its crew when it hit a mine at Fanad Head *en route* to Halifax, Nova Scotia. Some 121 crew members survived. The *Laurentic* was carrying the 1917 equivalent of £5million in gold and a reported £3million in silver coins to pay for arms for the British war effort. Grave or Memorial Reference: South. 3NN. 12 East. Cemetery: Arklow Cemetery, Co. Wicklow.

KENNY, Patrick: Rank: Sailor. Regiment or Service: Mercantile Marine. Unit: SS *Algiers* (London). Date of death: 26 February 1917.

Age at death: 37.

Supplementary information: Son of Thomas and Sarah Kenny, of 15 Tinahack, Arklow, Co. Wicklow. Steamship Algiers was sunk by a German submarine 3 miles south of the Owers light vessel. Eight of the crew died. Grave or Memorial Reference: He has no known grave but is listed on the Tower Hill Memorial UK.

KENNY, Simon: Rank: Lance Corporal. Regiment or Service: South African Infantry. Unit: 2nd Regt. Date of death: 12 April 1917. Age at death: 36. Service No: 8070.

Supplementary information: Son of Martin and Julia Kenny, of Ballyrichard, Arklow, Co. Wicklow. Grave or Memorial Reference: I.A.28. Cemetery: Browns Copse Cemetery in Reoux, France.

KENT, Walter: Rank: Private (Lance Corporal). Regiment or Service: Royal Irish Regiment. Unit: 2nd Bn. Date of death: 4 July 1916. Age at death: 36. Service No: 4898. Born in Duncannon, Co. Wicklow. Enlisted in Carrigtwohill, Co. Cork. Killed in action.

Supplementary information: Son of Mrs Mary Ellen Kent, of Duncannon, New Ross, Co. Waterford. Husband of Alice Kent, of Main Street, Carrigtwohill, Co. Cork. Grave or Memorial

The gravestone of Lawrence Kevin Kelly.

Reference: He has no known grave but is listed on Pier and Face 3.A. on the Thiepval Memorial in France.

KENYON, Patrick: Rank: Private. Regiment or Service: York and Lancaster Regiment. Unit: A Company, 8th Bn. Date of death: 1 July 1916, the first day of the Battle of the Somme. Age at death: 35. Service No: 17029. Born in Bray. Enlisted in Sheffield. Killed in action.
Supplementary information: Son of James Henry Kenyon. Husband of Shirley Augusta Kenyon, of Lower Street, Leeds, Maidstone. Grave or Memorial Reference: IV.C.30. Cemetery in Blighty Valley Cemetery, Authuile Wood in France.

KEOGH, Peter: Rank: Sailor. Regiment or Service: Merchant Navy. Unit: SS *Canford Chine* (Swansea). Age at death: 20. Date of death: 8 February 1941.
Supplementary information: Son of William Keogh, and of Elizabeth Keogh, of Arklow, Co. Wicklow. *Canford Chine* was captured by sunk by German Submarine U35 and sunk with gunfire 5miles off the Spanish coast. U35 was taken to England after the war and broken up in 1920 in Blyth. Grave or Memorial Reference: He has no known grave but is listed on panel 23 on the Tower Hill Memorial, UK.

KEOGH, T.: Rank: Gunner. Regiment or Service: Royal Field Artillery. Date of death: 13 October 1920. Age at death: 35. Service No: 12063.
Supplementary information: Son of the late Timothy Keogh. Husband of Annie Keogh, of Tower View, Glencormac, Bray, Co. Wicklow. Born at Tullow, Co. Carlow. Grave or Memorial Reference: C.A.35. Cemetery: Acton Cemetery UK.

KEOGH/KEHOE, William Patrick: Rank: Private. Regiment or Service: Australian Infantry, A. I. F. Service No: 1390. Unit: 4th Battalion, 2nd reinforcements embarked from Sydney, New South Wales, on board HMAT A48 Seang Bee on 11 February 1915. Born in Wicklow. Enlisted in Liverpool, New South Wales on 20 November 1914 aged 23. Weight: 13 st 6lbs. Height: 6'. Complexion: dark. Hair: dark brown. Eyes: blue. Religious denomination: Roman Catholic. Occupation on enlistment: policeman. Next of kin: father, John Kehoe, Dunbar, Co. Wicklow. Date of death: 5 November 1916. Age at death: 25. Wounded in Alexandria, 1 May 1915 by a shell to the thigh and treated in Adelaide hospital. Returned to duty five weeks later. Trained in Salisbury plain, Malta and also in the famous Bull Ring in Etaples in France. Served in Gallipoli from 5 January 1915 in camp Mustapha and afterwards in France. Suffered from Pyrexia in Anzac in Gallipoli and treated in Anzac Hospital. Wounded in action again on 3 November 1916 in France. Removed from the line by 35th Casualty Clearing Station to 27th Ambulance train for treatment. Died of wounds received in action at No 3 Stationary Hospital, Rouen in France. Wounds were gunshot wounds to the right arm, right wrist and right thigh. Williams estate was entitled to two pensions one Australian and one French. The French one was awarded to him on 2 November 1917 by the French Government. The death plaque and his medals were sent to his Father. Grave or Memorial Reference: O.I.F.1. Cemetery: St. Sever Cemetery Extension, Rouen in France.

KERR, Robert Goodman: Rank: Major, Temporary Major and also listed as Acting Lieutenant Colonel. Regiment or Service: Royal Inniskilling Fusiliers. Unit: 7th Bn attached to the 9th Bn Royal Irish Fusiliers. Date of death: 11 July 1918. Age at death: 28. He won the Military Cross and is listed in the *London Gazette*.

Supplementary information: Husband of Mrs C.J. Kerr, of Hillside, Delgany, Co. Wicklow. Grave or Memorial Reference: II.F.8. Cemetery: Bertenacre Military Cemeteru, Fletre in France.

KEYES/KEYS, Henry William: Rank: Private. Regiment or Service: Royal Inniskilling Fusiliers. Unit: 9th Bn. Date of death: 2 March 1915. Service No: 19357. Born in Delgany, Co. Wicklow. Enlisted in Dublin. Died at home. Age at death: 18.

Supplementary information: Son of George Alexander and Elizabeth Keys, of Beaumont, Delgany, Greystones, Co. Wicklow. Grave or Memorial Reference: Screen Wall. H.531. Cemetery: Belfast City Cemetery UK.

KILBRIDE, Edward: Rank: Private. Regiment or Service: Irish Guards. Unit: 1st Bn. Date of death: 29 October 1914. Service No: 4520. Born in Tomacork, Co. Wicklow. Enlisted in Enniscorthy, Co. Wicklow. Killed in action. Age at death: 24.

Supplementary information: Son of Edward and Mary Kilbride, of Bullingate, Carnew, Co. Wicklow. From and article in the *Echo* newspaper,

Edward Kilbride, Coolmeelagh, Bunclody, formerly in the employment of Mr R W Hall Dare, J P, D L, was killed in action at the front. His father has been notified by the War Office. A number of other Bunclody men, at the front are missing. Martin Brien, Chapel lane, Bunclody, a private in the 18th R I Regiment, brother to Messrs James and Laurence Breen, well known in GAA circles was wounded at the battle of the Aisne and is at present in a hospital in Paris. Amongst those who went down with the "Good Hope" which was sunk by German cruisers in an engagement off the Chilian coast on Sunday, November 1st was Thos O'Leary, Patrick Street, Enniscorthy, a naval reservist who was called up at the outbreak of the war prior to which he was engaged as porter in the Munster and Leinster Bank. O'Leary, who leaves a wife and child was for years a member of the Catholic Working men's Club and of the band and later of the A.O.H.

Grave or Memorial Reference: He has no known grave but is listed on Panel 11 on the Ypres (Menin Gate) Memorial in Belgium.

KILEEN/KILLEEN, Michael Joseph: Rank: Lance Corporal. Regiment or Service: Connaught Rangers. Unit: 6th Bn. Date of death: 31 January 1917. Age at death: 22. Service No: 10551. Born in Bray, Co. Wicklow. Enlisted in Dublin while living in Dublin. Died. Son of Michael Joseph and Julia Killeen, of 30 Cadogan Road, Fairview, Dublin. Twice wounded. Grave or Memorial Reference: V.C.34. Cemetery: Lillers Communal Cemetery, Souchez in France.

KING, Francis Irving: Rank: Private. Regiment or Service: Northumberland Fusiliers. Unit: 9th Bn. Date of death: 23 April 1917. Age at death: 26. Service No: 29/505. Born in Nockbride, Co. Wicklow. Enlisted in Huddersfield. Killed in action.
Supplementary information: Son of William and Maria King, of Ballygarrett, Newtownmountkennedy, Co. Wicklow. Grave or Memorial Reference: XXX. D.1. Cemetery: Cabaret-Rouge British Cemetery, Souchez in France.

KING, Henry Stuart: Rank: Sub-Lieutenant. Regiment or Service: Royal Navy. Unit: HMS *Indefatigable*. Date of death: 31 May 1916. Age at death: 19.

Supplementary information: Son of Francis A.S. and Olivia E. King, of Cliftonville, Bray, Co. Wicklow. During the Battle of Jutland the German Battlecruiser *Van Der Tann* fired 11-inch shells at *Indefatigable*. The first two entered 'X' magazine area and blew out the bottom of the ship and she began sinking by the stern. More 11-inch shells from the *Van Der Tann* destroyed 'A' turret and also blew up the forward magazine and she then sank. There were only two survivors of her crew of 1,017 men. The *Van Der Tann* was scuttled in Scapa flow in June 1919. Grave or Memorial Reference: 10. Grave or Memorial Reference: He has no known grave but is listed on Plymouth Naval Memorial, UK.

KING, William Olenthus: Rank: Sergeant. Regiment or Service: South Lancashire Regiment. Unit: 7th Bn. Date of death: 9 September 1916. Service No: 8561. Born in Arklow, Co. Wicklow. Enlisted in St Helen's in Lancs while living in Boston, Mass. Killed in action. Grave or Memorial Reference: I.H.12. Cemetery: Berksl Cemetery Extension in Belgium.

KINSELLA, J.: Rank: Private. Regiment or Service: Leinster Regiment. Secondary Regiment: Labour Corps. Secondary Unit: transferred. to (363753). Age at death: 41. Date of Death: 16 April 1919. Service No: 4014.

Supplementary information: Husband of Margaret Rinsella, of Shankill, Co. Dublin. Grave or Memorial Reference: B.81.1. Cemetery: Little Bray (St. Peter's) Catholic Cemetery, Wicklow.

KINSELLA, Michael: Rank: Private. Regiment or Service: Irish Guards. Unit: 2nd Bn. Date of death: 13 September 1917. Age at death: 40. Service No: 10558. Born in Greystones, Co. Wicklow. Enlisted in Bray, Co. Wicklow. Died of wounds.

Supplementary information: Son of John and Catherine Kinsella, of Greystones, Co. Wicklow. Grave or Memorial Reference: XI.B.7. Cemetery: Harlebeke New British Cemetery in Belgium.

KINSELLA, Patrick: Rank: Private. Regiment or Service: Royal Irish Fusiliers. Unit: 9th Bn. Formerly he was with the Royal Irish Rifles where his number was 22581. Date of death: 2 October 1918. Service No: 42506. Born in Ferns, Co. Wexford. Enlisted in Glasgow while living in Parkhead in Glasgow. Killed in action. Age at death: 30.

Supplementary information:

Postal rates for tobacco.

Son of John and Mary Kinsella of Ballycooge, Woodenbridge, Co. Wicklow. Husband of Mary Kinsella of 129 Brook Arklow. Co. Wicklow. Grave or Memorial Reference: He has no known grave but is listed on Panel 140 to 141 on the Tyne Cot Memorial in Belgium.

KINSELLA, Patrick: Rank: Private. Regiment or Service: Irish Guards. Unit: 1st Bn. Date of death: 30 September 1916. Age at death: 30. Service No: 8114. Born in Woodenbridge, Co. Wicklow.

Enlisted in Dublin. Killed in action.

Supplementary information: Son of John and Mary Kinsella, of Ballycooge, Woodenbridge, Co. Wicklow. Husband of Mary Kinsella, of 129 Brook, Arklow, Co. Wicklow. Grave or Memorial Reference: He has no known grave but is listed on Panel 140 to 141 on the Tyne Cot Memorial in Belgium.

KIRWIN/KERWIN, Matthew: Rank: Private. Regiment or Service: Irish Guards. Unit: 2nd Bn.

Date of death: 19 May 1916. Service No: 7230. Born in Enniscorthy. Enlisted in Dublin while living in Arklow, Co. Wicklow. Died of wounds. Grave or Memorial Reference: VI.D.42. Cemetery: Lijssenthoek Military Cemetery in Belgium.

KNOX, Francis William White: Rank: Private. Regiment or Service: Royal Inniskilling Fusiliers. Unit: 12th Bn. Date of death: 27 April 1916. Age at death: 37. Service No: 27861. Born in Delgany, Co. Wicklow. Enlisted in Bray while living in Greystones. Died of wounds at home.

Supplementary information: Son of Francis W. White Knox and Mrs A.C. Knox. Born at Kilmannock, Co. Wexford (From the Commonwealth Wargraves Commission). Grave or Memorial Reference: 5. 172. Cemetery: Breandrum Cemetery, Enniskillen, Co. Fermanagh.

L

LAMB, John Thompson: Rank: Sergeant (Pilot). Regiment or Service: Royal Air Force Volunteer Reserve. He was one of the four crewmen from 50 Squadron based in Waddington that lost their way returning from a cancelled raid (Convoy AD730) on Berlin. They flew a Hampden Bomber. Age at death: 20. Date of death: 17 April 1941. Service No: 754628.

Supplementary information: Son of Stanley and Hannah Lamb, of Carlisle. Grave or Memorial Reference: N.E. Corner. Cemetery: Blessington (St Mary) Church of Ireland Churchyard, Co. Wicklow. See page 178.

LAMBERT, William: Rank: Boatswain (Bosun). Regiment or Service: Mercantile Marine Unit: SS *Dowlais* (Cardiff). Age at death: 33. Date of death: 3 December 1917. The SS *Dowlais* was a defensively armed ship and was torpedoed by a German submarine off Cape De Fer in the Atlantic Ocean. There were no survivors of the twenty-six crew members. The ship was based in Cardiff.

Supplementary information: Son of Thomas and Elizabeth Lambert. Husband of Ann Lambert (*née* Loughlin), of 2 Old Chapel Ground, Arklow, Co. Wicklow. Born at Liverpool. Grave or Memorial Reference: He has no known grave but is listed on the Tower Hill Memorial UK.

La NAUZE, George Mansfield: Rank: Lieutenant. Regiment or Service: Royal Irish Rifles. Unit: 1st Bn. Date of Death: 9 May 1915. Age at Death: 23. Killed in Action. Supplementary information from Jimmy Taylor. Born 22 December 1891 at Manor, Highgate, Co. Fermanagh. The son of Thomas Story and Edith Emma (*née* Deering), La Nauze. Educated at Corrig School, Kingstown, Co. Dublin, and the Abbey Grammar School, Tipperary. Father's occupation: 'Private Gentleman'. Applied for a commission in 4th RIR 19 April 1911. Single. Permanent address: Island View, Clifden, Co. Galway. Occupation: none. Height 5'7½". Weight: 132 pounds. Chest: 33½–36". He entered 4th RIR as a 2/Lt. 20 May 1911, being promoted to

The gravestone of John Thompson Lamb.

Lt., 13 February 1913. Letter from OC 4th RIR, Newtownards, 29 July 1913, to Staff Capt. No. 11 District, advised that La Nauze had secured a position in Malaya and wanted to try it before severing connections with the 4th Bn. When war broke out he was employed in the Malay States but, returning as soon as possible, was sent to Holywood, near Belfast, to rejoin his battalion on 31 October 1914, remaining there at duty until 16 March 1915. He then proceeded to France, joining 1st RIR 20 March 1915. Killed in action 9 May 1915. He was first wounded, and while waiting for a stretcher to be taken to a hospital, a shell burst, killing him instantly. He had taken command of his company a short time previously. The WO telegram to his mother, 13 May, stated wounded, degree not known. Another telegram to her, 4 June, revised this to wounded and missing. There is a WO form on the file and seems to be a direct form of enquiry to the German Government, undated, asking if La Nauze was a POW. A German ink-stamp on the rear, and a stamped reply stated he was not on any POW list. The WO wrote to his mother on 6 May 1916, asking if she has had any further news; if not then death on or since 9 May 1915 would have to be presumed for official purposes. She replied saying that she had news from a Major Kelets who had spoken to George on the battlefield after he had been wounded but had been unable to have him moved to safety. Shortly thereafter a shell burst nearby and the Major presumed him dead. A statement by 6657 Cpl Carstairs, 14 November 1915, on leave at Boulogne, reported that La Nauze was wounded in the German front line trench and must have been taken prisoner or died after the battalion was driven back. Carstairs was in same platoon and was La Nauze's observer. Death accepted for official purposes 16 May 1916. A WO letter to C-in-C., Forces in Ireland, 10 November 1916, noted that George joined for duty, 2 November 1914, from the Malay Federated States, and enquired if he had permission to reside abroad, and if so, under what authority. The Irish Command forwarded the original 1913 paperwork that approved the move abroad, 11 October 1916.

Irish Life 14 December 1917:

Inspector C.D. La Nauze of the Royal North West Mounted Police, Canada, has just returned from a long patrol of two and a half years in the Arctic in search of the murderers of two

French priests who were murdered in 1913 by the Eskimos. Inspector La Nauze and his men were successful ... He is the only surviving son of Mrs G. Scott Mansfield of Hollywood, Glenealy, Co. Wicklow. His two brothers were killed in action in France in May, 1915.

His sister, A. De La Nauze served with the VAD. The RUR Museum holds all three sets of medals. File ref: WO339/59630 132968. Grave or Memorial Reference: He has no known grave but is listed on Panel 9 on Ploegsteert Memorial in Belgium.

LANEGAN, William: Rank: Private. Regiment or Service: Irish Guards. Unit: 1st Bn. Date of death: 18 September 1916. Age at death: 24. Service No: 3900. Born in Baltinglass, Co. Wicklow. Enlisted in Dublin. Died of wounds.

Supplementary information: Son of Elizabeth Lanegan, of 150 James's Street, Dublin. Grave or Memorial Reference: II.E.69. Cemetery: La Neuville British Cemetery, Corbie in France.

LANGRILL, John: Rank: Private. Regiment or Service: Connaught Rangers. Unit: 5th Bn. Date of death: 31 March 1915. Service No:

3861. Born in Ballinastone, Co. Wicklow. Enlisted in Naas while living in Stratford-on-Slaney, Co. Wicklow. Died at home.

Supplementary information: Husband of J. Fluskey (formerly Langrill), of Ballingcrow, Stratford-on-Slaney, Co. Wicklow. Grave or Memorial Reference: 1211. Cemetery: The Curragh Military Cemetery, Co. Kildare.

LANGTON, John: Rank: Rifleman. Regiment or Service: Kings Royal Rifle Corps. Unit: 17th Bn. Date of death: 24 October 1917. Service No: R/30433. Born in Bray, Co. Wicklow. Enlisted in Holloway in Middlesex while living in Bray. Died of wounds. Grave or Memorial Reference: XXII.A.11. Cemetery: Lijssenthoek Military Cemetery in Belgium.

LANGTON, Patrick Joseph: Rank: Private. Regiment or Service: King's Own Scottish Borderers. Unit: 1st Bn. He was previously with the Fife and Forfar Yeomanry where his number was 3256. Date of death: 11 April 1918. Age at death: 33. Service No: 41037. Born in Bray, Co. Wicklow. Enlisted in Flixton Park, Suffolk while living in Lambeth. Killed in action.

Supplementary information: Son of the late Martin and Elizabeth

Langton, of Bray. He has no known grave but is listed on Panel 5 on Ploegsteert Memorial in Belgium.

LAWLESS, James: Rank: Private. Regiment or Service: Royal Dublin Fusiliers. Unit: 2nd Bn. Date of death: 23 October 1916. Age at death: 26. Service No: 20380. Born in Greystones, Co. Wicklow. Enlisted in Greystones. Killed in action.

Supplementary information: Son of Andrew and Mary Lawless, of Blacklion, Greystones, Co. Wicklow. From a snippet in a Wicklow newspaper, 'Private James Lawless, Dublin Fusiliers, is reported missing since October. He is a son of Mrs Lawless, Coolgad, Greystones.' Grave or Memorial Reference: He has no known grave but is listed on Pier and Face 16.C. on the Thiepval Memorial in France.

LAWLESS, John: Rank: Private. Regiment or Service: Royal Dublin Fusiliers. Date of death: 1918. Died of wounds in Ballymurrin, Co. Wicklow. Born in Ballymurrin, Co. Wicklow. They are not in *Soldiers who Died in the Great War* nor are they in the Commonwealth Wargraves Commission Database. The above information is from Ireland's Memorial Records held in WWI Memorial Gardens in Islandbridge in Dublin.

LAWLESS, Thomas: Rank: Private. Regiment or Service: Royal Dublin Fusiliers. Date of death: 1918. Died of wounds in Ballymurrin, Co. Wicklow. Born in Ballymurrin, Co. Wicklow. No further information is available John and Thomas Lawless. They are not in *Soldiers Died in the Great War* nor are they in the Commonwealth Wargraves Commission Database. The above information is from Ireland's Memorial Records held in WWI Memorial Gardens in Islandbridge in Dublin.

LAWLESS, Peter: Rank: Private. Regiment or Service: Royal Dublin Fusiliers. Unit: 9th Bn. Date of death: 9 September 1916. Age at death: 20. Service No: 25013. Born in Wicklow. Enlisted in Wicklow while living in Kilbride, Co. Wicklow. Killed in action.

Supplementary information: Son of Michael Lawless, of Ballymurrin, Co. Wicklow. Grave or Memorial Reference: He has no known grave but is listed on Pier and Face 16C on the Thiepval Memorial in France.

LAWRENCE, Henry: Rank: Private. Regiment or Service: Machine Gun Corps. Unit:

Infantry. He was previously with the Royal Irish Regiment where his number was 8543. Date of death: 28 October 1916. Age at death: 22. Service No: 43312. Born in Bray, Co. Wicklow. Enlisted in Dublin while living in Bray. Killed in action.

Supplementary information: Son of Mrs Lawrence, of Wingfield, Bray, Co. Wicklow. He has no known grave but is listed on Pier and Face 5.C. and 12.C. on the Thiepval Memorial in France.

LAWRENCE, William: Rank: Private. Regiment or Service: Royal Dublin Fusiliers. Unit: 8th Bn. Date of death: 27 April 1916. Age at death: 28. Service No: 24563. Born in Hacketstown, Co. Carlow. Enlisted in Dublin while living in Moyne, Co. Wicklow. Killed in action.

Supplementary information: Son of Thomas Lawrence, of Slieverue, Ballinglen, Co. Wicklow. He has no known grave but is listed on Panel 127 to 129 on the Loos Memorial in France.

LAWRENSON, Reginald Robert: Rank: Shown as Lieutenant Colonel, Major and Temporary Acting Lieutenant Colonel. Regiment or Service: West India Regiment. Secondary Regiment: Highland Light Infantry. Secondary Unit: attd. 18th Bn. Died of Wounds. Age at death: 46. Date of death: 27 April 1918. Awards: DSO and Bar.

Supplementary information: Son of Ralph and Clarinda Lawrenson. Husband of Jessie Lawrenson, of Hillhead, Glasgow. Born at Shillelagh, Co. Wicklow. Educated at Trinity College, Dublin, and Royal Military College, Sandhurst. Grave or Memorial Reference: XXVIII.K.8. Cemetery: Etaples Military Cemetery in France. He is also commemorated on St Thomas's Roll of Honour in St Thomas Church, Cathal Brugha Street, Dublin.

LEDWIDGE, John: Rank: Rifleman. Regiment or Service: Royal Irish Rifles. Unit: 'D' Coy. 2nd Bn. Date of death: 26 November 1915. Age at death: 22. Service No: 6609. Died of Wounds. Born in Bray. Enlisted in Dublin.

Supplementary information: Son of Mrs Mary Ledwidge, of 1 Hudson's Terrace, Bray, Co. Wicklow. Grave or Memorial Reference: I.E.42. Cemetery: Bailleul Communal Cemetery Extension (Nord) in France.

LEE, Patrick: Rank: Private. Regiment or Service: Kings Liverpool Regiment. Unit: 18th Bn.

Date of death: 23 September 1917. Service No: 34538. Born in Kildare. Enlisted in Seaforth in Lancashire while living in Tankardstown, Co. Wicklow. Died of wounds. Grave or Memorial Reference: I.B.16. Cemetery: Outtersteene Communal Cemetery Extension, Bailleul in France.

LEE, Robert: Rank: Sergeant. Regiment or Service: Royal Irish Rifles. Unit; 2nd Bn. Date of Death: 27 October 1914. Service No: 9111. Born: 12 July 1888 in Wicklow. Enlisted in Lisburn, Co Down on 11 August 1908. Served in the S.R. and 3rd R.I.R. Killed in Action. Extract from the war diary from 27 October 1914 Neuve Chapelle. See page 184.

The trenches to the left of A&C Coys being reoccupied by our own troops, the enemy about 7am got round on left flank and rear, after these two Coy had suffered very severely from shrapnel, howitzer and rifle fire and Capt Dixon had sent repeated ... for support. He was obilged to ... these 2 Coys ... the village of Neuve Chapelle (250 yards in rear) to prevent the enemy getting round in the rear of the Brigade.

Only two officers and about forty-six NCOs and men succeeded in getting back out of a total of five officers and about 250 NCOs and men. Capt Davis being killed, Lieut Mulcamy-Morgan wounded and missing and Jonsson missing, all these were Special Reserve Officers. The fighting strength of the Battalion was under 200. The Batt that evening went into Billets at Richebourg St Vaast. Capts Drought, Jonsson, Davis and Lieut Eldred Inniskilling Fusiliers joined the Battalion.

Supplementary information: Son of Sergeant Joseph Lee, Royal Inniskilling Fusiliers and Annie Lee (*née* McGee). He has no known grave but is listed on Panels 42 and 43 on the Le Touret Memorial in France.

LEGGETT, Robert: Rank: Private. Regiment or Service: Irish Guards. Unit: 2nd Bn. Date of death: 31 July 1917. Service No: 10804. Born in Crosspatrick, Co. Wicklow. Enlisted in Tinahely. Died of wounds. Grave or Memorial Reference: I.H.32. Dozingham Military Cemetery in Belgium.

LEMATHY, William: Rank: Private. Regiment or Service: Royal Dublin Fusiliers. Unit: 2nd Bn. Date of death: 23 October 1916. Age at death: 23. Service No: 8640. Born in Ashford, Co. Wicklow. Enlisted in Dublin while living in Wicklow. Killed in action.

Supplementary information: Son of John and Jane Lemathy (*née* Falkner), of 44 Capel Street, Dublin. Grave or Memorial Reference: He has no known grave but is listed on Pier and Face 16.C. on the Thiepval Memorial in France.

LENNON, Daniel: Rank: Private. Regiment or Service: Irish Guards. Unit: 2nd Bn. Date of death: 31 July 1917. Age at death: 37. Service No: 8331. Born in Dunlavin, Co. Wicklow. Enlisted in Naas, Co. Kildare while living in Bow, Middlesex. Killed in action.

Supplementary information: Son of James and Mary Lennon, of Dunlavin, Co. Wicklow. Grave or Memorial Reference: I.B.4. Cemetery: Artillery Wood Cemetery in Belgium.

LEONARD, Ronald George William: Rank: Private. Regiment or Service: Royal Berkshire Regiment Unit: 1st/4th Bn. Age at

death: 21. Date of death: 11 April 1916. Service No: 3058.

Supplementary information: Son of Stuart and Mary Leonard, of Baronstown, Grangecon, Co. Wicklow. Enlisted in reading. Died of Wounds. Grave or Memorial Reference: I.C.5. Cemetery: Hebuterne Military Cemetery in France.

LEONARD, William: Rank: Private. Regiment or Service: Irish Guards. Unit: 2nd Bn. Date of death: 27 June 1917. Age at death: 26. Service No: 9390. Died of Wounds. Born in Manor Kilbride, Co. Dublin. Enlisted in Kingstown, Co. Dublin.

Supplementary information: Son of Christopher and Alice Leonard, of High Street, Wicklow. Husband of Bridget Leonard, of Upper Cullen, Kilbride, Wicklow. Grave or Memorial Reference: II.E.22. Cemetery: Mendingham Military Cemetery in Belgium.

Robert Lee.

LEWIS, George: Rank: Private. Regiment or Service: Irish Guards. Unit: 2nd Bn. Date of death: 15 September 1916. Age at death: 23. Service No: 8313. Born in Wicklow. Enlisted in Dublin. Killed in action.

Supplementary information: Son of George and Elizabeth Lewis, of 7 Annesley Square, North Strand, Dublin. He has no known grave but is listed on Pier and Face 7.D. on the Thiepval Memorial in France.

LINDE, Henry Eyre: Rank: Second Lieutenant. Regiment or Service: Royal Inniskilling Fusiliers. Unit: 7th Bn. Age at death: 23. Date of death: 24 June 1917. Died of Wounds.

Supplementary information: Son of Mrs Florence Jebb Linde, of Hillside, Delgany, Co. Wicklow. Grave or Memorial Reference: XII.B.6. Cemetery: La Laiterie Military Cemetery in Belgium.

LISNEY, Leslie Vernon: Rank: Lieutenant. Regiment or Service: Royal Irish Fusiliers. Secondary Regiment: North Staffordshire Regiment. Age at death: 27. Date of death: 16 July 1943. Service No: 153422.

Supplementary information: Son of Harry and Amy Lisney, of Bray, Co. Wicklow. Amy Florence Elizabeth Wells. Born: 13 September 1880 in Ireland. Date of death: 27 January 1961 at Bray.

LIVINGSTONE, George: Rank: Lance Corporal. Regiment or Service: Royal Irish Rifles. Unit: 8th Bn. Date of death: 2 July 1916. Age at death: 28. Service No: 15164. Born in Donnybrook, Co. Dublin. Enlistd in Belfast while living in Ashford, Co. Wicklow. Killed in action.

Supplementary information: Son of Frank and Ellen Livingstone. Grave or Memorial Reference: II.C.16. Cemetery: Cayeux Military in France.

LOVE, James Patrick: Rank: Rifleman. Regiment or Service: New Zealand Rifle Brigade. Unit: 4th Bn. Date of death: 23 November Service No: 41192. Killed in action. Age at death: 32.

Supplementary information: Son of Michael and Bridget Agnes Love of 16 Chief Street, Belfast. Born at Rathdangan, Wicklow. Information taken from the Nominal Ross of the New Zealand Expeditionary Force. First known rank: Rifleman. Occupation before enlistment: Bushman. Next of kin: Mrs M. Love. Body on Embarkation: New Zealand Rifle Brigade. Embarkation Unit: Reinforcements H Company.

Of the four Lynham brothers that went to war only three returned.

Embarkation Date: 16 February 1917. Place of Embarkation: Wellington, New Zealand. Transport: HMNZT 78. Vessel: *Navua*. Destination: Devonport, England. Nominal Roll Number: 55. Page on Nominal Roll: 33. He has no known grave but is listed on the Special Memorial IX.AA.12. Cemetery: Buttes New British Cemetery , Polygon Wood in Belgium.

LOVE, Thomas: Rank: Lance Corporal. Regiment or Service: Irish Guards. Unit: 1st Bn. Date of death: 8 October 1915. Service No: 6209. Born in Dublin. While living in Tathdangan, Co. Wicklow. Killed in action. Grave or Memorial Reference: I.F.14. Cemetery: St Mary's A.D.S. Cemetery, Haisnes in France.

LOVEROCK, Menyn Coote: Rank: Private. Regiment or Service: South African Infantry.

Unit: 3rd Regt. Date of death: 19 July 1916. Age at death: 41. Service No: 983.

Supplementary information: Son of Mrs M.B. Loverock, of Church Hill, Wicklow. Native of Finnea, Granard, Co. Longford. Grave or Memorial Reference: II.I.8. Cemetery: Delville Wood Cemetery, Longueval in France.

LOWE, Christopher: Rank: Rifleman. Regiment or Service: Royal Irish Rifles. Unit: 7th Bn. Date of death: 7 June 1917. Age at death: 22. Service No: 6674. Born in Rathdrum, Co. Wicklow. Enlisted in Dublin while living in Rathdrum, Co. Wicklow. Killed in action.

Supplementary information: Son of Daniel and Jane Lowe, of Rathdrum, Co. Wicklow. Grave or Memorial Reference: A.25. Cemetery: Irish House Cemetery in Belgium.

LOWE, Frank: Rank: Private. Regiment or Service: Household Cavalry and Cavalry of the Line. Unit: 4th Dragoon Guards (Royal Irish), 'C' Sqdn. Date of death: 10 May 1915. Age at death: 28. Service No: 3966. Born in Hertford City, Connecticut, U.S.A. Enlisted in Dublin while living in Rathdrum, Co. Wicklow. Killed in action.

Supplementary information: Son of Daniel Lowe, of Rathdrum. Grave or Memorial Reference: E.31. Cemetery: Potijze Chateau Lawn Cemetery in Belgium.

LYNCH, Patrick: Rank: Private. Regiment or Service: Royal Army Service Corps. Unit, 615th M.T. Company. Date of death: 16 May 1918. Age at death: 44. Service No: M/279006. Born in Mount Kennedy, Wicklow. Enlisted in Dublin while living in Foxrock, Co. Dublin. Died at home.

Supplementary information: Husband of Mary Teresa Lynch of 11 Brighton Cottages, Foxrock Co. Dublin. Grave or Memorial Reference: W.U.28. Cemetery: Deans Grange Cemetery in Dublin.

LYNHAM, Allan: Rank: Private. Regiment or Service: Royal Dublin Fusiliers. Unit: 2nd Bn. Date of death: 23 October 1916. Age at death: 20. Service No: 21135. Born in Rathdrum, Co. Wicklow. Enlisted in Dublin while living in Rathdrum. Killed in action.

Supplementary information: Son of Isaac Thomas and Marian Hannah Lynham, of Brewery House, Rathdrum. He has no known grave but is listed on Pier and Face 16C on the Thiepval Memorial in France.

M

MACMAHON, Herbert Henry: Rank: Lance Corporal. Regiment or Service: Royal Dublin Fusiliers. Unit: 10th Service Battalion. Date of death: 13 November 1916. Service No: 26424. Born in Bray, Co. Wicklow. Enlisted in Belfast while living in Hollyrood, Co. Down. Killed in action.

Supplementary information from De Ruvigny's Roll of Honour: Second Son of Revd Henry Herbert MacMahon, Methodist Minister of Dromore, Co. Down by his wife Emily, daughter of the late Theodore Cronhelm of Dublin, Solicitor. Born in Bray, 3 February 1892. Educated in Wesley College and Trinity College Dublin where he graduated with a B.A. in April 1915, being subsequently an accepted candidate for the Methodist Ministry and a Divinity Student at the Methodist College Belfast, where he was reading for his B.D. degree. Enlisted in the Royal Dublin Fusiliers in March 1916; served with the Expeditionary Force in France and Flanders from August and was killed in action at the battle of the Ancre 13 November following, while gallantly making an attack on the enemy trenches. Grave or Memorial Reference: He has no known grave but is listed on Pier and Face 16.C. on the Thiepval Memorial in France.

MADDEN, John: Rank: Rifleman. Regiment or Service: Royal Irish Rifles. Unit: 2nd Bn. Date of death: 27 October 1914. Age at death: 24. Service No: 7902. Born in Dublin. Enlisted in Dublin while living in Bray, Co. Wicklow. Killed in action.

Supplementary information: Son of Mrs Bridget Madden, of 42 Portugal Street, Glasgow. Extract from the war diary for this day; 27 October 1914 Neuve Chapelle,

The trenches to the left of A&C Coys being reoccupied by our own troops, the enemy about 7am got round on left flank and rear, after these two Coy had suffered very severe ... from shrapnel, howitzer and rifle fire and Capt Dixon had sent repeated ... for support. He was obilged to ... these 2 Coys ... the village of Neuve Chapelle (250 yards in rear) to prevent

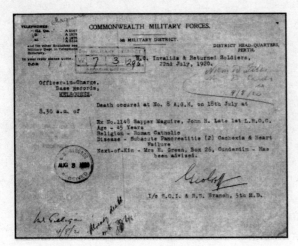

Death announcement of
John Henry Maguire.

the enemy getting round in the rear of the Brigade. Only 2 officers and about 46 NCOs & men succeeded in getting back out of a total of 5 officers and about 250 NCOs & men. Capt Davis being killed, Lieut Mulcamy-Morgan wounded & missing and … Jonsson missing, all these were Special Reserve Officers. The fighting strength of the Batt was under 200. The Batt that evening went into Billets at Richebourg St. Vaast. Capts Drought, Jonsson, Davis and Lieut Eldred Inniskilling Fusiliers joined the Batt.

Grave or Memorial Reference: He has no known grave but is listed on Panels 42 and 43 on the Le Touret Memorial in France.

MAGUIRE / McGUIRE, John: Rank: Private. Regiment or Service: Black Watch (Royal Highlanders. Unit: 8th (Service) Bn. Age at death: 23. Date of Death: 12 May 1916. Service no: S/4182. Born in Wicklow. Enlisted in Dunfermline, Fifeshirewhile. Killed in action.

Supplementary information: Son of John McGuire; husband of Elizabeth McGuire, of 2 Dundonald Terrace, Low Valleyfield, Newmills, Dunfermline. Native of Ireland. Grave or Memorial Reference: I.G.3. Cemetery, Rifle House Cemetery in Belgium.

MAGUIRE, John Henry: Rank: Sapper. Regiment or Service: Australian Engineers, A.I.F. Unit: 16th Battalion, 8th Reinforcement. Date of death: 18 July 1920. Service No: (there were three) 1148, W1385A and 109. Born in Wicklow. Transferred to the Tunnelling Corps with the Australian

Engineers as a Sapper. Embarked from Adelaide, South Australia on board RMS *Morea* on 26 August 1915 and from Freemantle, Western Australia on board HMAT A68 *Anchises* on 2 September 1915. Discharged from service 'Debility following Pleurisy aggrevated by service' with good conduct on 15 August 1917. Re-enlisted on 19 October 1917 in Freemantle in while living in Tammin, W.A. Occupation on enlistment: farmer. Age: 42. Height: 5'10". Hair: dark. Eyes: brown. Complexion: dark. Religious denomination:Church of England. (Death certificate says Roman Catholic). Enlisted into the Railway Corps at Blackberry Hill on 22 November 1917. Joined the Railway Operating Company in France on 28 March 1918. Transferred to Permanent Staff at the general base depot 8 September 1918 and then to the HQ Coy on 28 October 1918. Died in No 8 Australian General Hospital on 18 July 1920 at 8.30am. Age at death: 45. Cause of death was Subacute Pancreatitis, Cachexia and heart failure. His next of kin was listed as Mrs H. Green, Box 26, Cunderdin.

Supplementary information: There is a letter in his records from a lady he listed as his friend. He lived with this lady and her husband and he wanted them to be notified should anything happen to him.

27-6-21

To the Officer in Charge, Base records, Vic Barracks, Melb.

P. S. You will note I am no relative just a friend of the late John H Maguire.

Dear Sir.

Re; the late 1148 Sapper J. H. Maguire, Bly(?) Unity.

I do not know of any living relative of the above late soldier. He and my husband were close friends for the past 11 or 12 years and during that time he had not been in touch with any relative to our knowledge. I know his parents and Grandparents are dead for years (they having died in Ireland). He always made his home with us and when he returned from the front he was 5 months with us. Then went to Perth to get instructed in Intense Culture he having made up his mind to try potato and onion growing in the Collie district and it was from the Collie hospital he was sent to the base hospital at Freemantle where he died after being operated on. He got them to wire to me but did not get it in time to see him alive, as we live 15 miles out from Cunderdin(?) and over 100 miles from Perth. So poor fellow was just buried as my husband got to Freemantle. He made his will in my favour when going to the war but I did not collect a penny. He told them at the base hospital I was his next of kin and the four articles of clothing he had with him was handed over to my husband but his military coat and soldiers clothes were not to be found. I went to the curator of Interstate Estates to see if I could draw the sum of £11 in the deceased soldiers name as I had all his papers and bank book give to me from the base and they kept all his papers including his discharge and told me I could claim nothing as there was no will made. He probably expected us down to see him and fix things up but they told me at the Curators office that the will he made on going to the front was no good to me so I did not bother any further. He had his gratuity paper filled in but not sent in. I did not know how he was off for money when in Collie Hospital, so sent him £1 in case he required anything but that letter was not among his things when I got there.

So now I have given you all the information I can I am yours faithfully.

M. A. Green.

As far as one can tell from his records his medals were not sent to anyone and his pension was not claimed. Grave or Memorial Reference: R.C.CC.619.

Cemetery: Freemantle Cemetery. Australia.

MAHON, Patrick: Rank: Private. Regiment or Service: Royal Dublin Fusiliers. Unit: 2nd Bn. Date of death: 31 July 1915. Service No: 8754. Born in Wicklow. Enlisted in Dublin while living in Kildare. Died. Grave or Memorial Reference: I.B.9. Cemetery, Bois Guillaume Communal Cemetery in France.

MAINEY, Gerard: Rank: Able Seaman. Regiment or Service: Royal Navy. Unit: HMS. *Mahratta*. Age at death: 41. Date of death: 25 February 1944. Service No: D-JX 126431.

Supplementary information: Son of James and Elizabeth Mainey, of Seaforth, Lancashire. Husband of Cathrine Mary Mainey, of Arklow, Co. Wicklow. The Distroyer HMS *Mahratta* was sunk by German Submarine U990. She exploded and sank within minutes. The ship was involved in Operation 'Gearbox IV' which was to re supply the Spitzbergen Garrison. Only 16 of the 236 crew could be saved from the freezing waters. Grave or Memorial Reference: He has no known grave but is listed on Panel 87, Column 1. Grave or Memorial Reference: Panel 87, Column 1 on the Plymouth Naval Memorial, UK.

MALLEN, William James: Rank: Second Lieutenant (TP). Regiment or Service: Royal Dublin Fusiliers. Unit: 11th Bn. attd. 8th Bn. Date of death: 16 August 1917. Age at death: 18. Killed in action.

Supplementary information: Son of John and Margaret Mallen, of Grangecon, Co. Wicklow. Grave or Memorial Reference: He has no known grave but is listed on Panel 144 to 145 on the Tyne Cot Memorial in Belgium.

MALONE, Patrick: Rank: Private. Regiment or Service: Leinster Regiment. Unit: 2nd Bn. Date of death: 29 March 1916. Age at death: 41. Service No: 350. Born in Wicklow. Enlisted in Inverkeithing. Killed in action.

Supplementary information: Son of Mary Byrne (formerly Malone), of Pound Street, Wicklow, and the late Thomas Malone. Grave or Memorial Reference: III.A. 3. Cemetery: Berks Cemetery Extension in Belgium.

MALONE, Thomas: Rank: Private. Regiment or Service: Machine Gun Corps (Infantry). Formerly he was with the Leinster Regiment where his number was 3955. Unit: 15th Bn. Date of death: 24 March 1918. Age at death: 39. Service No: 53681.

Supplementary information: Son

of the late John and Margaret Malone. Husband of Bridget Malone, of Main Street, Baltinglass, Co. Wicklow. Grave or Memorial Reference: He has no known grave but is listed in Bay 10 on the Arras Memorial in France.

MANGAN, Francis: Rank: Sapper. Regiment or Service: Corps of Royal Engineers. Unit: 56th Field Company (Royal Engineers). Date of death: 16 January 1915. Service No: 22503. Born in Arklow, Co. Wicklow. Enlisted in Manchester while living in Bagenalstown, Co. Carlow. Killed in action. Grave or Memorial Reference: Enclosure No. 2 IV.B.4. Cemetery, Bedford House Cemetery in Belgium.

MANIFOLD, William: Rank: Fireman and Trimmer. Regiment or Service: Merchant Navy. Unit: SS *Sulaco* (Liverpool). Age at death: 54. Date of death: 19 October 1940.

Supplementary information: Son of William and Jane Manifold. Husband of Mary Manifold, of Arklow, Co. Wicklow. Steamship *Sulaco* was torpedoed and sunk by German Submarine U124, 360 miles west by south of Rockall. There was only one survivor from the 66 crew and that was the cook James Thompson Harvey. The Submarine U124 was sunk by depth

John Manley.

Steamship *Sulaco*.

charges laid down by a British Sloop and a Corvette on 2 March 1943 west of Oporto. All hands lost. William has no known grave but is listed on panel 104 on the Tower Hill Memorial, UK.

MANLEY, John: Rank: Private. Regiment or Service: Royal Dublin Fusiliers. Unit: 1st Bn. Date of death: 16 August 1916. Age at death: 29. Service No: 11054. Born in Bray, Co. Wicklow. Enlisted in Bray. Killed in action. Son of Mrs C. Manley, of 36 St Kevin's Square, Bray. Grave or Memorial Reference: III.H.1. Cemetery: White House Cemetery, St Jean-Les-Ypres in Belgium.

MANLEY, Herbert John: Rank: Gunner. First Rank; Driver. Regiment or Service: New Zealand Field Artillery. Date of death: 2 May 1915. Service No: 2/330. Born in Rathdrum. Enlisted while living in 33 Daniel Street, Wellington. Killed in action in Gallipoli.

Supplementary information: Next of kin: Mrs M. Manley (mother), 33 Daniel Street, Wellington, New Zealand. Embarked with the main body of troops from

Wellington, New Zealand on the ship Limerick or Arawa bound for Suez, Egypt on 16 October 1914. He is mentioned in Volume 1, page 480 in the *Nominal Rolls of New Zealand Expeditionary Force*. Grave or Memorial Reference: 72. From De Ruvigny's Roll of Honour. Son of the late John Manley, of Dundrum, Co. Wicklow for over thiry years Relieving Officer under Rathdrum Board of Guardians (who died 11 December 1910), by his wife, Maria, daughter of Arch Manning Greenane. Born Rathdrum, Co. Wicklow, 20 June 1892.' Educated: Rathdrum High School; went to New Zealand with his mother and brothers and sisters after his father's death in 1910, and after the outbreak of war joined the Expeditionary Force, 2 October 1914, and was killed instantaneously in action at Gallipoli, 2 May 1915, being shot through the heart. He was buried in a gully near the sea, close to the spot where he fell, and a wooden cross was erected by his comrades. Grave or Memorial Reference: He has no known grave but is listed on the Lone Pine Memorial, Turkey.

MARA, Edward: Rank: Private. Regiment or Service: Labour Corps. Unit: 1st Bn. He was previously with the Royal Dublin Fusiliers where his number was 20279. Date of death: 2 March 1918. Service No: 119034. Born in Rathnew, Co. Wicklow. Enlisted in Wicklow while living in Rathnew, Co. Wicklow. From the 'Abergele and Pensarn Visitor' March 1918,

Early on Saturday morning the body of a soldier on the Denbeighshire side of the Clwyd Bridge. From his disc and documents found on the body its was ascertained that he was Pte Edward Mara, attached to the Labour Company in France. His pass showed that he left France on Friday and was on his way to Rathlow [sic] in Ireland. He had evidently fallen out of the Hollyhead express during the night. At the inquest held on Monday, P. C. Manuel Davies said he examined the body and found a deep incised wound on the side of the head, and the left hip and right arm were broken. The identification disc on the deceased gave his name as Edward Mara, and his paybook showed that he attested on July 27th, 1915, at Dublin in the Royal Dublin Fusiliers, but was now attached to a Labour Company of the Royal Flying Coprs. His pass was from France to Rathlow, Ireland. There were several Treasury and French notes in the clothes of the deceased. The jury returned a

The gravestone of Edward Mara.

verdict of death through misadventure, and asked the Coroner to convey their sympathy to the relatives.

Grave or Memorial Reference: R.C. ground 4. I. 1103. Cemetery, Rathnew Cemetery, Wicklow.

MARTIN, Christopher: Rank: Private. Regiment or Service: Irish Guards. Unit: 1st Bn. Date of death: 27 August 1918. Age at death: 19. Service No: 11782. Born in Ashford, Co. Wicklow. Enlisted in Dublin while living in Newcastle, Co. Wicklow. Killed in action.
Supplementary information: Son of Arthur and Margaret Martin, of Ballyvolan, Newcastle. Grave or Memorial Reference: IV.D.12. Cemetery: Mory Abbey Military Cemetery, Mory in France.

MASON, Henry: Rank: Private. Regiment or Service: Canadian Infantry (Central Ontario Regiment). Unit: 4th Bn. Date of death: 8 October 1916. Age at death: 32. Service No: 406572. He won the Military Medal and is listed in the *London Gazette.* Born 16 January 1886 in Roundwood, Co. Wicklow. Enlisted 14 April 1915 in Hamilton. Occupation on enlistment: labourer. Height: 5'8½". Complexion: fair. Eyes: blue. Hair: black. Religion: Roman Catholic.

Next of kin listed as Patrick Mason (Father) Aughrim, Co. Wicklow.
Supplementary information: Son of Patrick and Mary Mason, of Aughrim. Grave or Memorial Reference: He has no known grave but is listed on the Vimy Memorial in France.

MASSY-MILES, Harry Godfrey: Rank: Captain. Regiment or Service: Royal Army Medical Corps. Secondary Regiment: London Regiment (Post Office Rifles). Secondary Unit: attd. 1st/8th Bn. Age at death: 32. Date of death: 26 April 1918. Died of wounds in 8th General Hospital, Rouen in France. Awards: Military Cross.
Supplementary information: Son of the Revd Joseph Henry and Adelaide Mary Miles. Husband of Charlotte Elizabeth J. Massy-Miles, of Meath Convalescent Home, Dublin Road, Bray, Co. Wicklow. Born in Dublin. T/Capt. Harry Godfrey Massy-Miles R.A.M.C. *London Gazzette* 26 July 1918 (edn 30813).

For conspicuos gallantry and devotion during several days of severe fighting, when he kept in close touch with the battalion, working unceasingly, without rest during the whole period, dressing the wounded including the French. He showed great initiative in establishing forward R.A.P.'s reconoitoring their sites beforehand under heavy hostile shellfire, thus greatly assisting the rapid evacuation of casualties. His courage and cheerfulness throughout a period of great strain were beyond praise.

Grave or Memorial Reference: Officers, B.1.12. Cemetery: St Sever Cemetery, Rouen in France.

MASON, Henry: Rank: Private. Regiment or Service: Royal Dublin Fusiliers. Unit: 9th Bn. Date of death: 31 December 1915. Service No: 14572. Born in Bray, Co. Wicklow. Enlisted in Dublin while living in Bray. Killed in action. Grave or Memorial Reference: He has no known grave but is listed on Panel 10 on Ploegsteert Memorial in Belgium.

MATES, John: Rank: Private. Regiment or Service: Royal Dublin Fusiliers. Unit: 1st Bn. Date of death: 7 August 1915. Age at death: 22. Service No: 19580. Born in Ballindarrig, Co. Wicklow. Enlisted in Bray. Died of wounds. Killed in action in Gallipoli.
Supplementary information: Son of John and Annie Mates, of Castletimon, Co. Wicklow. Grave or Memorial Reference: He has no known grave but is listed on Panel 190 to 196 on the Helles Memorial in Turkey.

MATES, Patrick: Rank: Private. Regiment or Service: Royal Inniskilling Fusiliers. Unit: 8th Bn. He was previously with the Royal Dublin Fusiliers where his number was 19264. Date of death: 15 July 1916. Age at death: 26. Service No: 25218. Born in Barndarrig, Co. Wicklow. Enlisted in Dublin while living in Wexford. Killed in action.
Supplementary information: Son of John and Annie Mates, of Barndarrig, Wicklow. Grave or Memorial Reference: VII.H.2. Cemetery: Cabaret Rouge British Cemetery, Souchez in France.

MATTHEWS, James L.: Rank: Private. Regiment or Service: Irish Guards. Unit: 2nd Bn. Date of death: 14 April 1918. Service No: 8520. Born in Kilcoole, Co. Wicklow. Enlisted in Wicklow while living in Rathmines. Died of wounds. Grave or Memorial Reference: V.A.34. Cemetery: Longuenesse (St Omer) Souvenir Cemetery in France.

MAUNSELL, Douglas Slade: Rank: Lieutenant. Regiment or Service: Royal Munster Fusiliers.

Unit: 2nd Bn. attd. 1st Bn. Date of death: between 5 September 1916. and 6 September 1916. Age at death: 31. Killed in action.

Supplementary information: Born 22 April 1885. Son of Major Arthur Munro Maunsell (late 2nd Bn. Royal Munster Fusiliers), and May Isabel Maunsell, of 10 Galtrine Road, Bray, Co. Wicklow. From De Ruvigny's Roll of Honour; 104th Foot, The Royal Munster Fusiliers. Second son of Maor Arthur Munro Maunsell, late 2nd Battn, The Royal Munster Fusiliers, of 10 Galtrim Road, Bray, by his wife, May. Daughter of Charles Thomson. Born: Belfast, 22 April 1885. Educated at Royal School, Armagh. Joined the 4th Battn, The Royal Dublin Fusiliers in 1911. Gazetted 2nd Lieut, 2nd battn The Royal Munster Fusiliers, 30 December 1914 and attached to the 1st Battn. The Royal Irish Rifles; gazetted Lieut 2nd Battn, The Royal Muster Fusiliers, 28 August 1915. Served with the Expeditionary Force in France and Flanders from November 1914. He was invalided home in September 1915, and did light duty in Cork. Served in Dublin during the rebellion in April 1916. Returned to France 1 September, following, and was killed in action at Guillemont, four hours after joining his battalion there on 5 September. Buried at Guillemont. Lieut Maunsell belonged to an old Limerick family, which had many distinguished soldiers from the eleventh century, when it came from France. Grave or Memorial Reference: He has no known grave but is listed on Pier and Face 16.C. on the Thiepval Memorial in France.

MAUNSELL, John William: Rank: Lieutenant. Regiment or Service: Australian Infantry, A.I.F. Unit: 5th Bn. Born: 4 December 1889. Date of death: 9 August 1918. Age at death: 29. Enlisted aged 25 in Melbourne on 13 March 1915 and was listed as a single man at that time. Four days later he was promoted to a Corporal and then to Sergeant on 9 November 1915. His occupation on enlistment was a Government Servant and also a tea and rubber planter. Height: 6'2?". Weight: 13st 2lbs, Eyes: brown. Hair: black. Complexion: medium. Religion: Church of England. Tattoo on right forearm Planters Rifle Corps (Volunteers). He was a student at United Service College, England and also at Harrow. When he arrived in Australia from Wicklow he was 19 years old and obtained work as a rubber planter. Killed in action.

Supplementary information: Son of Colonel A.J.S. Maunsell and Augusta Maunsell. Husband of Mildred Maunsell of Kooringa, South Australia. Born in County

Wicklow, Ireland. Nephew of Major General W.S.B. Boyce. Medal entitlements; British War Medal and the Victory Medal. Embarked from Melbourne, Victoria on board HMAT A33 *Ayrshire* on 3 June 1916 with the 18th Reinforcements and landed in Devonport and in December 1916 proceed to the Battlefields of France. Rapidly rising through the ranks he was Gazetted as Second Lieutenant 6 March 1916 and promoted to full Lieutenant in March 1917. He was wounded in September 1917 with a gunshot to the wrist in Ypres, the only other hospitalisation was for scabies which was common at the time. Next of kin was listed as his father Lt Col A.J.S. Maunsell, 4th Royal Warwickshire Regt. Kingswood, Castle Avenue, Dover, Kent. Also listed was Miss Ethel M. Smith of 101 Gipps Street, East Melbourne who was to receive any information about him. In a letter to the records she states that she was his fiance. After his death his father informed authorities to contact a Mrs Mildred Maunsell, Korringa, Burra, South Australia who he said was his son's wife. Mildred sent them a certificate of marriage proving her relationship to him and she received his personal effects, medals and pension rights in 1918. Originally he was buried in a temporary grave in Bayonvillers British Cemetery however in 1920 he was exhumed

and reburied. Grave or Memorial Reference: IV.B.1. Cemetery: Harbonnieres on the Somme in France. He is listed on the Burra and District Roll of Honour and on the Haileybury (College) Register Roll of Honour.

MAY, John: Rank: Able Seaman. Regiment or Service: Merchant Navy. Unit: SS *Egyptian* (Liverpool). Age at death: 22. Date of death: 6 March 1943.

Supplementary information: Son of John and Annie May, of Arklow, Co. Wicklow. SS *Egyptian* was torpedoed at 2am in the morning by German Submarine U230 in the Atlantic. She was on a voyage from Lagos to New York as part of a convoy with a cargo of oil seed, rubber, palm oil, and tin ore. Of the forty-eight crew members only three survived. U230 was scuttled on 21 August 1944 off Toulon during the allied invasion of Southern France. Grave or Memorial Reference: He has no known grave but is listed on panel 37 on the Tower Hill Memorial, UK.

McCABE, Francis James: Rank: Petty Officer (Air Mechanic). Regiment or Service: Royal Navy. Unit: HMS *Avenger*. Age at death: 31. Date of death: 15 November 1942. Service No: FAA-FX. 75878.

Supplementary information: Son of Daniel and Sara McCabe, of Bray, Co. Wicklow. Sunk by German Submarine U155. Its torpedo struck *Avenger's* bomb room which, astonishingly, ran across the middle of the ship from one side to the other and lay above the oil fuel tanks. It contained about thirty 500lb bombs, seventy 250lb-bombs, 120, 40lb-bombs, and 100 depth charges.

At 0315, a vivid reddish flash appeared on the Starboard side of AVENGER, stretching the whole length of the ship and lasting for about 2 seconds. This flash made a perfect silhouette of the ship, and was followed by a pall of black smoke. After the flash, nothing more was seen of AVENGER, but one or two small twinkling lights were observed in the water, obviously from floats. HMS ULSTER MONARCH passed over the position of AVENGER within 3 minutes and nothing was seen.

U155 and her crew survived the war. It was scuttled in June 1945 in Scotland during Operation Deadlight where most of the surviving U-boats were sent to the bottom. Francis has no known grave but is listed in Bay 3, Panel 4 on the Lee-On-Solent Memorial, UK.

McCARTHY, John: Rank: Private. Regiment or Service: Royal Army Service Corps. Unit: 68th Aux. Petrol Coy. Date of death: 17 May 1918. Service No: M/350339. Born in Roundwood, Co. Wicklow. Enlisted in Dublin while living in Enniskerry. Died of wounds. Grave or Memorial Reference: II.D.D. Cemetery: Bac-Du-Sud British Cemetery, Bailleulval in France

McCLEAN, John: Rank: Greaser. Regiment or Service: Merchant Navy. Unit: MV *British Vigilance* (London). Age at death: 48. The Motor Vessel MV *British Vigilance* was a tanker and while in convoy near it was damaged by German Submarine U514. The Submarine was later sent to the bottom off the Sappanish coast by eight rockets, an acoustic torpedo, and several depth charges. She was lost with all hands. Date of death: 3 January 1943.
Supplementary information: Son of John and Elizabeth McClean. Husband of Mary Bridget McClean, of Wicklow. Grave or Memorial Reference: He has no known grave but is listed on Panel 21 of the Tower Hill Memorial, UK.

McCLUSKEY, John: Rank: Private. Regiment or Service: Royal Irish Fusiliers. Unit: 7th/8th

Bn. He was previously with the Royal Dublin Fusiliers where his number was 14706. Date of death: 17 August 1917. Service No: 21337. Born in Dublin. Enlisted in Dublin while living in Powerscourt, Co. Wicklow. Killed in action. Grave or Memorial Reference: I.B.23. Cemetery: Potijze Chateau Grounds Cemetery in Belgium.

McCOLL, Laurence: Rank: Driver. Regiment or Service: Royal Horse Artillery and Royal Field Artillery. Unit, 'C' Battery, 102nd Brigade. Date of death: 27 August 1917. Service No: 38555. Born in Avoca, Co. Wicklow. Enlisted in Dublin. Died of wounds. Grave or Memorial Reference: IV.E.11. Cemetery: Dozingham Military Cemetery in Belgium.

McCORMACK, Michael: Rank: Private. Regiment or Service: Royal Dublin Fusiliers. Unit: 2nd Bn. Date of death: 5 July 1916. Service No: 17002. Born in Rathdrum, Co. Wicklow. Enlisted in Cork while living in Bagnalstown. Killed in action. Grave or Memorial Reference: He has no known grave but is listed on Pier and Face 16.C. on the Thiepval Memorial in France.

McCORMACK/McCOR-MICK, Thomas: Rank: Private. Regiment or Service: Royal Dublin Fusiliers. Unit: 9th Bn. Date of death: 9 September 1916. Service No: 27258. Born in Bray, Co. Wicklow. Enlisted in Bray. Killed in action. He has no known grave but is listed on Pier and Face 16.C. on the Thiepval Memorial in France.

McCULL, John: Rank: Seaman. Regiment or Service: Royal Naval Reserve. Unit: SS *Mavisbrook*. Age at death: 22. Date of death: 17 May 1918. Service No: 4839A.

Supplementary information: Son of Arthur and Annie McCull, of 9 Abbey Lane, Arklow, Co. Wicklow. The Steamship *Mavisbrook* was a 3,152- ton British Cargo Steamer and was only six years old when she was sent to the bottom by the German Submarine U-50. Eighteen of her crew died did not survive including the Master. She sank fifty miles south-east by S 1/1 S from Cabo de Gata in the Mediterranean Sea. Grave or Memorial Reference: He has no known grave but is listed on the Plymouth Naval Memorial UK. Grave or Memorial Reference: VII.H.49. Cemetery: Warlencourt British Cemetery in France.

McDIARMID, Hugh: Rank: Private. Regiment or Service:

God save Ireland !

"God save Ireland———."

When you sing these words you think you really mean them.

But since the War began, what have you done to help make them a reality?

If you are an Irishman between 19 and 40, physically fit and not already serving your Country as a sailor or a soldier, or in the munition factory, there is but one way for you to help to save Ireland from the Germans—

you must join an Irish Regiment and learn to sing "God save Ireland" with a gun in your hands.

Join To-day

GOD SAVE THE KING!
GOD SAVE IRELAND!

Enlistment Handbill.

Queens Own Cameron Highlanders. Unit: 1ˢᵗ Bn. Date of death: 22 November 1916. Age at death: 27. Service No: S/11257. Enlisted in Edinburgh, Midlothian while living in Shillelagh. Killed in action.

Supplementary information: Son of Hugh and Margaret McDiarmid, of 21 Boswell Terrace, Wardie, Edinburgh. Native of Shillelagh, Co. Wicklow. From De Ruvigny's Roll of Honour: 5ᵗʰ Service Battalion. The Queen's Own (Cameron Highlanders), son of Hugh McDiarmid, late Head Gamekeeper to the Earl Fitzwilliam, Coolattin, Shillelagh, by his wife, Margaret. Daughter of W. Orr. Born: Shillelagh, 30 January 1889. Educated: Shillelagh and Edinburgh. Enlisted 1 September 1914; served with the Expeditionary Force in France and Flanders from May, 1915. He was wounded at Loos, 25 September 1915 and invalided to England. He rejoined his Regiment on recovery, 19 August 1916, and was killed in action near Bapaume, 21 November, following, by a shell. Buried at Le Sars. Grave or Memorial Reference: VII.H.9. Cemetery: Warlencourt British Cemetery in France.

McDIARMID, William Orr: Rank: Pte. Regiment or service: Wellington Regiment. New Zealand Expeditionary Force. Unit: 1st Battalion. Date of Death: 7 April 1916. Service No.: 10/1890.

Supplementary information: Son of Hugh and Margeret Mc Diarmid of 74 Bonaly Road, Edinburgh, Scotland. Born at Shillelagh Co. Wicklow. Information taken from the Nominal Roll of the New Zealand Expeditionary Force. First known rank: Private. Next of kin: Hugh McDiarmid, Coollatin Co. Wicklow. Marital status: Single. Enlistment address: Hurleyville, Patea, New Zealand. Military district: Wellington. Body on Embarkation: 4th Reinforcements. Embarkation Unit: Wellington Infantry Battalion. Embarkation date: 17 April 1915 in Wellington. Vessel: *Willochra* or *Knight Templar* or *Waitomo*. Destination: Suez, Egypt. Page on Nominal Roll: 440. Last Unit Served: Wellington Infantry Regiment. Place of Death: United Kingdom. Date of Death: 7 April 1916. Killed in action. He has no known grave but is listed on the Screen Wall. Cemetery: Walton and Weybridge (Walton-on-Thames) Cemetery UK.

McDONALD, J.: Rank: Private. Regiment or Service: Royal Munster Fusiliers. Unit: 1st Bn. Age at death: 18. Date of death: 3 September 1919. Service No: 32537.

Supplementary information: Son of Mrs Mary Anne McDonald, of 4, Wexford Road, Arklow. Grave or Memorial Reference: South. 3.U.6 East. Cemetery: Arklow Cemetery, Co. Wicklow.

McDONALD, James: Rank: Corporal. Regiment or Service: East Surrey Regiment. Unit: 2nd Bn. Date of death: 29 September 1915. Service No: 4015. Born in Delgany, Bray, Co. Wicklow. Enlisted in Fulham in Middlesex while living in Kensington in Middlesex. Killed in action. Grave or Memorial Reference: He has no known grave but is listed on Panel 60 on the Loos Memorial in France.

McDONALD, James: Rank: Gunner. Regiment or Service: Royal Horse Artillery and Royal Field Artillery. Unit: 30th Div. Ammunition Col. Date of death: 19 April 1916. Age at death: 18. Service No: 100549. Born in Coolkenno, Co. Wicklow. Enlisted in Naas. Son of Edward and Annie McDonald, of Tulloclay, Tullow, Co. Carlow. Grave or Memorial Reference: South. 3.U.6. East. Cemetery: Argoeuves Communal Cemetery in France.

The gravestone of J. McDonald.

McDONALD, John: Rank: Private. Regiment or Service: East Kent Regiment. Unit: 7th Bn. Date of death: 3 May 1917. Service No: G/13234. Born in Kilguade, Co. Wicklow. Enlisted in Bray while living in Kilpedder, Co. Wicklow. Killed in action.

Supplementary information: Son of Owen and Mary McDonald, of Kilfidder, Greystones, Co. Wicklow. Grave or Memorial Reference: He has no known grave but is listed on bay 2 of the Arras Memorial.

McDOWELL, William: Rank: Private. Regiment or Service: Leinster Regiment. Unit: 2nd Bn. Date of death: 9 September 1916. Service No: 2907. Born in Bray, Co. Wicklow. Enlisted in Dublin while living in Bray. Killed in action. Grave or Memorial Reference: He has no known grave but is listed on Pier and Face 16.C. on the Thiepval Memorial in France.

McEVOY, John: Rank: Private. Regiment or Service: Royal Dublin Fusiliers. Unit: 2nd Bn. Date of death: 21 March 1918. Service No: 25272. Born in Wicklow. Enlisted in Wicklow. Killed in action. Grave or Memorial Reference: He has no known grave but is listed in Panels 79 to 80 on the Pozieres Memorial in France.

McEVOY, Michael: Rank: Private. Regiment or Service: Royal Dublin Fusiliers. Unit: 2nd Bn. Date of death: 26 April 1915. Age at death: 20. Service No: 11428. Born in Dublin. Enlisted in Dublin while living in Wicklow. Killed in action.

Supplementary information: Son of Peter and Elizabeth McEvoy, of 3 Castle Street, Wicklow. Grave or Memorial Reference: He has no known grave but is listed on Panel 44 and 46 on the Ypres (Menin Gate) Memorial in Belgium.

McFADDEN/MACFADDIN, George Loftus: Rank: Private. Regiment or Service: Irish Guards. Unit: 1st Bn. Date of death: 3 June 1915. Age at death: 18. Service No: 4834. Born in Kilmanagh, Co. Kilkenny. Enlisted in Dublin while living in Arklow, Co. Wicklow. Died of wounds at home. Son of the late Revd T.H. MacFaddin and Ellen MacFaddin, of Kilmanagh, Co. Kilkenny. Grave or Memorial Reference: O. 280. Cemetery: Shorncliffe Military Cemetery, UK.

McFARLAND, Vivian John Alexander: Rank: Private. Regiment or Service: Royal Inniskilling Fusiliers. Unit: 3rd Company, 9th Bn. Date of death: 28 June 1916. Service No: 16258. Born in Bray, Co. Wicklow. Enlisted in Finner Camp, Donegal while living in Bray. Died of wounds.

Supplementary information: Youngest son of William Harvey McFarland and Lillian McFarland, of Pembroke House, Main St, Bray, Co. Wicklow. Grave or Memorial Reference: I.A.4. Cemetery: Puchevillers British Cemetery in France. He is also listed in the Rathmichael Roll of Honour and on the Rathmichael Church of Ireland War Memorial in Shankill, Co. Dublin.

McGILLIGAN, Michael Aidan: Rank: Flight Lieutenant (Pilot). Regiment or Service: Royal Air Force. Unit: 16 Sqdn. Age at death: 25. Date of death: 8 June 1944. Service No: 111245.

Supplementary information: Son of Michael and Mary Georgina McGilligan, of Greystones, Co. Wicklow. Flying a Spitfire PR XI PA929 during a PR sortie. He crashed near Redhill on return from sortie; believed to have lost control lost in cloud. He is also listed in Fighter Command Losses. Vol. 3.N.L.R. Franks. Grave or Memorial Reference: Grave 59. Cemetery: Reigate (Redstone) Cemetery, UK.

McGOWAN, Harry: Rank: Rifleman. Regiment or Service: Royal Irish Rifles. Unit: 18th Bn and 23rd Entrenching Battalion late 14th Bn. Date of death: 24 March 1918. Service No: 5720. Born in Holyfort, Co. Tipperary. Enlisted in Wicklow while living in Arklow, Co. Wicklow. Killed in action. Grave or Memorial Reference: He has no known grave but is listed in Panels 74 to 76 on the Pozieres Memorial in France.

McGRATH, John: Rank: Driver. Regiment or Service: Royal Engineers. Unit: 495th Field Coy. Date of death: 12 November 1918, the day after the war ended. Age at death: 39. Service No: 367883.

Supplementary information: Son of the late Thomas McGrath, of Bray. Husband of Margaret Carroll (formerly McGrath), of 50 Ardeer Square, Stevenston, Ayrshire. Grave or Memorial Reference: C.121. Cemetery: Alexandria (Hadra) War memorial Cemetery in Egypt.

McGREGOR, Alfred: Rank: Corporal. Regiment or Service: Royal Irish Regiment. Unit: 7th Bn. He was previously with the South Irish Horse where his number was 1391. Date of death: 21 March 1918. Age at death: 30. Service No: 25553. Born in Bray, Co. Wicklow. Enlisted in Dublin while living in Bray. Killed in action. Grave or Memorial Reference: He has no known grave but is listed in Panels 30 and 31 on the Pozieres Memorial in France.

McGREGOR, Alexander: Rank: Lance Corporal. Regiment or Service: Queens own Cameron Highlanders. Unit: 1st Bn. Date of death: 14 September 1914. Age at death: 18. Service No: 9571. Born in Bray. Enlisted in Stratford, Warwickhire while living in Plaistow, London. Killed in action. Son of Alexander and Isabella McGregor, of 42 Beaufoy Road, Plaistow, Essex. Grave or Memorial Reference: 5.1.3. Cemetery: Chauny Communal Cemetery British Extension in France.

McGUINNESS, John: Rank: Private. Regiment or Service: Royal Dublin Fusiliers. Unit: 2nd Bn. Date of death: 24 May 1915. Age at death: 17. Service No: 5725. Born in Stratford, Co. Wicklow. Enlisted in Naas while living in Stratford. Killed in action.
Supplementary information: Son of John McGuinness, of Stratford-on-Slaney, Co. Wicklow. Enlisted in August 1914. He has no known grave but is listed on Panel 44 and 46 on the Ypres (Menin Gate) Memorial in Belgium.

McGUINNESS, Myles: Rank: Acting Lance Corporal. Regiment or Service: Royal Munster Fusiliers. Unit: 2nd Bn. Date of death: 10 January 1917. Age at death: 20. Service No: 10369. Born in Rathdrum, Co. Wicklow. Enlisted in Kinsale, Co. Cork while living in Rathdrum. Killed in action.
Supplementary information: Son of John and Bridget McGuinness, of Greenane, Rathdrum, Co. Wicklow. Grave or Memorial Reference: He has no known grave but is listed on panel 143 to 144 on the Tyne Cot memorial in Belgium.

McINERNEY, Thomas: Rank: Private. Regiment or Service: Leinster Regiment. Unit: 2nd Bn. Date of death: 16 May 1915. Service No: 8719. Born in Arklow, Co. Wicklow. Enlisted in Sheffield. Killed in action.
Supplementary information: Son of Mrs M. McInerney, of Killwran, Broadford, Co. Clare. Grave or Memorial Reference: C.10. Cemetery: Ferme Buterne Military Cemetery in France.

McKENNA, John: Rank: Serjeant. Regiment or Service: Gordon Highlanders. Unit: 1st Bn. Date of death: 18 August 1916. Age at death: 24. Service No: S/3450. Born in Dublin. Enlisted in

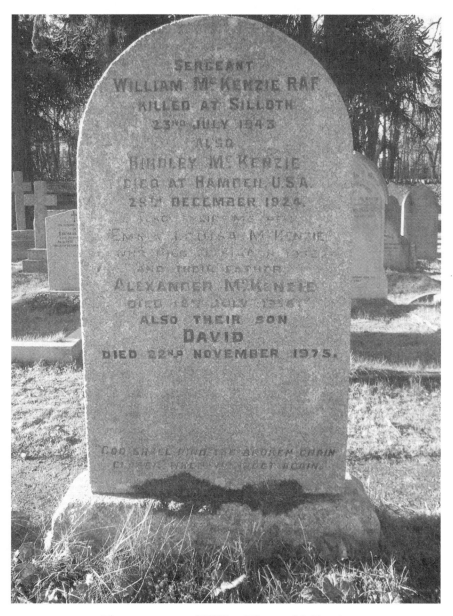

The gravestone of William Thomas McKenzie.

Hamilton. Killed in action.

Supplementary information: Son of Margaret Bourke (formerly McKenna) and John McKenna, of Newbridge, Killarney Road, Bray, He has no known grave but is listed on Pier and Face 15.B. and 15.C. on the Thiepval Memorial in France.

McKENZIE, William Thomas: Rank: Sergeant. Regiment or Service: Royal Air Force Volunteer Reserve. Date of death: 23 July 1943. Age at death: 29. Service No: 1525454. Died when he walked into the rotating propeller of Wellington Bomber HE305 at 3.30am in the morning. Possibly at Wigton.

Supplementary information: Son of Alexander and Emma McKenzie, of Bray. Grave or Memorial Reference: U-68. Cemetery: Powerscourt (Church of Ireland) Churchyard, Co. Wicklow.

McLENNAN, Farquhar John: Rank: Second Lieutenant. Regiment or Service: Gordon Highlanders. Unit: 1st Bn. Date of death: 18 August 1916. Age at death: 24. Killed in action.

Supplementary information: Son of John McLennan, of Killough House, Bray, Co. Wicklow. He has no known grave but is listed on Pier and Face 15.B. and 15.C. on the Thiepval Memorial in France.

McLOUGHLIN, Terence: Rank: Gunner. Regiment or Service: Royal Garrison Artillery. Unit: 35th Heavy Battery. Date of death: 19 May 1918. Service No: 17735. Enlisted in Dublin while living in Mineview, Wicklow. Died. Grave or Memorial Reference: Q.III.K.12. Cemetery: St Sever Cemetery Extension, Rouen in France.

McNULTY, Henry Lawrence: Rank: Private. Regiment or Service: Royal Dublin Fusiliers. Unit: 6th Bn. Date of death: 8 October 1916. Service No: 20294. Born in Dublin. Enlisted in Canning Town while living in Enniskerry. Died of wounds. Grave or Memorial Reference: I.A.112. Cemetery: Lahana Military Cemetery in Greece.

McQUINN, Patrick Joseph: Rank: Lance Corporal. Regiment or Service: Irish Guards. Unit: 2nd Bn. Date of death: 2 July 1916, second day of the battle of the Somme. Age at death: 24. Service No: 6914. Born in Abbeydorney, Co. Kerry. Enlisted in Dublin while living in Newcastle, Co. Wicklow. Killed in action.

Supplementary information: Son of John and Anne McQuinn, of Abbeydorney, Co. Kerry. Husband of Martha McQuinn. Grave or Memorial Reference: II.H.18.

Cemetery: Essex Farm Cemetery in Belgium.

MEADE, K.: Rank: Private. Regiment or Service: Royal Dublin Fusiliers Age at death: 34. Date of death: 21 December 1918. Service No: 30943 Grave or Memorial Reference: In south-west part. Cemetery: Manor Kilbride Old Graveyard, Co. Wicklow.

MEAGAN / MEGAN, Christopher: Rank: Private. Regiment or Service: Royal Dublin Fusiliers. Unit: 9th Bn. Date of death: 16 September 1916. Age at death: 21. Service No: 17729. Born in Rathdrim, Co. Wicklow. Enlisted in Arklow while living in Rathdrum. Died of wounds.
Supplementary information: Son of Edward and Mary Megan, of Ballyhad, Rathdrum, Co. Wicklow. Grave or Memorial Reference: B.19.7. Cemetery: St Sever Cemetery, Rouen in France.

MEGAN, Lawrence: Rank: Private. Regiment or Service: Royal Dublin Fusiliers. Unit: 10th Bn. Date of death: 13 November 1916. Service No: 26835. Born in Enniskerry, Co. Wicklow. Enlisted in Dublin while living in Navan, Co. Meath. Killed in action. Grave

or Memorial Reference: VII.B.5. Cemetery: Ancre British Cemetery, Beaumont-Hamel in France.

MEREDITH, John: Rank: Private. Regiment or Service: Machine Gun Corps (Infantry). He was previously with the North Lancashire Regiment where his number was 11378. Date of death: 2 July 1916. Age at death: 35. Service No: 16983. Born in Wicklow. Enlisted in Bolton while living in Wicklow. Killed in action.
Supplementary information: Son of John and Ann Meredith, of 62 Raglan Street, Garston, Liverpool. Native of Wicklow. Grave or Memorial Reference: II.A.8. Cemetery: Bully-Grenay Communal Cemetery, British Extension in France.

MESSITT, John: Rank: Private. Regiment or Service: Royal Dublin Fusiliers. Unit: 2nd Bn. Date of death: 18 October 1918, three weeks before the war ended. Age at death: 23. Service No: 19787. Born in Bray, Co. Wicklow. Enlisted in Bray. Killed in action. Grave or Memorial Reference: I.A.112. Cemetery: Highland Cemetery, Le Chateau in France.

MEYER, Ernest Samuel: Rank: Private. Regiment or Service:

The gravestone of K. Meade.

Canadian Infantry (Manitoba Regiment). Unit: 8th Bn. Date of death: 9 August 1918. Service No: 830185. Age at death: 33. Born 24 April 1886 in Bray, Co. Wicklow. Enlisted on 23 December 1915 in Winnipeg while living at 22 Carmen Ave, Ewlmwood, Winnipeg. Occupation on enlistment: credit manager. Height: 5'9". Complexion: fair. Eyes: blueish-grey. Hair: fair. Religion: Church of England. Next of kin listed as Mrs Ethel Kay Mayer of 22 Carmen Ave, Ewlmwood, Winnipeg.

Supplementary information: Son of Thomas and Sarah Meyer, of Bray, Co. Wicklow. Husband of Ethel M. Meyer, of 1517 Fernwood Road, Victoria, British Columbia. Grave or Memorial Reference: A.20. Cemetery: Manitoba Cemetery, Caix in France.

MIDDLETON, Thomas William: Rank: Ordinary Seaman. Regiment or Service: Royal Navy. Unit: HMS *Marshall South*. Age at death: 28. Date of death: 24 September 1916. Service No: J/42510.

Supplementary information: Son of the late Mr and Mrs Thomas W. Middleton, of Baltinglass, Co. Wicklow. Grave or Memorial Reference: I.C.2. Cemetery: Dunkirk Town Cemetery in France.

MITCHELL, David Carroll: Rank: Second Lieutenant. Regiment or Service: Royal Fusiliers (City of London Regiment). Unit: 1st Bn. Age at death: 21. Date of death: 16 March 1941. Service No: 95247.

Supplementary information: Son of Major Christopher C. Mitchell, D.S.O, M.C, and Star Mitchell, of Ballynure, Co. Wicklow. Grave or Memorial Reference: 4.C.1. Cemetery: Keren War Cemetery in Eretrea, East Africa.

MITCHELL, John: Rank: Able Seaman. Regiment or Service: Mercantile Marine. Unit: Motor Vessel *Arabis* (London). Age at death: 48. The Motorship Arabis was built in 1914 and was torpedoed and sunk by a German Submarine 210 miles west of Unshant. Nineteen men and the Captain died.

Supplementary information: Son of the late Thomas and Winifred Mitchell (*née* Flanagan). Born at Wicklow. He has no known grave by is listed on the Tower Hill Memorial UK.

MOLE, Nigel Brook: Rank: Flight Lieutenant. Regiment or Service: Royal Air Force. Unit: 269 Sqdn Age at death: 24. Date of death: 24 October 1940. Service No: 37779.

Supplementary information: Son of Harold Brook Mole and Rose Mary Mole, of Tinahely, Co. Wicklow. Took off 0711hrs in Hudson I P5132 UA-F. Failed to return. Believed to have been shot down by Ltn Deutschle of 6/JG77. Grave or Memorial Reference: He has no known grave but is listed on panel 4 on the Runnymede Memorial, UK. He is also listed in the Coastal Command Pilots Roll of Honour.

MONRO, Charles: Rank: Acting Company Sergeant Major. Regiment or Service: Argyll and Southern Highlanders. Unit: 2nd Bn. Date of death: 21 October 1914. Service No: 5287. Born in Wicklow, Co. Wicklow. Enlisted in Stirling while living in Carrigart, Co. Donegal. Killed in action. Grave or Memorial Reference: He has no known grave but is listed on Panel 9 and 10 on Ploegsteert Memorial in Belgium.

MOODY, Patrick: Rank: Private. Regiment or Service: Royal Irish Fusiliers. Unit: 7th Bn. Date of death: 9 September 1916. Service No: 13198. Born in Ashford, Co. Wicklow. Enlisted in Wicklow. Killed in action. Grave or Memorial Reference: He has no known grave but is listed on Pier and Face 15.A. on the Thiepval Memorial in France.

MOODY, William Patrick: Rank: Private 2nd Class. Regiment or Service: Royal Air Force. Unit: Recruits Training Wing (Blandford). Date of death: 3 November 1918. Age at death: 18. Service No: 309651.
Supplementary information: Son of William and Charlotte Moody, of Summer Hill, Wicklow. Grave or Memorial Reference: 74. Cemetery: Blandford Cemetery UK.

MOONEY, John Edward: Rank: Private. Regiment or Service: Northumberland Fusiliers. Unit: 1st Bn. Date of death: 08 November 1914. Age at death: 34. Service No: 296. Born in Wicklow, Co. Wicklow. Enlisted in Manchester.
Supplementary information: Brother of Mrs C. Oldham, of 6 Church Street , Oldham. Grave or Memorial Reference: He has no known grave but is listed on Panel 8 and 12 on the Ypres (Menin Gate) Memorial in Belgium.

MOORE, Alexander: Rank: Chief Steward. Regiment or Service: Mercantile Marine. Unit: SS *Garron Head* (Belfast). The

Steamship Garron Head was sunk by a German Seamine 40 miles from Bayonne in France. 28 of the crew died. The Captain survived. Date of death: 16 November 1917. Age at death: 37.

Supplementary information: Son of Thomas and Catherine Moore. Husband of Kathleen Isabella Moore (*née* Maguire), of 3 Orwell Terrace, Ballygomartin Road, Belfast. Born at Rathdrum, Co. Wicklow. Grave or Memorial Reference: He has no known grave but is listed on the Tower Hill Memorial UK.

MOORE, Edward: Rank: Private. Regiment or Service: Royal Highlanders. (The Black Watch). Unit: 1st Bn. Date of death: 25 January 1915. Age at death: 25. Service No: S/3838. Born in Stratford, Co. Wicklow. Enlisted in Lochgelly, Fifeshire. Killed in action.

Supplementary information: Son of Mrs Mary Moore, of Stratford-on-Slaney, Grangecon, Co. Wicklow. Grave or Memorial Reference: He has no known grave but is listed on Panel 24 and 26 on the Le Touret Memorial in France.

MOORE, Henry Geoffrey Hamilton: Rank: Second Lieutenant. Regiment or Service: Royal Irish Regiment. Unit: 2nd Bn. Date of death: 20 October 1914. Age at death: 20. Killed in action.

Supplementary information: Son of J.H. Hamilton Moore and Ethel Florence Moore, of Dromin, Delgany, Co. Wicklow. Grave or Memorial Reference: He has no known grave but is listed on Panel 11 and 12 on the Le Touret Memorial in France.

MOORE, James: Rank: Private. Regiment or Service: Royal Dublin Fusiliers. Unit: 2nd Bn. Date of death: 2 January 19. Age at death: 23. Service No: 5519. Born in Baltinglass, Co. Wicklow. Enlisted in Naas while living in Ballyhook, Co. Wicklow. Died of wounds.

Supplementary information: Son of Thomas and Kate Moore (*née* Wade), of Ballyhook, Stratford-on-Slaney, Co. Wicklow. Grave or Memorial Reference: VI.G.9. Cemetery: Berlin south-western Cemetery in Germany.

MOORE, Morgan Edward Jellett: Rank: Lieutenant. Regiment or Service: Royal Irish Rifles. Unit: 2nd Bn. Date of death: 24 March 1918. Age at death: 24. Died of wounds as a prisoner of war. He won the Military Cross and is listed in the *London Gazette*.

Supplementary information: Son

of Edward and Nina Moore, of *The Haven*, Teignmouth, Devon. Educated at Aravon Bray, Co. Wicklow, Trinity College, Glenalmond, and King's College, Cambridge. Born at Letterkenny, Co. Donegal. Grave or Memorial Reference: VI.E.9. Cemetery: Grand-Seraucourt British Cemetery in France. He is also listed on the Avaron School Memorial in Christ Church in Bray.

MOOREHOUSE, George: Rank: Lance Corporal. Regiment or Service: Royal Irish Fusiliers. Unit: 1st Bn. He was previously with the Royal Inniskilling Fusiliers where his number was 23536. Date of death: 1 October 1918. Age at death: 23. Service No: 49806. Born in Nun's Cross, Co. Wicklow. Enlisted in Dublin while living in Enniskerry. Killed in action also listed as wounded and missing, reported killed.

MORAN, Aloysius: Rank: Private. Regiment or Service: Royal Dublin Fusiliers. Unit: 2nd Bn. Date of death: 25 October 1916. Service No: 8855. Born in Bray, Co. Wicklow. Enlisted in Dublin. Died of wounds. Grave or Memorial Reference: II.B.25. Cemetery: Grove Town Cemetery, Meulte in France.

MORGAN, John: Rank: Private. Regiment or Service: Royal Dublin Fusiliers. Unit: 2nd Bn. Date of death: 26 April 1915. Age at death: 29. Service No: 9450. Born in Barnderry, Co. Wicklow. Enlisted in Dublin. Killed in action.

Supplementary information: Son of Thomas and Winifred Morgan, of 2 Beech View Terrace, Glasnevin, Dublin. Grave or Memorial Reference: He has no known grave but is listed on Panel 44 and 46 on the Ypres (Menin Gate) Memorial in Belgium.

MORRIS, George Herbert: Rank: Private. Regiment or service: Gloucestershire Regiment. Unit: 2nd Bn. Date of death: 7 February 1915. Age at death: 22. Service No: 11889. Born in Baltinglass, Co. Wicklow. Enlisted in Camberwell while living in Belfast. Killed in action.

Supplementary information: Son of Joseph and Anna Maria Morris, of 32 Vicinage Park, Belfast. Grave or Memorial Reference: He has no known grave but is listed on Panel 44 and 11 on the Ypres (Menin Gate) Memorial in Belgium.

MORRISON, Donald Derek: Rank: Flight Lieutenant (Pilot). Regiment or Service: Royal Air Force Volunteer Reserve. Age at death: 22. Date of death: 25 January

Henry Morton.

1946. Service No: 153364.

Supplementary information: Son of Kenneth Melrose Morrison and Isobel Jane Morrison; stepson of Mr N.A. Hall, of Bray, Co. Wicklow. Grave or Memorial Reference: Sec. W. 7L. Grave 357. Cemetery: Darlington West Cemetery, UK.

MORTON, Henry: Rank: Private. Regiment or Service: Household Cavalry and Cavalry of the line (Including the Yeomanry and Imperial Camel Corps). Unit: 1st Sussex Yeomanry attached to the 42nd Division. Date of death: 13 November 1915. Age at death: 48. Service No: 1790. Born in Wicklow. Enlisted in Chichester while living in Prestwich in Manchester. Killed in action in Gallipoli.

Supplementary information: Son of Thomas and Mary Morton, of Wicklow. Veteran of the South African War. 20 Years Service with the 3rd Bn Grenadier Guards. Included on the Irish National War Memorial. From De Ruvigny's Roll of Honour. Son of the of the late Thomas Morton, who served twenty-one years in India with the 2nd Bengal Fusiliers, and received the good conduct medal and served afterwards for fifteen years on the staff of the old Wicklow Rifles. Born: Wicklow, 15 December 1867. Educated: Wicklow Church School; enlisted in the Royal Artillery, 15 June 1887. Transferred into the Grenardier Guards, 1 October following, and was posted to the 3rd battalion. He served through the South African War, 1899–1902, receiving the Queen's South African medal with six bars (Belmont, Modder River, Dreifontein, Johannesburg, Diamond Hill, Belfast) and the King's medal with two bars (1901 and 1902). He obtained his discharge at his own request in

September, 1906, after being with the Colours for nineteen years and eighty-seven days. When he was awarded the long service and good conduct medal. He was servant to capt, Weller-Poley, re-enlisted in the Sussex Yeomanry the day the war was declared. He went to the Dardinelles with the Expeditionary Force in September 1915 and was killed in action on 13 November, 1915. He was buried in Anglesea Gully, Gallipoli. Writing to his brother, Mr George Morton of 4 North Road, Prestwich, Manchester, Capt Weller-Poley, said; 'I feel that I have lost a true friend and trusted servant who can never be replaced.' And Mr Thomas Weller-Poley of Chichester. J. P., 'Your brother Henry had been with us so long and was so much liked and respected by everyone, that the news of his death is a genuine sorrow to us and to the whole establishment'. Grave or Memorial Reference: Sp. Mem. C.165. Cemetery: Twelve Tree Copse Cemetery, Gallipoli.

MULALLY/MULLALY, Miles: Rank:Private.Regiment or Service: Irish Guards. Unit: 2nd Bn. Date of death: 8 October 1917. Service No: 9733. Born in Blessington. Enlisted in Dublin. Killed in action. Grave or Memorial Reference: VII. B.20. Cemetery: Artillery Wood Cemetery in France.

MULCAHY-MORGAN, Edward Spread: Rank: Captain. Regiment or Service: Royal Irish Rifles. Son of John Edward Spread Mulcahy-Morgan, Lara House, Rathdrum, Co. Wicklow, by his wife, Susan, eldest daughter of the late William Bennett Campion KC, HM Sgt-at-Law. Educated at the Erasmus Smith Abbey Grammar School, Tipperary. Commissioned to 4th RIR, 5 April 1907, promoted Lt. 7 April 1910, and Capt., 3rd RIR, 10 October 1914. Wounded and missing, 27 October 1914, while serving with 2nd RIR. *Immortal Deeds*: 'When lying severely wounded in the back and arms by shell fire, he was only able to articulate: "Advance! Advance!" when approached by a non-commissioned officer who wished to help him.' His brother, Lt. Francis Campion Mulcahy-Morgan, 7th RIR, was born at Clondalkin, Co. Dublin 5 March 1895 (fourth son), and killed in action 6 September 1916.

Their father wrote to the War Office on 15 February 1916:

I am now proceeding to wind up the affairs of my other son Capt. E.S. Mulcahy-Morgan … I have since heard from several returned soldiers whom I have interviewed that he was fatally injured, which I regret to know is true or we would long since have heard from him. I shall be glad to know if you will issue a death certificate in his case also. We never received either his pay or (£50) allowance while he was on duty in Dublin or Kingstown.

They had three brothers, including Major William Edmund Victor and three sisters, Susan L., Martha K. and Albina I. Lara's House was sold in the 1930s, converted to a hotel but burned down in the 1950s. Killed in action. Grave or Memorial Reference: He has no known grave but is listed on Panel 42 and 43 on the Le Touret Memorial in France. He is also named on the Abbey Grammar School War Memorial.

MULCAHY-MORGAN, Francis Campion: Rank: Lieutenant. Regiment or Service: Royal Irish Rifles. Unit; 7th Bn.Killed in action. Date of Death; 6 September 1916. He was the fourth son of Mr Edward S .Mulcahy-Morgan, Lara House, Dundrum, Co. Wicklow, and a brother of Captain Edward Spread Mulcahy-Morgan, Royal Irish Rifles, and Captain T.W. Mulcahy-Morgan, Royal Irish Fusiliers and Royal Flying Corps.

From De Ruvigny's Roll of Honour: Son of John Edward Spread Mulcahy-Morgan, of Lara, Rathdrum, by his wife, Susan, eldest daughter of the late William Bennett Campion, K.C., H.M. Sergeant-at-Law and brother to Captain E.S.Mulcahy-Morgan (also killed in action). Born: Clondalkin, County Dublin, 5 March 1895. Educated at Partora Royal School, Enniskillen. Applied for a commission on the outbreak of the war. Gazetted 2nt Lieutenant, Royal Irish Rifles, 10 October 1914, and promoted Lieutenant, 30 December following. Served with the Expeditionary Force in France and Flanders from December, 1915 and was killed near Ginchy, 6th September, 1916 while leading his men on patrol in the enemy's lines. Grave or Memorial Reference: He has no known grave but is listed on Pier and face 15 A and 15 B on the Thiepval Memorial in France.

MULHALL, John: Rank: Private. Regiment or Service: Connaught Rangers. Unit: 'A' Coy. 2nd Bn. Date of death: 14 September 1914. Age at death: 22. Service No: 10621. Born in Booterstown, Co. Dublin. Enlisted in Dublin while living in Dublin. Killed in action.
Supplementary information: Son of Mrs Sarah Mulhall, of Sutton West, Ontario, Canada, and Patrick Mulhall, of Bray, Co. Wicklow. Grave or Memorial Reference: He

has no known grave but is listed on the La-Ferte-Sous-Jouarre Memorial in France.

MULLIGAN, Christopher: Rank: Lance Corporal. Regiment or Service: Irish Guards. Unit: 2nd Bn. Date of death: 8 October 1917. Service No: 11270. Born in Avoca, Co. Wicklow. Enlisted in Dublin. Killed in action. Grave or Memorial Reference: VIII. B. 18. Cemetery: Artillery Wood Cemetery in France.

MULVEY, William: Rank: Private. Regiment or Service: Royal Dublin Fusiliers. Unit: 9th Bn. Secondary Regiment: Labour Corps. Secondary Unit: transferred. to (228771) 657th H.S. Employment Coy. Age at death: 36. Date of death: 23 October 1918. Service No: 19093.

Supplementary information: Husband of Catherine Mulvey, of Casey's Cottages, Green Park Road, Bray. Grave or Memorial Reference: Ha. 47.7. Little Bray (St Peter's) Catholic Cemetery, Wicklow.

MURPHY, Colman O'Shaughnessy: Rank: Flying Officer (Pilot). Regiment or Service: Royal Air Force. Unit: 24 Sqdn. Age at death: 27. Date of death: 17 June 1940. Service No: 39892.

Supplementary information: Son of John J.L. Murphy and Anne Murphy, of Bray, Co. Wicklow. 24th Squadron

MURPHY, Edward: Rank: Gunner. Regiment or Service: Royal Horse Artillery and Royal Field Artillery. Unit: 'D' Bty. 38th Bde. Date of death: 23 July 1917. Unit: 'D' Bty. 38th Bde. Age at death: 32. Service No: 6007. Born in Bray, Co. Wicklow. Enlisted in Wicklow. Killed in action.

Supplementary information: Husband of Elizabeth Murphy, of Bray. Grave or Memorial Reference: I.N.14. Cemetery: Brandhoek Military Cemetery in Belgium.

MURPHY, James: Rank: Private. Regiment or Service: Royal Dublin Fusiliers. Unit: 6th Bn. Date of death: 9 October 1918. Age at death: 26. Age at death: 26. Service No: 9010. Born in Wicklow. Enlisted in Wicklow. Died in Egypt.

Supplementary information: Son of Christopher and Bridget Murphy, of Ballalley, Wicklow. Grave or Memorial Reference: B.01.82. Cemetery: Southampton (Hollybrook) Cemetery UK.

MURPHY, James: Rank: Fusilier. Regiment or Service: Royal Inniskilling Fusiliers. Age at death: 33. Date of death: 16 October 1945. Service No: 6409824.

Supplementary information: Son of Patrick and Mary Murphy. Husband of Frances Mary Murphy of North Bray. Grave or Memorial Reference: Grave Q.42. Little Bray (St Peter's) Catholic Cemetery, Wicklow.

MURPHY, James: Rank: Gunner. Regiment or Service: Royal Artillery. Unit: 1 Lt. Bty, 6 A.A. Regt. Age at death: 17. Date of death: 16 May 1940. Service No: 1438889.

Supplementary information: Son of Nicholas and Cathrine Murphy, of Arklow, Co. Wicklow. Grave or Memorial Reference: Grave 4. Cemetery: Kain Communal Cemetery in Belgium.

MURPHY, James: Rank: Gunner. Regiment or Service: Royal Horse Artillery and Royal Field Artillery. Unit: 33rd Battery, 33rd Brigade. Date of death: 22 July 1917. Age at death: 32. Service No: 31156. Born in Blessington, Wicklow. Enlisted in Dublin. Died of wounds in Ypres.

Supplementary information: Son of Mathew and Katherine Murphy, of Hempstown, Tinod, Co. Dublin.

Husband of Julia Murphy, of 3 Sheridan's Cottages, Dawson Street, Newbridge, Co. Kildare. Grave or Memorial Reference: I.A.112. Cemetery: Dickebusch New Military Cemetery Extension in Belgium.

MURPHY, John: Rank: Private. Regiment or Service: Royal Dublin Fusiliers. Unit: 2nd Bn. Date of death: 31 October 1918. Service No: 16254. Born in Rathnew, Co. Wicklow. Enlisted in Carlow while living in Rathnew. Died of wounds. He has no known grave but is listed on Panel 10 on the Viz-En-Artois Memorial in France.

MURPHY, John: Rank: Private. Regiment or Service: Royal Irish Fusiliers. Unit: 1st Bn. He was previously with the Royal Dublin Fusiliers where his number was 17010. Date of death: 17 June 1916. Service No: 21309. Born in Bray, Co. Wicklow. Enlisted in Bray while living in Kingstown, Co. Dublin. Died of wounds. Grave or Memorial Reference: V.E.38. Cemetery, Bethurne Town Cemetery in France.

MURPHY, John Anthony: Rank: Able Seaman. Regiment or Service: Royal Navy. Unit: HMS *Repulse*. Age at death: 18. Date of death: 10 December 1941. Service No: D-JX 162884.

Supplementary information: Son of John Murphy and of Anne Murphy (*née* Pearce), of Bray, Co. Wicklow. HMS *Repulse* was a Renown class Battlecruiser and sunk when attacked by 87 Japanese Aircraft based in Saigon. She managed to dodge 19 torpedoes by was eventually hit by 4 or 5 and sunk within 20 minutes. The story of the sinking is told in the book 'Suez to Singapore' Regarding the attach the Captain said "I found dodging the torpedoes quite interesting and entertaining, until in the end they started to come in from all directions and they were too much for me' The photograph above was taken by a Japanese aircraft during the attack. HMS *Repulse* on the bottom of the picture has just been hit, the ship on the top is the Battleship 'Prince of Wales' which also sank an hour afterwards. Grave or Memorial Reference: He has no known grave but is listed on panel 48, Column 1 on the Plymouth Naval Memorial, UK.

MURPHY, L.: Rank: Serjeant. Regiment or Service: Royal Garrison Artillery Unit: 85th Coy. Date of death: 20 April 1920. Age at death: 35. Service No: 25752.

Supplementary information: Son of James and Mary Murphy. Born at Newcastle, Co. Wicklow. Grave or Memorial Reference: D.52. Cemetery: Maala Cemetery in Yemen.

MURPHY, Mathew Peter Patrick: Rank: Assistant Steward. Regiment or Service: Merchant Navy. Age at death: 17. Date of death: 17 January 1941.

Supplementary information: Son of Michael J. and Mary B. Murphy, of Arklow, Co. Wicklow. Grave or Memorial Reference: He has no known grave but is listed on panel 6 on the Tower Hill Memorial, UK.

MURPHY, Michael: Rank: Rifleman. Regiment or Service: Royal Irish Rifles. Unit: 2nd Bn. Date of death: 26 October 1914. Age at death: 27. Service No: 7803. Born in Wicklow. Enlisted in Wicklow. Killed in action.

Supplementary information: Son of Francis Murphy and Mary Murphy, of High Street, Wicklow. Grave or Memorial Reference: He has no known grave but is listed on Panel 42 and 43 on the Le Touret Memorial in France.

MURPHY, Michael: Rank: Private. Regiment or Service: Manchester Regiment. Unit: 1st Bn. Date of death: 21 October 1917. Age at death: 21. Service

No: 3103. Born in Enniskerry, Co. Wicklow. Enlisted in Ashton-Under-Lyne, Lancashire while living in Enniskerry. Drowned in Mesopotamia.

Supplementary information: Son of John and Alicia Murphy, of Cloon, Enniskerry, Co. Wicklow. From De Ruvigny's Roll of Honour: 1ˢᵗ Battalion, (63 Foot the Manchester regiment). Third son of John Murphy, of Cloon, Enniskerry, by his wife, Alicia, daughter, of Henry Box, of Glencullen, Co. Dublin. Born: Cloon, Enniskerry, 26 April 1896. Educated: Castletown, near Enniskerry; worked on a farm. Enlisted in the Manchester regt, 12 August 1914. Served with the Mediterranean Expeditionary Force at Gallipoli from 15 July 1915. He was present at the landing at Suvla Bay; was wounded 9 August and invalided home. On recovery rejoined his regiment in Mesopotamia, and was droned 21 October 1917. While on active service. Grave or Memorial Reference: He has no known grave but is listed on Panel 31 and 64 on the Basra Memorial in Iraq.

MURPHY, Owen: Rank: Private. Regiment or Service: Royal Dublin Fusiliers. Unit: 1ˢᵗ Bn. Date of death: 28 February 1917. Age at death: 32. Service No: 20189. Born in Newtownmountkennedy, Co. Wicklow. Enlisted in Ashford while living in Wicklow. Killed in action.

Supplementary information: Husband of Kathleen Murphy, of Newtownmountkennedy, Co. Wicklow. Grave or Memorial Reference: He has no known grave but is listed on Pier and face 16.C. on the Thiepval Memorial in France.

MURPHY, Patrick: Rank: Corporal. Regiment or Service: Royal Dublin Fusiliers. Unit: 9ᵗʰ Bn. Date of death: 9 September 1916. Age at death: 42. Service No: 13386. Born in Bray, Co. Wicklow. Enlisted in Kilsyth (Scotland) while living in Bray. Killed in action.

Supplementary information: Husband of Mary Murphy, of 13 Dargan Street, Bray. Grave or Memorial Reference: XVD.20. Cemetery: Terlincthun British Cemetery, Wimille in France.

MURPHY, Thomas: Rank: Private. Regiment or Service: Royal Dublin Fusiliers. Unit: 8ᵗʰ Bn. Date of death: 11 August 1917. Service No: 20350. Born in Bray, Co. Wicklow. Enlisted in Bray. Killed in action. Grave or Memorial Reference: He has no known grave but is listed on Panel 44 and 46 on the Ypres (Menin Gate) Memorial in Belgium.

MURPHY, William: Rank: Private. Regiment or Service: Leinster Regiment. Unit: 1st Bn. Date of death: 13 September 1916. Service No: 4158. Born in Bolling, Co. Wicklow. Enlisted in Glasgow while living in Glasgow. Died at sea.

Supplementary information: Brother of Thomas Murphy, of Main Street, Glenborg, Lanarkshire. Grave or Memorial Reference: X.D. 10A. Cemetery: Etaples Military Cemetery in France.

MURRAY, Anthony: Rank: Able Seaman. Regiment or Service: Mercantile Marine. Unit: SS *Denebola* (London). The Steamship denebola was sunk by the German Submarine UB 86 near Gurnards Head 5½ miles south-west of St Ives. Torpedoed without warning the ship was laden with a cargo of coal she was bringing from Swansea to Rouen. Date of death: 17 August 1918. Age at death: 33.

Supplementary information: Son of Mary-Anne and John Murray (*née* Longbrill), of 13 Old Chapel Ground, Arklow, Co. Wicklow. Grave or Memorial Reference: He has no known grave but is listed on the Tower Hill Memorial UK.

MURRAY, John: Rank: Private. Regiment or Service: Labour Corps. He was previously with the Royal Army Service Corps where his number was 141415 and T4/141415. Date of death: 13 July 1918. Age at death: 45. Service No: 310583. Born in Rathdrum, Co. Wicklow. Enlisted in Little Bray while living in Bray.

Supplementary information: Son of Mary Murray. Husband of Elizabeth Murray, of 21 Maitland Street, Dargle Road, Bray, Co. Wicklow. Grave or Memorial Reference: V.E.26. Cemetery: Pernes British Cemetery in France.

MURRAY, Patrick: Rank: Private. Regiment or Service: Royal Dublin Fusiliers. Unit: 9th Bn. Date of death: 17 May 1916. Age at death: 19. Service No: 19292. Born in Avoca, Co. Wicklow. Enlisted in Dublin while living in Wicklow. Died of wounds.

Supplementary information: Son of Patrick and Julia Murray, of Coolgorrow. Grave or Memorial Reference: Plot 2. Row K. Grave 2C. Cemetery: Le-Treport Military Cemetery in France.

MURRAY, Richard: Rank: Private. Regiment or Service: Royal Irish Fusiliers. Unit: 7/8th Bn. Age at death: 21. Date of death: 12 January 1917. Service No: 18561. Born in Bray, Co. Wicklow. Enlisted in Bray. Killed in action.

Supplementary information: Son of Edward and Eliza Murray, of 4 Casey's Cottage, Little Bray, Co. Wicklow. Grave or Memorial Reference: X.35. Cemetery: Kemmel Chateau Military Cemetery in Belgium.

MURRAY, William: Rank: Private. Regiment or Service: Royal Dublin Fusiliers. Unit: 6th Bn. Date of death: 8 October 1918. Age at death: 27. Service No: 27974. Born in Rathdrum, Co. Wicklow. Enlisted in Naas while living in Rathdrum. Killed in action.

Supplementary information: Brother of Miss Kathleen Murray, of River View Cottage, Ballyhad, Rathdrum, Co. Wicklow. Grave or Memorial Reference: C.6.

Cemetery: Beaurevoir British Cemetery in France.

MUTCH, Edward George: Rank: Lance Corporal. Regiment or Service: Devonshire Regiment. Unit: 1st Bn. Date of death: 5 September 1916. Age at death: 23. Service No: 9551. Born in Wicklow. Enlisted in Exceter while living in Plymouth. Killed in action.

Supplementary information: Son of Elizabeth Clarke (formerly Mutch), of 58 Clare Buildings, Coxside, Plymouth, and William Mutch. He has no known grave but is listed on Pier and Face 16.C. on the Thiepval Memorial in France.

First World War enlistment posters.

IRISHMEN AVENGE THE LUSITANIA

JOIN AN **IRISH REGIMENT** TO-DAY

Can You any longer resist the Call?

IS **YOUR** HOME WORTH FIGHTING FOR?

IT WILL BE TOO LATE TO FIGHT WHEN THE ENEMY IS AT YOUR DOOR SO **JOIN TO-DAY**

Mr. **JOSEPH DEVLIN**, M.P. AND THE **IRISH BRIGADE**

"May every good fortune, success and blessing attend the colours of the Irish Brigade, whose valour, I hope, will be crowned with the laurels of glory worthily earned in the arena of a great conflict on behalf of a righteous cause . . . . .

"When they come back again, they will be welcomed not only as soldiers of the Allies, but as friends of liberty who have raised the dignity and prestige and glory of Ireland to a higher position than it ever occupied before . .

IRISHMEN DO YOUR DUTY IN THIS RIGHTEOUS CAUSE AND **JOIN THE IRISH BRIGADE**

JUMP INTO YOUR PLACE IN THE

SPORTSMAN'S COMPANY

199

OF THE **IRISH CANADIAN RANGERS** OVERSEAS BATTALION Headquarters: 91 STANLEY ST. MONTREAL. Under Lt.Col. H.J.TRIHEY.

N

NAYLOR, Bartholmew: Rank: Lance Corporal. Regiment or Service: Royal Dublin Fusiliers. Unit: 10th Bn. Date of death: 13 November 1916. Age at death: 22. Service No: 26061. Born in Bray, Co. Wicklow. Enlisted in Bray. Killed in action.

Supplementary information: Son of Mrs Mary Anne Naylor, of Newcourt Cottage, Bray, Co. Wicklow. Grave or Memorial Reference: He has no known grave but is listed on Pier and Face 16.C. on the Thiepval memorial in France.

NAYLOR, Samuel: Rank: Sailor. Regiment or Service: Merchant Navy. Unit: MV *Walmer Castle* (London). Age at death: 24. Date of death: 21 September 1941.

Supplementary information: Son of William and Esther Naylor, of Bray, Co. Wicklow. Samuel has no known grave but is listed on panel 116 on the Tower Hill Memorial, UK.

NEILL, Charles: Rank: Private. Regiment or Service: Royal Dublin Fusiliers. Unit: 1st Bn. Date of death: 21 March 1918. Service No: 21541. Born in Enniskerry, Co. Wicklow. Enlisted in Bray. Killed in action. Grave or Memorial Reference: He has no known grave but is listed in Panels 79 and 80 on the Pozieres Memorial in France.

NEILL, Thomas: Rank: Private (Signaller). Regiment or Service: Royal Dublin Fusiliers. Unit: 2nd Bn. Date of death: 8 November 1918. Age at death: 21. Service No: 27967. Born in Bray, Co. Wicklow. Enlisted in Ardeer (Scotland), while living in Stevenson (Scotland). Killed in action.

Supplementary information: Son of Michael and Kate Neill, of 26 Station Square, Stevenston, Ayrshire. Buried in the north-east part of Floursies Churchyard in France.

NESTOR, Patrick: Rank: Chief Petty Officer (Coastguard). Regiment or Service: HM Coastguard. Unit: Wicklow Head Coast Guard Station. Date of death:

The gravestone of Patrick Nestor.

11 May 1915. Service No: 123748. Grave or Memorial Reference: R.C. ground 3.D.1457. Cemetery: Rathnew Cemetery, Co. Wicklow.

NEWSOME. G.: Rank: Private. Regiment or Service: South African Infantry. Unit: 4th Regt. Date of death: 30 October 1918. Age at death: 39. Service No: 20532.

Supplementary information: Son of William and Fanny Newsome, of Rathnew, Co. Wicklow. Grave or Memorial Reference: I.F.6. Cemetery: Brookwood Military Cemetery UK.

NEWTON, George Perceval: Rank: Private. Regiment or Service: Royal Dublin Fusiliers. Unit: 2nd Bn. Date of death: 27 August 1914. Age at death: 30. Service No: 8619. Born in Ballybeg, Co. Wicklow. Enlisted in Wicklow while living in Ballybeg. Killed in action.

Supplementary information: Son of George Glascott Newton (late Major Suffolk Regt.) and Anne Westby Newton, of Ballybeg. Grave or Memorial Reference: I.C.22. Cemetery: Honnechy British Cemetery in France.

NICHOLSON, Richard: Rank: Able Seaman. Regiment or

Service: Mercantile Marine. Unit: SS *Solway Queen* (Aberdeen). The Steamship Solway Queen was sunk by a German submarine 7 miles west of Black Head, Wigtownshire carrying a cargo of coal. The Captain and ten of her crew died. The Submarine U-101 was commanded by Carl Siegfried Ritter Von Georg. Ten days after the war ended the submarine surrendered and was broken up in Morcombe in 1920.

Supplementary information: Son of Annie Price (formerly Nicholson), and the late Thomas Nicholson. Husband of Alice Nicholson (*née* Kearns), of 4 King's Hill, Arklow, Co. Wicklow. Born at Arklow. Age at death: 29. Grave or Memorial Reference: He has no known grave but is listed on the Tower Hill Memorial, UK. See **KEARON, Thomas Randolph** another Wicklow man who also died with him on that day.

NICHOLSON, Robert Howlett: Rank: Private. Regiment or Service: Royal Dublin Fusiliers. Unit: 10th Bn. Date of death: 13 November 1916. Service No: 25472. Born in Bray, Co. Wicklow. Enlisted in Dublin. Killed in action. Grave or Memorial Reference: I.C.46. Cemetery: Ancre British Cemetery, Beaumont-Hamel in France.

NOBLETT, Robert James: Rank: Private. Regiment or Service: Royal Inniskilling Fusiliers. Unit: 2nd Bn. Date of death: 1 April 1917. Age at death: 27. Service No: 28188. Born in Carnew, Co. Wicklow. Enlisted in Wicklow. Killed in action.

Supplementary information: Son of Edward and Mary Noblett, of 147 The Mount, Belfast. Grave or Memorial Reference: I.A.112. Cemetery: Savy British Cemetery in France.

NOCTOR, John Patrick: Rank: Gunner. Regiment or Service: Royal Field Artillery, Territorial Force. Unit: 25th Bde. Date of death: 27 November 1917. Age at death: 21. Service No: 686647. Born in Garston in Lancs. Enlisted in Liverpool. Died of wounds.

Supplementary information: Son of James and Ann Noctor, of Coolroe, Tinahely, Co. Wicklow. Grave or Memorial Reference: XIV.E.24. Cemetery: Dozingham Military Cemetery in Belgium.

NOCTOR, Patrick: Rank: Private. Regiment or Service: Royal Dublin Fusiliers. Unit: 9th Bn. Date of death: 1 July 1916, first day of the Battle of the Somme. Service No: 13508. Born in Wicklow. Enlisted in Wicklow. Killed in action. Ireland's Memorials Records has his date of death down as 1 October 1916.

Supplementary information: Son of Patrick and Mary Noctor. Husband of Mary Noctor, of High Street, Wicklow. Grave or Memorial Reference: Y.25. Cemetery: Kemmel Chateau Military Cemetery in Belgium.

NOLAN, Charles: Rank: Gunner. Regiment or Service: Royal Horse Artillery and Royal Field Artillery. Unit: 'D' Battery, 77th Brigade. Date of death: 6 September 1916. Service No: 30479. Born in Enniskerry, Wicklow. Enlisted in Dublin. Died of wounds. Grave or Memorial Reference: He has no known grave but is listed on Pier and Face 1A and 8A on the Thiepval Memorial in France.

NOLAN, James: Rank: Private. Regiment or Service: Royal Dublin Fusiliers. Unit: 6th Bn. He was previously with the Lancers where his number was 5423. Date of death: 4 October 1916. Service No: 25917. Born in Bray, Co. Wicklow. Enlisted in Saltcoats while living in Bray. Died of wounds in the Balkans. Grave or Memorial Reference: 1689. Cemetery; Mikra British Cemetery, Kalamaria in Greece.

Philip Nolan.

NOLAN, John: Rank: Private. Regiment or Service: Connaught Rangers. Unit: 5th Bn. Date of death: 13 September 1915. Service No: 3911 and 5/3911. Born in Baltinglass, Co. Wicklow. Enlisted in Linlithgow, while living in Linlithgow. Died in Gallipoli. Grave or Memorial Reference: F. 126. Cemetery: Alexandria (Chatby) Military and War Cemetery in Egypt.

NOLAN, Patrick: (Alias. Family name is **O'TOOLE**). Rank: Private. Regiment or Service: Connaught Rangers. Unit: 1st Bn. Date of death: 15 April 1916. Age at death: 36. Service No: 9131. Born in Bray, Co. Wicklow. Enlisted in Naas while living in Dublin. Died of wounds in Mesopotamia. Son of William and Mary O'Toole. Husband of Frances O'Toole, of 12 George's Place, Temple Street, Dublin. Grave or Memorial Reference: He has no known grave but is listed on Panel 40 and 64 on the Basra Memorial in Iraq.

NOLAN, Patrick: Rank: Private. Regiment or Service: Irish Guards. Unit: 1st Bn. Date of death: 26 March 1918. Age at death: 38. Service No: 5196. Born in Tinahely, Co. Wicklow. Enlisted in Dublin.

Killed in action.

Supplementary information: Son of James and Mary Nolan, of Lehaunstown, Cabinteely, Co. Dublin. Grave or Memorial Reference: III.K.8. Cemetery: Bucquoy Road Cemetery, Ficheux in France.

NOLAN, Philip: Rank: Lance Sergeant. Regiment or Service: Irish Guards. Unit: 2nd Bn. Date of death: 20 June 1916. Age at death: 28. Service No: 6786. Born in Dunlavin, Co. Wicklow. Enlisted in Dublin while living in Freynestown, Co. Wicklow. Killed in action.

Supplementary information: Son of Philip and Julia Nolan, of Freynestown, Dunlavin, Co. Wicklow. From an article in the a Wicklow Newspaper:

Irish Guardsman Killed in action.

The news of the death of Sergeant Philip Nolan, Irish Guards, son of the late Mr Philip Nolan, Fryanstown, Dunlavin, has occasioned general and sincere regret. Deceased who was only 29 years old, served his time in the Henry Street warehouse, Dublin, and subsequently joined the RIC, serving in Carlow, Mayo and Belfast. Volunteering for active service he was sent to the front early last year, returning for a brief holiday just a month ago. The following affecting letter was received by his poor mother from the Chaplain of the Irish Guards; June 25th. -Dear Mrs Nolan- You will, perhaps, have heard the news of the sad loss of your dear son. I know that God alone can comfort you in your grief, and that all words of mere human sympathy are of no avail. Still there is something that as a priest and Chaplain to the Irish Guards that I can tell you, which at least may sooth any anxiety you may feel as to his fitness to appear before God. We had Mass every morning for seven mornings before going to the trenches on this fateful occasion, and on the very morning of our departure there was General Communion, General Absolution and the Holy Father's Blessing and Plenary Indulgence, all of which your son received. So however great is your sorrow at his loss, do not doubt that he was well prepared to appear in the sight of God. He was a steady, good living man, liked and respected by all who knew him, and a good soldier. He made the offering of his … coming out here, and God has thought fit to accept it. He did his duty and, and thus, fulfilling Gods will "obedient" like his Divine Master, "unto death" May God comfort you in your

great affliction, and may Our Lady, the Mother of all Sorrows, be with you in your grief. With most heartfelt sympathy.
Yours sincerely in J.C., S.S. Knapp, Chaplain.

Grave or Memorial Reference: He has no known grave but is listed on Panel 11 on the Ypres (Menin Gate) Memorial in Belgium. See page 233.

NOLAN, Thomas: Rank: Private. Regiment or Service: Irish Guards. Unit: 1st Bn. Date of death: 9 October 1917. Age at death: 28. Service No: 8934. Born in Kiltegan, Co. Wicklow. Enlisted in Cork while living in Kiltegan. Killed in action.

Supplementary information: Son of Mrs Margaret Nolan, of Feddan, Kiltegan. Grave or Memorial Reference: He has no known grave but is listed on Panel 10 to 11 on the Tyne Cot Memorial in Belgium.

NORDELL, Michael: Rank: Private. Regiment or Service: Royal Dublin Fusiliers. Unit: 8th Bn. Date of death: 25 September 1916. Age at death: 34. Service No: 26578. Born in Bray, Co. Wicklow. Enlisted in Edinburgh while living in Glasgow. Died of wounds.

Supplementary information: Son of Charles and Mary Nordelle. Grave or Memorial Reference: II.F.231. Cemetery: Bailleul Communal Cemetery Extension (Nord) in France.

NOTELY/NOTLCY, Henry: Rank: Private. Regiment or Service: Royal Irish Fusiliers. Unit: 1st Bn. Date of death: 11 May 1917. Age at death: 23. Service No: 24837. Born in Ballymore-Eustace, Co. Kildare. Enlisted in Maryborough, Queen's County while living in Dublin. Killed in action.

Supplementary information: Son of Mr and Mrs James Notley, of Ballymore Eustace, Co. Wicklow. Husband of Mary Jane Notley, of 16 Middle Gardiner Street, Dublin. Grave or Memorial Reference: C.26. Cemetery: Roeux British Cemetery in France.

O

O'BRIEN, Harold George: Rank: Private. Regiment or Service: Royal Dublin Fusiliers. Unit: 'B' Coy. 7ᵗʰ Bn. Date of death: 16 August 1915. Age at death: 30. Service No: 17960. Born in Monkstown, Co. Dublin. Enlisted in Dublin. Killed in action in Gallipoli.

Supplementary information: Son of John and Catherine Elizabeth O'Brien, of Kiltimon Cottage, Ashford, Co. Wicklow. Grave or Memorial Reference: He has no known grave but is listed on Panel 190 to 196 on the Helles memorial in Turkey.

O'BRIEN, John: Rank: Private. Regiment or Service: Royal Dublin Fusiliers. Unit: 5ᵗʰ Bn. Date of death: 5 May 1916. Service No: 25275. Born in Tinahely, Co. Wicklow. Enlisted in Shillelagh, Co. Wicklow. Died at home. Grave or Memorial Reference: 590. Cemetery: Curragh Military Cemetery, Co. Kildare.

O'BRIEN, Matthew: Rank: Private. Regiment or Service: East Lancashire Regiment. Unit: 8ᵗʰ Bn.

Date of death: 15 July 1916. Service No: 16665. Born in Aughrim, Co. Wicklow. Enlisted in Oldham in Lancashire while living in Aughrim. Killed in action. Grave or Memorial Reference: He has no known grave but is listed on Pier and Face 6.C. on the Thiepval Memorial in France.

O'BRIEN, Michael: Rank: Ordinary Seaman. Merchant Navy. Unit: SS *Tregenna* (St. Ives) Age at death: 26. Date of death: 17 September 1940.

Supplementary information: Son of Patrick and Mary O'Brien, of Arklow, Co. Wicklow. SS *Tregenna* had left Halifax with a cargo of steel. During a severe north-west gale she was picked off by German Submarine U65 and a single torpedo into her bow sent her to the bottom south of Rockall. Thirty-three of the crew went down with her. Only four survived and they were the ones on watch. In April 1941 U65 was depth charged and sent to the bottom. Michael has no known grave but is listed on Panel 110 on the Tower Hill Memorial, UK.

O'BRIEN, Patrick: Rank: Fireman and Trimmer. Regiment or Service: Merchant Navy Unit: SS *Samala* (Liverpool) Age at death: 19. Date of death: 30 September 1940.

Supplementary information: Son of Denis and Kathleen O'Brien, of Wicklow. Sunk by German Submarine U37 with the loss of her entire crew of sixty-five. Grave or Memorial Reference: He has no known grave but is listed on panel 91 on the Tower Hill Memorial, UK.

O'BRIEN, Thomas Christopher: Rank: Private. Regiment or Service: Hampshire Regiment. Unit: 1st Bn. Age at death: 20. Date of death: 4 October 1944 Service No: 14443992.

Supplementary information: Son of William and Elizabeth O'Brien, of Rathnew, Co. Wicklow, Irish Republic. Grave or Memorial Reference: 9.B.7. Cemetery: Armhem Oosterbeek War Cemetery in Holland.

O'CARROLL, K.: Rank: Fireman. Regiment or Service: Mercantile Marine Reserve. Unit: HMS *Eaglet*. Date of death: 21 November 1918. Service No: 898499.

Supplementary information: Son of Mrs R O'Carroll, of Bray. Grave or Memorial Reference: D.A.52.

Cemetery, Little Bray (St Peter's) Catholic Cemetery, Wicklow.

O'CONNOR, Arthur: Rank: Private. Regiment or Service: Royal Munster Fusiliers. Unit: 2nd Bn. Date of death: 9 September 16. Service No: 6802. Born in Bray, Co. Wicklow. Enlisted in Limerick. Killed in action. Grave or Memorial Reference: He has no known grave but is listed on Pier and Face 16.C. on the Thiepval Memorial in France.

O'CONNOR, James: Rank: Private. Regiment or Service: Irish Guards. Unit: 2nd Bn. Date of death: 30 September 1915. Service No: 4424. Born in Ferns, Co. Wexford. Enlisted in Dublin while living in Arklow. Killed in action. Grave or Memorial Reference: He has no known grave but is listed on Panel 9 and 10 on the Loos Memorial in France.

O'CONNOR, John: Rank: Private. Regiment or Service: Royal Dublin Fusiliers. Unit: 1st Bn. Date of death: 3 December 1915. Service No: 21771. Born in Newtownmountkennedy, Co. Wicklow. Enlisted in Athlone. Killed in action in Gallipoli. Grave or Memorial Reference: III.B.7. Cemetery: Hill 10 in Turkey.

O'CONNOR, Thomas: Rank: Private. Regiment or Service: Welsh Regiment. Unit: 16th Bn. Date of death: 7 July 1916. Service No: 32520. Born in Arklow, Co. Wicklow. Enlisted in Bridgend. Killed in action. Grave or Memorial Reference: He has no known grave but is listed on Pier and Face 7A and 10A on the Thiepval Memorial in France.

O'DONNELL, M: Rank: Able Seaman. Regiment or Service: Mercantile Marine. Unit: SS *Auckland Castle* (Newport). Age at death: 51. Date of death: 24 August 1918.

Supplementary information: Husband of Maria O'Donnell, of 27 Bell Street, North Shields. Born at Arklow. Grave or Memorial Reference: He has no known grave but is listed on the Tower Hill Memorial, UK.

O'DONOHOE/O'DON-OUGHUE, James: Rank: Private. Regiment or Service: Royal Army Ordnance Corps. Unit: 3rd Company. Date of Death: 7 November 1918. Service No: S/7447. Born in Wicklow. Enlisted in Dublin. Grave or Memorial Reference: Div.62.II.I.1. Cemetery: Ste Marie Cemetery, Le Havre in France.

O'DOWD, Daniel: Rank: Private. Regiment or Service: Pioneer Corps. Age at death: 52. Date of death: 2 June 1943. Service No: 13007599.

Supplementary information: Son of Michael and Anne O'Dowd. Husband of Mary O'Dowd, of Kilternan. Grave or Memorial Reference: Grave S.21. Little Bray (St. Peter's) Catholic Cemetery, Wicklow.

O'FARRELL, Maurice: Rank: Corporal. Regiment or Service: Royal Munster Fusiliers. Unit: 6th Bn. Date of death: 16 December 1915. Service No: 197. Born in Wicklow. Enlisted in Barry, Glamorgan while living in Dublin. Died of wounds in Greek Macedonia. Grave or Memorial Reference: 20. Cemetery: Salonika (Lembet Road) Military Cemetery in Greece.

O'GRADY, Dermot: Rank: Second Engineer Officer. Regiment or Service: Merchant Navy Unit: SS *Albert C. Field* (St. Catherines, Ontario) Age at death: 44. Date of death: 20 July 1946.

Supplementary information: Son of William and Henrietta O'Grady, of Wicklow. Husband of Mary Ellen O'Grady, of Wicklow. The Canadian cargo steamship *Albert C. Field* was sunk by a torpedo

The gravestone of Dermot O'Grady.

from a German Aircraft and rests in 32feet of water just off Anvil Point. She was carrying a cargo of ammunition. Grave or Memorial Reference: Grave 731. Cemetery: Rathnew Cemetery, Co. Wicklow.

O'GRADY, J.: Rank: Colour Serjeant. Regiment or Service: Machine Gun Corps (Infantry). Date of death: 7 April 1919. Service No: 166247. Grave or Memorial Reference: R.C. ground 3.G.1406. Cemetery: Rathnew Cemetery, Co. Wicklow.

O'NEILL, Christopher: Rank: Able Seaman. Regiment or Service: Merchant Navy Unit: MV *Melbourne Star* (London) Age at death: 47. Date of death: 2 April 1943.

Supplementary information: Son of Michael and Ann O'Neill, of Birkdale, Southport, Lancashire. Husband of Annie O'Neill, of Arklow, Co. Wicklow. MV *Melbourne Star* was damaged *en route* to Malta by the German Submarine U129 but made it to port. U129 was scuttled in 1944. It was raised afterwards and broken up in 1946. Grave or Memorial Reference: He has no known grave but is listed on Panel 69 on the Tower Hill Memorial, UK.

O'NEILL, Leo Michael: Rank: Private. Regiment or Service: Bedfordshire and Hertfordshire Regiment Unit: 6th Bn. Age at death: 33. Date of death: 27 July 1944. Service No: 5948634.

Supplementary information: Born in Salford. Enlisted while living in London. Son of Michael and Mary O'Neill, of Greystones, Co. Wicklow. Grave or Memorial Reference: Plot P.P. Grave 40034. Cemetery: Croyden (Mitchham Road) Cemetery, UK.

O'NEIL/O'NEILL, Michael: Rank: Private. Regiment or Service: Royal Dublin Fusiliers. Unit: 2nd Bn. Date of death: 18 March 1917. Service No: 20341. Born in lusk, Co. Dublin. Enlisted in Dunlavin, Co. Wicklow while living in Freynestown, Co. Wicklow. Died. Grave or Memorial Reference: III.B.12. Cemetery: Bailleul Communal Cemetery Extension (Nord) in France.

O'REILLY, Frank Power: Rank: Lieutenant. Regiment or Service: Royal Navy Unit: HMS *Invincible*. HMS *Invincible* was sunk during the battle of Jutland. Age at death: 29. Date of death: 31 May 1916.

Supplementary information: Son of Terence and Angela O'Reilly, of Croghan Lodge, Avoca, Co. Wicklow. Native of Dublin.

Grave or Memorial Reference: 11. Memorial: Portsmouth Memorial, UK.

O'REILLY, George: Rank: Rifleman. Regiment or Service: Royal Irish Rifles. Unit: 1st Bn. Date of death: 1 July 1916, first day of the Battle of the Somme. Service No: 2862. Born in Bray, Co. Wicklow. Enlisted in Naas, Co. Kildare. Killed in action. Grave or Memorial Reference: He has no known grave but is listed on Pier and Face 15 A and 15 B on the Thiepval Memorial in France.

O'ROURKE, James: Rank: Private. Regiment or Service: Coldstream Guards. Date of death: 12 March 1917. Service No: 18568. Born in Danard, Co. Wicklow. Enlisted in Blackpool. Killed in action. Grave or Memorial Reference: III.A.29. Cemetery: Combles Communal Cemetery Extension in France.

O'ROURKE, Patrick Jerry: Rank: Aircraftman 1st Class. Regiment or Service: Royal Air Force Volunteer Reserve Age at death: 30. Date of death: 5 November 1945 Service No: 1254281.
Supplementary information: Son of Edward and Margaret O'Rourke.

Husband of Elizabeth Mary O'Rourke, of Bray, Co. Wicklow. Grave or Memorial Reference: Grave B.61. Cemetery: Little Bray (St Peter's) Catholic Cemetery, Dublin.

ORMSBY, John Yeadon: Rank: Lieutenant Colonel. Regiment or Service: Royal Artillery. Age at death: 41. Date of death: 22 November 1941 Service No: 573.
Supplementary information: Son of Colonel Thomas Ormsby, D.S.O. and of Lucy Ormsby (*née* Thompson). Husband of Louise Gwendolyn Ormsby (*née* Lynch), of Bray. Grave or Memorial Reference: 4.F.4. Cemetery: Asmara War Cemetery, Eritrea.

ORR, Alexander William Burrell: Rank: Private. Regiment or Service: Royal Fusiliers (City of London Regiment). Unit: 20th (Public Schools Batt) Bn. Date of death: 14 February 1916. Service No: 5393 and PS/5393. Born in Enniskerry. Enlisted in Belfast while living in Belfast. Killed in action. Grave or Memorial Reference: LI.6.D. Cemetery: Cambrin Churchyard Extension in France.

O'SULLIVAN, Arthur Moore: Rank: Captain. Regiment or Service: Royal Irish Rifles. Unit:

Arthur Moore O'Sullivan.

Motor Vessel
Melbourne Star.

1st Bn. Date of death: 9 May 1915. Age at Death: 36. Killed in Action. Awards: Mentioned in Despatches.

Supplementary information: From De Ruvigny's Roll of Honour: Son of the late Patrick O'Sullivan, Advocate-General, Madras Presidency. By his wife Sydney Jane (Auburn, Greystones, Co Wicklow) daughter, of William Daniel Moore, MD. Educated: Bedford Grammer School and Hertford College, Oxford. Enlisted in the Oxfordshire L.I. in 1900. Gazetted 2nd Lieut, in the Royal Irish Rifles, 23 July 1902, and promoted to Lieut, 9 July 1906. Capt 11 March 1910. Was Adjutant of his regiment from 1 January 1910 to 31 December 1912. Served in the South African War, 1900–01; took part in the operations in Cape Colony, Orange River Colony, and the Transvaal, April, 1900 to 1901. Was employed with the West African Frontier Force, 1 October 1905 to 22 November 1907. He went to France with the Expeditionary Force in November 1914, and was killed in action at Fromelles, 9 May 1916. Capt O'Sullivan was mentioned in Sir John (now Lord) French's Despatch of 31 May 1915, for gallant and distinguished service. Supplementary information from Jimmy Taylor;

Born at Octacamund, India, 19 August 1878.

Quis Separabit, vol. III, no.1, described the preparations for leaving Aden:'I can still see "Amos" [Captain A.M. O'Sullivan[, our PMC, singing "We're going to war, we're going to b—y war" whilst he and the Mess Staff lightly tossed mess property and mess plate into the boxes. This "lightly tossing" cost us in 1919 £300 for repair of silver.' It was he who fired his revolver at midnight, 25/26 December 1914, to signal the end of the Christmas truce in his part of the line. Wounded by machine gun fire while cutting barbed wire, 11 March 1915. Killed in action 9 May 1915. Royal Irish Rifles Graveyard, Laventie, Pas de Calais I.C.1. Medals sent to his sister, Miss M.E. O'Sullivan, 9 Fairview Road, Norbury. File destroyed. Grave or Memorial Reference: I.C.1. Cemetery: Royal Irish Rifles Graveyard, Laventie in France.

O'TOOLE, J.: Rank: Private. Regiment or Service: Royal Dublin Fusiliers. Unit: Depot. Date of death: 27 November 1919. Age at death: 25. Service No: 20361.

Supplementary information: Son of Mrs O'Toole, of 8 Bond Street, Wicklow. Grave or Memorial Reference: Roman Catholic.

ground 3.E.1439. Cemetery: Rathnew Cemetery in Wicklow.

O'TOOLE, Patrick: (Served as **NOLAN**). Rank: Private. Regiment or Service: Connaught Rangers. Unit: 1st Bn. Date of death: 15 April 1916. Age at death: 36. Service No: 9131. Born in Bray, Co. Wicklow. Enlisted in Naas while living in Dublin. Died of wounds in Mesopotamia.

Supplementary information: Son of the late William and Mary O'Toole. Husband of Frances O'Toole, of 12 George's Place, Temple Street, Dublin. Grave or Memorial Reference: He has no known grave but is listed on Panel 40 and 64 on the Basra Memorial in Iraq.

OVINGTON, Anthony: Rank: Corporal. Regiment or Service: Royal Dublin Fusiliers. Unit: 10th Bn. Date of death: 13 November 1916. Service No: 25463. Born in Woodfield, Co.Wicklow. Enlisted in Armagh while living in Baltinglass, Co. Wicklow. Killed in action. Grave or Memorial Reference: He has no known grave but is listed on Pier and Face 16 C on the Thiepval Memorial in France.

OWENS, James: Rank: Private. Regiment or Service: Royal

The gravestone of J. O'Toole.

Dublin Fusiliers. Unit: 1st Bn. Date of death: 30 April 1915. Age at death: 24. Service No: 10959. Born in Ashford, Co. Wicklow. Enlisted in Wicklow. Died of wounds. Killed in action in Gallipoli.

Supplementary information: Son of John and Mary Owens, of Rathmore, Ashford, Co. Wicklow. rave or Memorial Reference: Panel 190 to 196. Grave or Memorial Reference: He has no known grave but is listed on Panel 190 to 196. on the Helles Memorial in Turkey.

P

PARKES, Robert: Rank: Private. Regiment or Service: East Lancashire Regiment. Unit: 2nd Bn. Date of death: 3 July 1915. Service No: 8695. Died of wounds. Born in Rathnew.
Supplementary information: Son of Robert and Ellen Parkes, of Dublin. Grave or Memorial Reference: II.G.148. Cemetery: Sailly-Sur-La-Lys-Canadian Cemetery in France.

PASLEY, George Gerald: Rank: Second Lieutenant. Regiment or Service: Royal Flying Corps. Age at death: 19. Date of death: 19 December 1917.
Supplementary information: Son of Mrs M. Pasley, of 'The Mount', Tinahely. Grave or Memorial Reference: In north-west part. Cemetery: Kilcommon Church of Ireland Churchyard, Tinahely, Co. Wicklow.

PASLEY, John Vincent: Rank: Acting Lance Corporal. Regiment or Service: Military Police Corps Unit: No.1 Troop Mounted Military Police. Attached Traffic Control. Date of death: 5 March 1919. Age at death: 22. Service No: P/13078. Born in Lugduff. Enlisted in Tinahely while living in Tinahely.
Supplementary information: Son of Mr J. George and Margaret J. Pasley, of 'The Mount', Tinahely, Co. Wicklow. Grave or Memorial Reference: III.B.14. Cemetery: Cologne Southern Cemetery.

PERROTT, William George Lecky: Rank: Bombardier. Regiment or Service: Royal Artillery Unit: 5 Searchlight Regt. Age at death: 28. Date of death: 5 March 1943 Service No: 835997.
Supplementary information: Son of William and Matilda Perrott, of Woodenbridge, Co. Wicklow. Commandeered by Lt-Col.J.Bassett, R. A, 35 L.A.A. Dying on Balili Island with 516 other gunners, was laid to rest at 12 mile north of Port Moresby, Papua New Guinea. Grave or Memorial Reference: He has no known grave but is listed on Column 8 of the Singapore Memorial.

PETERS, George Charles Boyce: Rank: Flying Officer

(Pilot). Regiment or Service: Royal Air Force. Unit: 79 Sqdn. Age at death: 27. Date of death: 29 September 1940. Service No: 40593.

Supplementary information: Son of George Henry Boyce and Marion Peters, of Aldwick, Sussex. His aircraft, a Hurricane X P5177 was shot down off Cork 1830hrs. He is listed in Fighter Command Losses. Vol. 1.N.L.R. Franks. Grave or Memorial Reference: Grave 2252. Cemetery: Rathnew Cemetery, Co. Wicklow.

PHIBBS, Christopher: Rank: Driver. Regiment or Service: Royal Horse Artillery and Royal Field Artillery. Unit 'D' Battery, 88th Brigade. Date of death: 3 August 1916. Age at death: 21. Service No: 86379. Born in Wicklow. Enlisted in Warrington in Lancashire. Killed in action.

Supplementary information: Son of Mr P. and Mrs A. Phibbs, of 9 Antrobus Street, Warrington. Grave or Memorial Reference: VI.R.2. Cemetery; Danzig Alley British Cemetery, Mametz in France.

PHILLIPS, Andrew: Rank: Sailor. Regiment or Service: Mercantile Marine. Unit: SS *William Middleton* (Sunderland). Date of death: 28 September 1917. Age at death: 30.

Supplementary information: Son of Patrick and Ann Phillips. Husband of Margaret Ann Phillips (*née* Breen), of 18 Clarence Street, North Strand, Dublin. Born at Wicklow. Grave or Memorial Reference: He has no known grave but is listed on the Tower Hill memorial UK.

PHILLIPS, W.: Rank: Leading Stoker. Regiment or Service: Royal Naval Reserve. Unit: HMS *Vivid*. Age at death: 40. Date of death: 3 June 1917. Service No: 1795U.

Supplementary information: Husband of Annie Phillips, of 1 Ferry Bank, Arklow. Grave or Memorial Reference: South. 3MM.7 East. Cemetery: Arklow Cemetery, Co. Wicklow.

PHILP, Richard Thomas: Rank: Sergeant (W. Op.-Air Gnr.). Regiment or Service: Royal Air Force Volunteer Reserve Unit: 102 Sqdn. Age at death: 20. Date of death: 15 August 1941. Service No: 997009.

Supplementary information: Son of William Frederick and Elizabeth Philp, of Bray, Co. Wicklow. Aircraft based in Topcliffe (Whitley V Z6829.DY) was shot down by a night-fighter (Ofw Paul Gildner, 4. /NJG1) and crashed at 0448 hrs in Waddenzee of Terschelling during

Advertisement for War Bonds.

operation Hannover. Four bodies recovered and buried together. Remains of three of the bodies were buried in a single coffin. One of the crew escaped but was captured the next day. The dead are listed in 'Bomber Command Losses'. Vol. 2 WR. Chorley. Grave or Memorial Reference: Joint grave 32. Cemetery: Terschelling (West-Terschelling) General Cemetery in Holland.

PLUNKETT, John: Rank: Lance Corporal. Regiment or Service: Royal Dublin Fusiliers. Unit: 2nd Bn. Date of death: 1 July 1916, first day of the Battle of the Somme. Service No: 11685. Born in Rathnew, Co. Wicklow.

Enlisted in Naas while living in Rathnew. Killed in action. Grave or Memorial Reference: I.D.29. Cemetery: Sucrerie Military Cemetery in France.

POLLARD, Henry: Rank: Private. Regiment or Service: Royal Dublin Fusiliers. Unit: 1st Bn. Date of death: 9 December 1918. Service No: 5654. Born in Baltinglass, Co. Wicklow. Enlisted in Carlow while living in Baltinglass. Died. Grave or Memorial Reference: II.E.8. Cemetery: Berlin South-Western Cemetery in Germany.

PORTER, William: Rank: Private. Regiment or Service:

Royal Munster Fusiliers. Unit: 7th Bn. Formerly he was with the Royal Dublin Fusiliers where his number was. 15765. Date of death: 15 August 1915. Age at death: 37 Service No: 5316. Born St Lawrence O'Toole, Dublin. Enlisted in Dublin.

Supplementary information: Husband of Mary Agnes Porter, of Lough Dan, Roundwood, Co. Wicklow. Grave or Memorial Reference: He has no known grave but is listed on Panel 185 to 190 on the Helles Memorial in Turkey.

PORTER, William: Rank: Able Seaman. Regiment or Service: Royal Navy Unit: HMS *Glorious*. Age at death: 26. Date of death: 8 June 1940 Service No: D-JX 134981.

Supplementary information: Son of William and Mary Porter, of Annamoe, Co. Wicklow. HMS *Glorius* was an Aircraft Carrier and sunk with 2 of her two escorting destroyers by two German Battlecruisers in the Norwegian Sea. Over 1,500 men died when they went down. Grave or Memorial Reference: He has no known grave but is listed on Panel 38, Column on the Plymouth Memorial, UK.

PRESTON, Arthur John Dillon: Rank: Captain. Regiment or Service: Royal Dublin Fusiliers. Unit: 6th Bn. Date of death: 15 August 1915. Age at death: 29. Awards: Mentioned in Despatches.

Supplementary information: Member of the Peerage. Husband of Sylvia Wyke Preston, of Clowbryn, Greystones, Co. Wicklow. From De Ruvigny's Roll of Honour: Son of Major Arthur John Preston, of Swainston, Co. Meath, late Duke of Wellingtons Regt. B.A. from Trinity College, Dublin. J.P. Counties Durham and Meath, by his wife Gertrude Mary, daughter of Richard Knight, of Bobbing Court, Co, Kent. Born: Luther House, Huddersfield, 16 November 1885. Educated: Malvern College. Gazetted 2nd Lieut to 3rd (Militia) Battalion of the Durham L. I. 5 October 1904. Posted to the 1st Bn Dublin Fusiliers, 2 March 1907, promoted Lieut, 15 Decemer 1909 and Capt, 2nd Bn, 7 June 1914. Served with the 1st Bn in Egypt where he joined the mounted infantry, winning at Cairo the Lloyd Lindsay Prize. At the outbreak of the European war he was ordered to Naas and afterwards to the Curragh to raise the 6th Service Battalion of the Royal Dublin Fusiliers with which he proceeded to the Gallilpoli Peninsula on 9 July. He took part in all the heavy fighting at Suvla Bay until 15 August when he fell in the moment of victory. The Colonel of his battalion, writing to

Arthur John Dillon Preston.

his widow, remarked;

I am sure all Ireland will soon hear of the charge of the Dublins and Munsters on that afternoon. Your husband (Capt Preston, second in command) was responsible for it and organise it splendidly, and in conjunction with Capt Whyte he brilliantly led it. It was a magnificent sight considering the charged up a hill through a hail of bombs and bullets. Capt, Preston got safely on the hill (capturing the trench), but in the counter attack was fatally wounded in the right breast. I was the last officer to speak to him, and told splendidly he had done. Personally, I feel his death very much. No man could have helped his colonel more than he, the success of the regt, was greatly due to him.

Capt, Whyte, Royal Dublin Fusiliers, wrote;

We closed on the Munsters, and all collected on some dead ground about 100 yards from there joking. When the word came that we were to clear the ridge we fixed bayonets, then we all started together, Dublins and Munsters, John Armstrong shouting "Come on boys." The Turks threw bombs and opened fire upon us as we neared the top, but we went straight on and rushed the trench. The Turks put up their hands.

I saw John stop his men who were just going to bayonet a Turkish officer. As you know, he was my best friend, and was loved by every one in the regt., officers, N.C.O's and men. The only consolation is that he died a glorious death, leading his men to victory, the death I am sure, he would have chosen.

Capt, Preston wrote to his wife on that fatal 15 August remarking; 'I have had six hours sleep and am full of buck and life.' Also to his father a five page letter. The battle had even then commenced in the valley below. It was written under strenuous circumstances, no change of clothes for five nights, and only six hours sleep, no chance of a wash, and exposed to the heat of a tropical sun, yet his last written words were 'Love to you all; I am very fit and quite happy.'

He and the Adjutant, Capt Richards, who fell at the same time, were buried side by side in the same grave close to the sea shore at Suvla Bay. A flat gravestone covers them with their remains engraved upon it under the words, 'In Victory.' He was mentioned for gallant and distinguished service in the field by Sir John Hamilton in his Despatch of 11 December 1915. While in Egypt he and Lieut Crozier sailed hundreds of miles up the White Nile from Khartoum, in a rough native boat, on which occasion they secured a fine bag of big game, including a lion, buffalo, elephant, hippo, and various specimens of antelope and deer. He was a keen sportsman, well-known with the Kildare and Meath hounds, and a fine cricketer and tennis player, and the best shot with revolver and rifle (tied) in his Battalion. Captain Preston at St Mary-Le-Bone Church, London 24 March 1914, Sylvia, daughter of Arthur James Billie of Tadworth, Co. Surrey, and had a son; John Nathaniel who was born on the 27 January 1915. Note: Captain Richards and Captain Preston fell together and were buried side by side however at this time they are both in different cemeteries, Captain Richards is now buried in Green Hill Cemetery which is also located in Turkey. Grave or Memorial Reference: Special Memorial 50. Cemetery: Azmak Cemetery in Suvla, Turkey.

PRESTON, Patrick: Rank: Private. Regiment or Service: Royal Dublin Fusiliers. Unit: 2nd Bn. Date of death: 24 May 1915. Age at death: 29. Service No: 8995. Born in Blessington, Co. Wicklow. Enlisted in Naas. Killed in action.

Supplementary information: Son of Patrick Preston. Husband of Mrs M. Wood (formerly Preston), of Rathashe Road, Naas, Co. Kildare. He has no known grave but is listed on Panel 44 and 46 on the Ypres (Menin Gate) Memorial in Belgium.

PRICE, Edward: Rank: Lance Corporal. Regiment or Service: Royal Dublin Fusiliers. Unit: 1st Bn. Date of death: 01 March 1917. Age at death: 22. Service No: 11244. Born in Roundwood, Wicklow. Enlisted in Dublin while living in Roundwood. Died of wounds.

Supplementary information: Son of Mrs Bridget Price, of Bolinass,

Ashford, Co. Wicklow. He has no known grave but is listed on Pier and Face 16.C. on the Thiepval Memorial in France.

PRICE, Ernest Dickinson: Rank: Lieutenant. Regiment or Service: Royal Irish Regiment. Unit: 3rd Bn. Secondary Regiment: Royal Irish Rifles. Secondary Unit: attd. 2nd Bn. Date of death: 19 March 1916. Age at death: 22. Died of Wounds.

Supplementary information: Son of Lt. Col. Ivon H. Price, D.S.O, Assistant Inspector General Royal Irish Constabulary, and Margaret E. Price, of Greystones, Co. Wicklow. Educated at St Columba's College and Trinity College, Dublin. Grave or Memorial Reference: XV.K.13. Cemetery: Cabaret-Rouge British Cemetery, Souchez in France and he is also commemorated on a marble plaque on the walls of the reading room in Trinity College, Dublin.

PRUNTY, Jack: Rank: Gunner. Regiment or Service: Royal Artillery/ Unit: 28. Field Regt. Age at death: 25. Date of death: 4 September 1942. Service No: 972725.

Supplementary information: Son of John and Ellen Prunty, of Bray, Co. Wicklow. Grave or Memorial Reference: XXIII.E.11. Cemetery: El Alamein War Cemetery in Egypt.

Q

QUAILE, John: Rank: Gunner. Regiment or Service: Royal Garrison Artillery. Unit: 143rd Siege Battery. Date of death: 30 September 1917. Age at death: 28. Service No: 78016. Born in Tinahely, Co. Wicklow. Enlisted in Glasgow. Killed in action.

Supplementary information: Son of Hugh and Julia Quaile, of Ballyshonogue, Tinahely. Grave or Memorial Reference: I.G.27. Cemetery: Ypres Reservoir Cemetery in Belgium.

QUIN, Terence: Rank: Private. Regiment or Service: Royal Irish Regiment. Unit: 6th Bn. Date of death: 5 April 1917. Service No: 3608. Born in Kilquade, Co. Wicklow. Enlisted in Roundwood, Co. Wicklow. Died. Grave or Memorial Reference: He has no known grave but is listed on Panel 33on the Ypres (Menin Gate) Memorial in Belgium.

QUINN, John: Rank: Rifleman. Regiment or Service: Royal Irish Rifles. Unit: 1st Bn. Date of death: 20 July 1915. Service No: 6257. Born in Arklow, Co. Wicklow. Enlisted in Dundalk, Co. Louth while living in Newry, Co. Down. Killed in action. Grave or Memorial Reference: K.36. Cemetery: Y Farm Military Cemetery, Bois-Grenier in France.

QUINN, Walter: Rank: Captain (Dental Surgeon). Regiment or Service: General List. Date of death: 11 July 1921. Age at death: 37.

Supplementary information: Only son of Mark W. Quinn, J.P, and Gertrude Quinn, of 3 Bayswater Terrace, Greystones, Co. Wicklow. Grave or Memorial Reference: II.N.17. Cemetery: Basra War Cemetery in Iraq.

R

RAYNE, John: Rank: Sergeant. Regiment or Service: Labour Corps. He was previously with the Northumberland Fusiliers where his number was 628. Date of death: 15 October 1917. Service No: 386442. Born in Hollywood, Wicklow. Enlisted in Newcastle-on-Tyne while living in Byker, Newcastle-on-Tyne. Killed in action.

REDMOND, Benjamin: Rank: Second Engineer Officer. Regiment or Service: Merchant Navy Unit: SS *Coast Wings* (London) Age at death: 32. Date of death: 27 September 1940.

Supplementary information: Son of Benjamin P. and Mary Jane Redmond, of Kilbride, Co. Wicklow. Husband of Mary I. Redmond, of Ballybrittas, Co. Leix. SS *Coast Wings* was an old Dutch cargo ship and in convoy OG-43 when she was struck by a torpedo from German Submarine U46. She was one of two ships sent to the bottom by the same Submarine that day. U46 was de-commissioned in Nesutadt in October 1943 and scuttled on 4 of May 1945. Grave or Memorial Reference: He has no known grave but is listed on Panel 31 of the Tower Hill Memorial, UK.

REDMOND, Charles: Rank: Private. Regiment or Service: Royal Dublin Fusiliers. Unit: 2nd Bn. Date of death: 24 May 1915. Service No: 9597. Born in Shillelagh. Enlisted in Carlow while living in Wicklow. Killed in action. Grave or Memorial Reference: He has no known grave but is listed on Panel 44 and 46 on the Ypres (Menin Gate) Memorial in Belgium.

REDMOND, John: Rank: Able Seaman. Regiment or Service: Merchant Navy. Unit: S. S. *Glenmaroon* (Belfast). Date of death: 7 December 1944.

Supplementary information: Son of Michael and Sarah Redmond; husband of Elizabeth Redmond, of Arklow, Co. Wicklow. SS *Glenmaroon* was struck by an enemy aircraft which set it on fire and it sank with the loss of three men. It was built in Paisley in 1917.

Grave or Memorial Reference: Sec. 7. R. C. Grave 2440. Cemetery: Barrow-in-Furness Cemetery, UK.

REDMOND, John Joseph: Rank: Private. Regiment or Service: Royal Munster Fusiliers. Unit: 6th Bn. Date of death: 2 July 1916. Age at death: 20. Service No: 3209. Born in Ashford, Co. Wicklow. Enlisted in Dublin while living in Bray, Co. Wicklow. Died in Greek Macedonia.

Supplementary information: Son of Patrick and Bridget Redmond, of Bray. Grave or Memorial Reference: 181. Cemetery: Salonika (Lembet Road) Military Cemetery in Greece.

REDMOND, Michael: Rank: Private. Regiment or Service: Royal Marine Light Infantry. Unit: HMS *Malaya.* Date of death: 1 June 1916. Age at death: 30. Service No: PO/687. Private Redmond died from wounds received during the Battle of Jutland the previous day. He is one of the very few Wicklow First World War Naval casualties to have a grave and not just a name on a memorial to those lost at sea or buried at sea. Although HMS *Malaya* was hit eight times by enemy guns during the Battle she was able to make it back to base. The ship was scrapped in 1948.

Supplementary information: Son of Michael Redmond, of 1 South Quay, Arklow, Co. Wicklow. Grave or Memorial Reference: O.32. Cemetery: Lyness Royal Naval Cemetery, Orkney, UK.

REDMOND, William Hoey Kearney: Rank: Major. Regiment or service: Royal Irish Regiment. Unit: 6th Bn. Age at Death: 56. Date of Death: 7 June 1917. Died of wounds received in an attack at Wytschaete Wood in Belgium after being injured by a shell. Mentioned in Despatches.

Supplementary information: Husband of Eleanor Redmond. Nationalist member of Parliament for Wexford from 1884. Awarded the Legion of Honour (France). Information taken from his records (WO339/19182) by Jimmy Taylor; Served as an officer in the Wexford Militia and the 3rd (Militia) Battalion, Royal Irish regiment from 24 December 1879 until 11 January 1882. Temporary commission as captain in 6th (Service) Battalion, Royal Irish Regiment 22 February 1915. Home address Glenbrook, Delgany, Co Wicklow and Palace Manshions, Kensington, London. War Office telegram to wife 8 June 1917 reports that he died of wounds 7 June 1917 and expresses sympathy. Death report dated 10 June 1917 shows died of wounds, 7 June 1917, 6th Royal Irish Regiment attached 16th

Divisional Company. Undated War Office memo reports burial 'at the south end of the garden of the hospice, Locre, SW of Ypres'. Letter to HQ Horse Guards Whitehall 21 June 1917 requests buglers of one Battlion Brigade of Guards to attend St Mary's Catholic Church, Clapham (London SW) 23rd June at 10am to sound Last Post at requiem Mass for Major Redmond. 'All expenses incurred will be refunded privately.' (Irish Guards preffered). Estate valued at £4018.2.9., against which there were debts of £1885.3.2 Whole estate to widow. Personal effects were taken directly to Mrs Redmond by the reverend M. O'Connell, S. C. F. 16th Division, whilst on leave. Mentioned in Despatches, *London Gazette*, 4 January 1917. French legion d'Honeur (Chevalier) *London Gazette* 14 July 1917. 1914-15 Star, British War Medal and Victory Medals, with oak leaf (MID). Willie was one of the rare people to be buried abroad during the First World War in a coffin. Grave or Memorial Reference: Close to Path leading to the Cemetery. Cemetery: Locre Hospice Cemetery in Belgium.

REID, William: Rank: Private. Regiment or Service: Leinster. Date of death: 9 June 1917. Age at death: 21. Service No: 3266. Born in Greystones, Co. Wicklow.

Enlisted in Kingstown, Co. Dublin while living in Sandymount, Dublin. Killed in action.

Supplementary information: Son of William Reid. Grave or Memorial Reference: He has no known grave but is listed on Panel 44 on the Ypres (Menin Gate) Memorial in Belgium.

RICHARDSON, William: Rank: Private. Regiment or Service: Royal Dublin Fusiliers. Unit: 1st Bn. Date of death: 28 June 1915. Service No: 17746 Enlisted in Dublin while living in Kilcool, Co. Wicklow. Killed in action.

REILLY, Peter Joseph: Rank: Private. Regiment or Service: Royal Irish Regiment. Unit: 7th Bn. Date of death: 5 November 1918. Service No: 6957. Born in St Andrews, Dublin. Enlisted in Dublin while living in Bray, Co. Wicklow. Died.

REILLY, Richard: Rank: Sergeant. Regiment or Service: King's Own Royal Regiment (Lancaster). Unit: 2nd Bn. Age at death: 32. Date of death: 3 February 1940. Service No: 3709469.

Supplementary information: Son of Richard and Margaret Reilly; husband of Elizabeth Reilly, of Tinahely, Co. Wicklow. Grave

Solicitors Memorial in the Law
Library, Four Courts, Dublin.

or Memorial Reference: 7.D.10.
Cemetery: Ismailia War Cemetery
in Egypt.

REILLY, William: Rank: Private.
Regiment or Service: Royal
Inniskilling Fusiliers. Unit: 9th Bn.
Date of death: 15 October 1918.
Age at death: 28. Killed in action.
Service No: 28007. Enlisted in
Navan.

Supplementary information: Son
of Thomas and Rebecca Reilly,
of Ardbraccan Quarry, Navan,
Co. Meath. Husband of Elizabeth
Reilly, of 'Milverton', Greystones,
Co. Wicklow. Grave or Memorial
Reference: III.C.18. Cemetery:

Dadizelele New British Cemetery
in Belgium.

REVELL, Robert Arthur:
Rank: Private. Regiment or
Service: Essex Regiment. Unit: 1st
Bn. Date of death: 12 June 1915.
Age at death: 25.

Supplementary information:
Son of Ellen Jane and John
Anthony Revell, of 7 Gattrine
Road, Bray, Co. Wicklow. Died
of wounds. Grave or Memorial
Reference: Q. 474. Cemetery:
Alexandria (Chatby) Military
and War Cemetery in Egypt he is
also commemorated on a marble
plaque on the walls of the reading

Clement Robertson.

room in Trinity College, Dublin.

RICE, Joseph: Rank: Private. Regiment or Service: Irish Guards. Unit: 2ⁿᵈ Bn. Date of death: 9 February 1916. Service No: 3426. Born in Bray, Co. Wicklow. Enlisted in Dublin. Died. Grave or Memorial Reference: A.8. Cemetery: Chipilly, Communal Cemetery in France.

Rath, Greystones, Co. Wicklow, and 51 Merrion Square, Dublin) and of Adelaide Prudentia Richards (*née* Roper). Grave or Memorial Reference: II.B.22. Cemetery: Green Hill Cemetery. He is also listed on the War Memorial in St Annes Church Dublin 2 and on the Solicitors Memorial on the wall beside the enquiries desk of the Law Library in the Four Courts in Dublin.

RICHARDS, William Reeves: Rank: Captain (Adjt). Regiment or Service: Royal Dublin Fusiliers. Unit: 6ᵗʰ Bn. Date of death: 15 August 1915. Age at death: 24. Killed in action. Awards: Mentioned in Despatches.
Supplementary information: Son of John William Richards, J.P. (of

RICHARDSON, William: Rank: Private. Regiment or Service: Royal Dublin Fusiliers. Unit: 1ˢᵗ Bn. Date of death: 28 June 1915. Age at death: 31. Service No: 17746. Enlisted in Dublin while living in Kilcoole, Co. Wicklow.
Supplementary information: Son of James and Mary Ann

Richardson, of Rathdrum, Co. Wicklow. Husband of Sarah Richardson, of 10 Purcell Terrace, Bray. Decorations 'two stripes'. Grave or Memorial Reference: VII.D.7. Cemetery: Twelve Tree Copse Cemetery in Turkey.

RIORDAN, Timothy: Rank: Private. Regiment or Service: Irish Guards. Unit: 1st Bn. Date of death: 17 September 1916. Service No: 6085. Born in Dunlavin, Co. Wicklow. Enlisted in Dublin. Killed in action. Grave or Memorial Reference: He has no known grave but is listed on Pier and Face 7 D on the Thiepval Memorial in France.

ROBERTSON, Clement: Rank; Captain. Regiment or Service: The Queen's (Royal West Surrey Regiment). Unit: 3rd Bn. Secondary Regiment: Attached to the Tank Corps. Date of death: 4 October 1917. Age at death: 28. Awards: Victoria Cross.
Supplementary information: Born at Pietermaritzburg, South Africa. Won the VC at Zonnebeke in Belgium on 4 October 1917. Son of Maj. John Albert Robertson (late R.A.), and Mrs Frances Octavia Caroline Robertson (*née* Wynne), of Struan Hill, Delgany, Co. Wicklow. The Victoria Cross was presented to his Mother by Brigadier General C. Williams,

Commanding Dublin District at the Royal Barracks (Collins Barracks) on 27 March 1918. From *The London Gazette*, No. 30433, dated 14 December 1917,

For most conspicuous bravery in leading his Tanks in attack under heavy shell, machine-gun and rifle fire. Capt. Robertson, knowing the risk of the Tanks missing the way, continued to lead them on foot, guiding them carefully and patiently towards their objective although he must have known that his action would almost inevitably cost him his life. This gallant officer was killed after his objective had been reached, but his skilful leading had already ensured successful action. His utter disregard of danger and devotion to duty afford an example of outstanding valour.

Supplementary information: from De Ruvigny's Roll of Honour. Fourth son of Major John Albert Robertson, of Struan Hill, Delgany, Co. Wicklow, by his wife, Frances Octavia Caroline, daughter, of Capt, John Wynne, of Wynneston, Co. Dublin. Born: Martixburg, Natal, South Africa, 15 November 1889. Educated Haileybury College, and Trinity College, Dublin, where he took an Engineering degree. He was an Engineer in the R.W.D., Egypt; returned to England on the outbreak of war in August 1914. He joined the University and Public Schools Battalion of the Royal Fusiliers in October. Gazetted 2nd Lt, The Queens (Royal West Surrey Regt); served with the Expeditionary Force in France and Flanders from May 1915, being appointed to the Tank Corps in January 1917. He was killed in action at Broodseinde, 4 October, following. His Commanding Officer wrote; 'It is impossible for me to attempt to express to you what a splendid example he has set for us all. I feel his loss very deeply myself, as he was such a splendid officer, and so popular with us all, officers and men alike.' He was posthumously awarded the V.C. Grave or Memorial Reference: Believed to be buried in III.F.7. Cemetery: Oxford Road Cemetery in Belgium. See page 261.

ROBINSON, James Arthur: Rank: Lieutenant Colonel. Regiment or Service: 13th Frontier Force Rifles. Unit: 6th Royal Bn. Age at death: 51. Date of death: 25 March 1944. Service No: A-1508 Awards: O.B.E.

Supplementary information: Son of Thomas and Isabella Caroline Robinson. Husband of Maud Loney Robinson, of Wicklow. Grave or Memorial Reference: 9.D.8. Cemetery: Karachi War Cemetery in Pakistan.

ROCHE, William John: Rank: Leading Seaman. Regiment or Service: Royal Navy. Unit: (RFR/PO/B/6862). HMS *Viknor*. Date of death: 13 January 1915. Age at death: 31. Service No: 214714.

Supplementary information: Son of Peter and Mary Roche, of Co. Wicklow. Husband of Mary Jane Roche, of 49 Ripley Grove, Copnor, Portsmouth. The ship sank with all hands after hitting a mine and many the bodies were washed up on the Irish and British shores. They were buried where they were found. William John Roche's body was not found. The bodies of 6 Viknor Sailors were washed up on the beach of Rathlin Island, Co. Antrim and are buried in St Thomas Churchyard in two graves 'Known only to God'. Grave or Memorial Reference: 7. Memorial: Portsmouth Naval Memorial, UK.

ROCHFORD, Patrick: Rank: Gunner. Regiment or Service: Royal Garrison Artillery. Unit, 184th Siege Battery. Date of death: 4 May 1918. Age at death: 35. Service No: 97387. Born in Rathdrum, Co. Wicklow. Enlisted in Wicklow while living in Rathdrum. Died of wounds, 'killed by a shell in Arras'.

Supplementary information: Son of the late Dennis and Mary Rochford, of Kingstown, Co. Dublin. Husband of Catherine Rochford, of 36 Upper Gardiner

HMS *Penelope*.

Street, Dublin. Grave or Memorial Reference: V.G.40. Cemetery; Duisans British Cemetery Extension in France.

ROCK, Robert Herbert: Rank: Marine. Regiment or Service: Royal Marines. Unit: HMS *Penelope*. Date of death: 18 February 1944. Service No: PO-X 5097.

Supplementary information: Son of George Alfred and Elizabeth Martha Rock, of Bray, Co. Wicklow. His brother George A. also fell. While returning to Anzio from Naples a torpedo from German Submarine U410 struck her in the engine room and sixteen minutes later another torpedo hit her in the aft boiler room which immediately sent her to the bottom with 656 of her crew. 415 of them died including the Captain. U410 was sunk near Toulon in France by American bomber planes during an air raid. Grave or Memorial Reference: He has no known grave but is listed on Panel 87, Column 3 on the Portsmouth Memorial, UK.

ROCK, George Alfred: Rank: Sergeant. Regiment or Service: Royal Ulster Rifles. Unit: 2nd Bn. The London Irish Rifles Age at death: 37. Date of death: between 20 January 1943 and 21 January 1943. Service No: 3765683.

Supplementary information: Son of George Alfred and Elizabeth Martha Rock, of Bray, Co. Wicklow. His brother Robert H. also fell. Grave or Memorial Reference: 2.C.6. Cemetery: Medjez-El-Bab War Cemetery in Tunisia.

ROONEY, Patrick: Rank: Private. Regiment or Service: Royal Dublin Fusiliers. Unit: 'C' Coy. 8th Bn. Date of death: 8 June 1917. Age at death: 24. Killed in action. Service No: 28723. Born in Tullow, Carlow. Enlisted in Dublin while living in Carlow.

Supplementary information: Son of William and Kate Rooney, of Donishall, Carnew, Co. Wicklow. He has no known grave but is listed on Panel 44 and 46 on the Ypres (Menin Gate) Memorial in Belgium.

ROSTERN, Jack: Rank: Sergeant (W. Op. /Air Gnr.) Regiment or Service: Royal Air Force Volunteer Reserve. Age at death: 26. Date of death: 24 February 1942. Service No: 1068192. Lost over the Irish Republic. The aircraft they were flying was a Lockheed Hudson V (Long Range) and had a four man crew. It crashed into the Irish Sea during terrible weather and the bodies of two of the crew (Sgt Jack Rostern 1068192 and Sgt Alexander Sherlock Beard) were picked up by a fishing vessel just off Cahore Point. One other body was found after the war.

Supplementary information: Son of Harold and Annie Rostern, of Radcliffe, Lancashire. Husband of Emily Rostern. Grave or Memorial Reference: Prot. Ground. Joint grave E. 75. Cemetery: Arklow Cemetery, Co Wicklow.

RUSSELL, Charles: (Alias. True name is **BARR, Charles**): Rank: Rifleman. Regiment or Service: Royal Irish Rifles. Unit: 1ˢᵗ Bn. He was previously with the North Irish Horse where his number was 2416. Date of death: 24 March 1918. Age at death: 19. Service No: 20187. Born in Malton, Yorks. Enlisted in Bray, Co. Wicklow while living in Rathdrum, Co. Wicklow. Killed in action. He has no known grave but is listed on the Pozieres Memorial in France.

RUTLEDGE, Richard John Joseph: Rank: Private. Regiment or Service: The Black Watch (Royal Highlanders). Unit: 8ᵗʰ (Service) Bn. Date of death: 13 October 1917. Service No: 202873. Born in Ashford, Co. Wicklow. Enlisted in Glasgow. Died of wounds. Grave or Memorial Reference: IX.F.4. Cemetery: Dozingham Military Cemetery in Belgium.

RYAN, L.: Rank: Gunner. Regiment or Service: Royal Field Artillery. Date of death: 4 September 1915. Service No: 6277.

Supplementary information: Alternative Commemoration. Buried in Kilcool Old Graveyard, Co. Wicklow and commemorated on the Special memorial in Glasnevin (or Prospect) Cemetery, Dublin.

RYAN, Patrick: Rank: Private. Regiment or Service: Royal Irish Regiment. Unit: 7th Bn. He was previously with the Royal Dublin Fusiliers where his number was 27279. Date of death: 16 August 1918. Age at death: 19. Service No: 26315. Born in Bray, Co. Wicklow. Enlisted in Kingstown, Co. Dublin. Died of wounds.

Supplementary information: Son of John and Ellen Ryan, of Towson's Cottages, Shankhill, Co. Dublin. Grave or Memorial Reference: III. C.15. Cemetery: Arneke British Cemetery in France.

RYDER, Bernard: Rank: Lance Corporal. Regiment or Service: Royal Dublin Fusiliers. Unit: 2nd Bn. Date of death: 23 October 1916. Age at death: 25. Service No: 9632. Born in Ballycross, Co. Wicklow. Enlisted in Dublin while living in Wicklow. Killed in action.

Supplementary information: Son of Mr and Mrs McDonald, of 1 Bergins Cottages, Castle Street, Bray, Co. Wicklow. He has no known grave but is listed on Panel 44 and 46 on the Ypres (Menin Gate) Memorial in Belgium.

RYDER, Richard: Rank: Rifleman. Regiment or Service: Kings Royal Rifle Corps. Unit: 2nd Bn. Date of death: 31 October 1914. Service No: 1979. Born in Wicklow. Enlisted in Wicklow. Died of wounds. Grave or Memorial Reference: He has no known grave but is listed on Panel 51 and 53 on the Ypres (Menin Gate) Memorial in Belgium.

S

SAUNDERS, William: Rank: Private. Regiment or Service: Northumberland Fusiliers. Unit: 'F' Company, 1st Bn. Date of death: 26 April 1914. Age at death: 30. Service No: 146. Born in Killcoole, Co. Wicklow. Enlisted in Dublin.

Supplementary information: Son of the late William and Bridget Saunders. Husband of Julia Saunders, of New Cottage, Killincarrick, Delgany, Co. Wicklow. Served in India. Grave or Memorial Reference: He has no known grave but is listed on Panel 5 and 6. on the Le Touret Memorial in France.

SCOTT, George: Rank: Gunner. Regiment or Service: Royal Garrison Artillery. Unit: B Siege Depot. Date of death: 8 January 1916. Service No: 7424. Born in Rathnew, Co. Wicklow. Enlisted in Maynooth, Co. Kildare while living in Kilcock, Co. Kildare. Died at home. Grave or Memorial Reference: C. K6. Cemetery: Bexhill Cemetery, UK.

SCOTT, Henry Donald: Rank: Warrant Officer (Pilot). Regiment or Service: Royal Air Force Volunteer Reserve. Unit: 19 Sqdn. Age at death: 23. Date of death: 18 August 1944. Service No: 981101.

Supplementary information: Son of J.E. Scott and Saidie Scott, of Greystones, Co. Wicklow. Henry was based in Ellon in Northern France and flew a Mustang. Grave or Memorial Reference: Coll. grave 10A. C. 7–10. Cemetery: Belgrade War Cemetery in Serbia and Montenegro.

SEGRAVE, William Henry: Rank: Lieutenant. Regiment or Service: Royal Flying Corps. Secondary Regiment: General List. Date of death: 12 February 1917. Age at death: 31. Killed.

Supplementary information: Son of Major O'Neal Segrave, D.S.O. and Beatrice Segrave, of Kiltyneon, Newtownmountkennedy, Co. Wicklow. Grave or Memorial Reference: C.16. Cemetery: Annitsford (St John) Roman Catholic Churchyard, UK.

SHANNON, Daniel: Rank: Rifleman. Regiment or Service:

A Christmas present from Princess Mary to all the soldiers at the front in 1914. It contained .303 bullet pencils, a Christmas card with a photo of the King and Queen and Princess and cigarettes or chocolate.

Royal Irish Rifles. Unit: 2nd Bn. Date of death: 12 October 1916. Age at death: 25 also listed as 27. Service No: 5235. Born in Arklow, Co. Wicklow. Enlisted in Wicklow. Killed in action or died of wounds near Thiepval.

Supplementary information: Son of Thomas and Margaret Shannon, of Drumdaughtergan, Rathdrum, Co. Wicklow. Grave or Memorial Reference: VI.B.22. Cemetery: Courcelette British Cemetery in France.

SHANNON, John: Rank: Private. Regiment or Service: Royal Dublin Fusiliers. Unit: 9th Bn. Date of death: 9 September 1916. Age at death: 38. Service No: 15579. Born in Sandycove, Co. Dublin. Enlisted in Dublin while living in Ashford, Co. Wicklow. Killed in action.

Supplementary information: Son of Thomas and Catherine Shannon, of Aghowle, Ashford, Co. Wicklow. Grave or Memorial Reference: He has no known grave but is listed on Pier and Face 16.C. on the

Thiepval Memorial in France.

SHAW, Francis: Rank: Private. Regiment or Service: Connaught Rangers. Unit: 6th Bn. Date of death: 2 August 1917. Age at death: 23. Service No: 10607. Born in Bray, Co. Wicklow. Enlisted in Dublin while living in Dublin. Killed in action.

Supplementary information: Son of the late Christopher and Kathrine Shaw. Twice wounded. Grave or Memorial Reference: He has no known grave but is listed on Panel 42 on the Ypres (Menin Gate) Memorial in Belgium.

SHAW, Godfrey Ambrose Samuel Wensley: Rank: First Radio Officer. Regiment or Service: Merchant Navy. Unit: SS *Tredinnick* (St. Ives) Age at death: 56. Date of death: 25 March 1942.

Supplementary information: Son of John Shaw, and of Alice Shaw (*née* de B. Sidley), of Bray, Co. Wicklow. SS *Tredinnick* was sunk by a torpedo (no further information available). Grave or Memorial Reference: He has no known grave but is listed on Panel 110 on the Tower Hill Memorial, UK.

SHERIDAN, Patrick: Rank: Lance Corporal. Regiment or Service: Royal Irish Regiment. Unit: 2nd Bn. Date of death: 24 May 1915. Age at death: 29. Killed in action. Service No: 7185. Born in St Mary's, Dublin. Enlisted in Gorey while living in Ballyrorey, Co. Wexford.

Supplementary information: Son of Mr and Mrs Sheridan, of Coolboy, Tinahely, Co. Wicklow. Grave or Memorial Reference: He has no known grave but is listed on Panel 33 on the Ypres (Menin Gate) Memorial in Belgium.

SHORTT/SHORT, Michael: Rank: Private. Regiment or Service: Connaught Rangers. Unit: 5th Bn. Date of death: 30 December 1915. Service No: 10603. Born in Enniskerry, Co. Wicklow. Enlisted in Dublin. Died of wounds in Salonika. Grave or Memorial Reference: 1793. Cemetery; Mikra British Cemetery, Kalamaria in Greece.

SHORTT, Patrick: Rank: Greaser. Regiment or Service: Lighthouse and Pilotage Authorities. Unit: The Commissioners of Irish Lights. SS *Isolda* (Dublin) Age at death: 44. Date of death: 19 December 1940.

Supplementary information: Son of Patrick and Emely Shortt; husband of Kathleen Shortt, of Bray, Co. Wicklow. SS *Isolda* left Rosslare harbour for maintenance work on the Barrels and Conningbeg lightships. She had a large EIRE painted on her side so it could be seen she was from a neutral country. It was Captained by Captain Bestic who had been an officer on the Titanic. The ship was bombed on three occasions in short succession by a German Aircraft. She sank near the Saltee Islands off Kilmore Quay and 6 of her crew died. Grave or Memorial Reference: He has no known grave but is listed on Panel 22 on the Tower Hill Memorial, UK.

SIMPSON, John: Rank: Corporal. Regiment or Service: Royal Dublin Fusiliers. Unit: 8th Bn. Date of death: 29 April 1916. Age at death: 30. Service No: 14477. Born in Shillelagh, Co. Wicklow. Enlisted in Dublin while living in Shillelagh. Killed in action.

Supplementary information: Son of the late Patrick and Mary Simpson. Grave or Memorial Reference: He has no known grave but is listed on Panel 127 to 129 on the Loos Memorial in France.

SINNOTT, John: Rank: Rifleman. Regiment or Service: Royal Irish Rifles. Unit: 1ˢᵗ Bn. Date of death: 26 October 1916. Age at death: 21. Service No: 2440. Born in Bray, Co. Wicklow. Enlisted in Bray, Co. Wicklow. Killed in action.

Supplementary information: Son of Mrs Mary A. Sinnott, of Fair View, Bray. Grave or Memorial Reference: He has no known grave but is listed on Pier and Face 15.A. and 15.B. on the Thiepval Memorial in France.

SINNOTT, Patrick: Rank: Private. Regiment or Service: Royal Fusiliers. Unit: 23ʳᵈ Bn. Date of death: 17 February 1917. Age at death: 24. Service No: G/61959. Formerly he was with the 5ᵗʰ Lancers Regiment where his number was G/23462. Killed in action. Born in Ashford, Co. Wicklow. Enlisted in Bray while living in Newcastle.

Supplementary information: Son of John and Elizabeth Sinnott, of Timore, Newcastle, Co. Wicklow. Grave or Memorial Reference: He has no known grave but is listed on Pier and Face 8.C.9.A. and 16.A. on the Thiepval Memorial in France.

SINUOTT, Patrick: Rank: Private. Regiment or Service:

Royal Munster Fusiliers. Unit: 6ᵗʰ Bn. Date of death: 2 July 1916. Service No: 3209. Born in Ashford, Wicklow. Enlisted in Dublin while living in Bray, Co. Wicklow. Died in Greek Macedonia. No further information on this man in any variant forms of his name.

SLOAN, Harold Fitzgerald: Rank: Surgeon Lieutenant. Regiment or Service: Royal Naval Volunteer Reserve. Unit: HMS *Javelin*. Age at death: 26. Date of death: 29 November 1940.

Supplementary information: Son of Harold Alexander Sloan and Mabel Fitzgerald Sloan, of Bray, Co. Wicklow. BA, MB, BCh. (Dublin). From the ships record of 29 November 1940;

Sighted enemy destroyers which had attacked convoy off Start Point sinking two ships. Took part in night action against KARL GASTNER, HANS LODY and RICHARD BEITZEN during which enemy ships fired torpedoes. Hit by torpedo forward and another aft causing extensive damage. Complete bow structure forward of gun mounting demolished and after structure were both demolished with extensive fire caused when magazine exploded. Major flooding of other compartments

Casualty form of
Arthur Chaloner
Smith.

and ship totally disabled. Only 155 feet of original 353 feet length of hull remained. 46 of ship's company lost their lives.'

Casualties were taken off by HMS *Jackal* and the other ships returned to scene after a fruitless chase of the German destroyers. Air attacks were driven off by RAF aircraft and ship taken in tow to Plymouth by a Falmouth tug escorted by HMS *Kashmir*. Grave or Memorial Reference: He has no known grave but is listed on Panel 44, Column 2 on the Portsmouth Memorial, UK.

SMULLEN, John: Rank: Private. Regiment or Service: Highland Light Infantry. Unit: 5th (City of Glasgow) Bn (Territorial). Date of death: 24 August 1918.

Age at death: 24. Service No: 29061. Born in Wicklow. Enlisted in Greenock, Renfrewshire while living in Wicklow. Killed in action. *Supplementary information:* Son of W. and Ellen Smullen, of Rathnew, Co. Wicklow. Grave or Memorial Reference: He has no known grave but is listed on Panel 9 and 10 of the Vis-En-Artois memorial in France.

SMITH, Arthur Chaloner: Rank: Private. Regiment or Service: Australian Infantry, A.I.F. Unit: 16th Bn, 8th Reinforcement. Date of death: 12 June 1917. Killed in action at Messines. Service No: 2707. Born in Bray, Co. Wicklow. Enlisted 23 May 1915 in Perth. Occupation on enlistment: Store Keeper. Age on enlistment, 42. Height: 5'10.5".

Weight: 173lbs. Hair: light brown. Eyes: blue. Complexion: fair. Next of kin: Wife: Aida Rebecca Smith of 122 Lake Street, Perth Western Australia. Religious denomination: COE. Served on the Western Front, Gallipoli, Egypt, Mudros, Alexandria, Heliopolis, Ghezireh, Tel-El-Kebir, Helouan, and Marseilles France.

Supplementary information: Embarked from Alexandria to join the Mediterranean Expeditionary Force, 18 October 1915. Sick to hospital, 17 December 1915; transferred by Hospital Ship 'Dunluce Castle' to Alexandria, 23 December 1915 (jaundice). Admitted to 2nd Auxiliary Hospital, Heliopolis, 24 December 1915. Ttransferred to Al Hayat Helouan, 5 January 1916. Discharged to duty, 13 January 1916. Rejoined unit, Tel el Kebir, 9 March 1916. Proceeded from Alexandria to join the British Expeditionary Force, 1 June 1916; disembarked Marseilles, 9 June 1916. Entitled to the 1914–15 Star, The Victory Medal and the British War Medal. His pension of 20 shillings per week was granted to his wife from 1 September 1917. Her new addresses were 155 Palmerstown Street, Perth and Ormiston College, Palmerstwon Street, Perth and 41 Glendowne Street, Perth. Grave or Memorial Reference: He has no known grave but is listed on Panel 7.17.2 3.25.27.29.31 on the Ypres (Menin Gate) Memorial in Belgium.

SMITH, Robert: Rank: Lance Corporal. Regiment or Service: Royal Dublin Fusiliers. Unit: 8th Bn. He won the Military Medal and is listed in the *London Gazette*. Date of death: 7 September 1916. Service No: 14548. Born in Rathnew, Co. Wicklow. Enlisted in Wicklow while living in Dublin. Killed in action. Grave or Memorial Reference: He has no known grave but is listed on Pier and Face 16.C. on the Thiepval Memorial in France.

SMYTH, Algernon Beresford: Rank: Captain. Regiment or Service: Kings own Yorkshire Light Infantry. Unit: 2nd Bn. Date of death: 15 November 1914. Born in Bray Head, 11 January 1884. Killed in action in Ypres 15 November 1914. Age at death: 30.

Supplementary information: Son of Devaynes Smyth, D.L, J P, of Bray Head, Bray, Co. Wicklow. Grave or Memorial Reference: He has no known grave but is listed on Panel 47 on the Ypres (Menin Gate) Memorial in Ypres (Ieper). West-Vlaanderen, Belgium. He is also commemorated on a window in Christ Church in Bray. The window was dedicated by his brother Charles Smyth and his Dorothy Devaynes. It says; 'To the

Glory of God, and in proud and ever living memory of Captain Algernon Beresford Smyth of the 2nd Battn Kings Own Yorkshire Light Infantry.' Mentioned in Despatches. He is also mentioned in the Haileybury Register 1862–1911.

SMYTH, Joseph: Rank: Private. Regiment or Service: Connaught Rangers. Unit: 1st Bn. Date of death: 10 June 1915. Age at death: 21. Service No: 10943. Born in Glenera, Enniskerry, Co. Wicklow. Enlisted in Dublin while living in Dublin. Died of wounds.

Supplementary information: Foster-son of Julia McAneny, of Lacken, Enniskerry, Co. Wicklow. Grave or Memorial Reference: VIII.A.77. Cemetery: Boulogne Eastern Cemetery in France.

SMYTHE, ALBERT Edward: Rank: Private. Regiment or Service: Irish Guards. Unit: 1st Bn. Date of death: 1 November 1914. Age at death: 18. Service No: 4480. Born in Old Leighlin, Co. Carlow. Enlisted in Carlow while living in Rathdrum, Co. Wicklow. Killed in action.

Supplementary information: Son of Edward Henry and Esther Hamilton Smythe, of Knockbawn, Enniskerry, Co. Wicklow. One of five sons who served in the Great War. Grave or Memorial Reference: He has no known grave but is listed on Panel 11 on the Ypres (Menin Gate) Memorial in Belgium.

SOAMES, Arthur John: Rank: Lance Corporal. Regiment or Service: Suffolk Regiment. Unit: 7th Bn. Age at death: 21. Date of death: 3 July 1916. Age at death: 21. Killed in action. Service No: 9237. Born in Bedford. Enlisted in Cambridge.

Supplementary information: Only son of Arthur Eady and Ellen Margaret Soames, of The Mall, Wicklow. Grave or Memorial Reference: He has no known grave but is listed on Pier and Face 1.C. and 2.A. on the Thiepval Memorial in France.

SOMERS, Christopher: Rank: Corporal and Acting Corporal. Regiment or Service: Royal Dublin Fusiliers. Unit: 2nd Bn. Date of death: 28 June 1918. Age at death: 33. Died of Wounds. Service No: 3/27177 and 27177. Born in Dublin. Enlisted in Belfast while living in Dublin.

Supplementary information: Husband of Catherine Somers, of 5 Panbroke Cottages, Main Street, Bray, Co. Wicklow. Grave or Memorial Reference: VIII. C.5. Cemetery: Niederzwhren

Daniel Somers.

Cemetery in Germany.

SOMERS, Daniel: Rank: Private. Regiment or Service: Irish Guards. Unit: 2nd Bn. Date of death: 28 October 1915. Service No: 7256. Born in Cloneyhorn, Co. Wicklow. Enlisted in Glasgow in Lanarkshire while living in Cloneyhorn. Died of Wounds. From the *Wicklow People*,

Private Somers Carnew. News was received at his home in Cloneyhorn, Carnew on Friday of the death in hospital in England as a result of wounds received in action of Private Daniel Somers of the Irish Guards. The brave young soldier, who has laid down his life for his country, was but 27 years of age. He was the son of respectable farming people and was beloved by his comrades for manly and estimable qualities. He was employed in Scotland, and answered the call about nine months ago when he joined the Guards Regiment. He was regarded as one of the best marksmen in his parish and combining with this accomplishment, and aptitude for acquiring quick proficiency in drill, he became competent as a trained soldier in a remarkably short space of time, and he was drafted out to France in September, his remarkable success in handling firearms being so recognised by the military authorities, that he was allotted the duties of sniper. About October 30 he received serious wounds in his left leg, arm and eye and was

Gravestone of Daniel Somers.

for treatment to Base holpital and subsequently to one of the London hospitals, where he succumbed to his wounds. The military authorities gave the most sympathetic attention to the wishes of his relatives, that the remains might be laid to rest in his native soil, and arrangements were made by which the coffin was despatched at the expense of the Government of Ireland. The remains arrived at Shillelagh railway station on Saturday evening, and notwithstanding extremely inclement weather, were awaited by and exceedingly large crowd, who displayed the utmost anxiety to pay their tribute of respect to the remains of the brave soldier, who was a universal favourite. The funeral, which took place in Tomacork on Sunday, which was very largely attended, formed yet another striking tribute to the respect and esteem in which the deceased and his family were held.

Buried in Tomacork Graveyard, Co. Wicklow.

SOMMERS, Kennedy William: Rank: Private. Regiment or Service: Royal Dublin Fusiliers. Date of death: 17 January 1917. Service No: 17716. Killed in action in the Dardinelles. Age at death: 26.

Born in Co. Wicklow. No further information is available on this man.

SPEARES, Harold Thorne: Rank: Second Lieutenant. Regiment or Service: Royal Inniskilling Fusiliers. Unit: 10th Bn. Date of death: 16 August 1917. Killed in action.

Supplementary information: Son of John Speares, of The Castle, Rathdrum, Co. Wicklow. Grave or Memorial Reference: He has no known grave but is listed on Panel 70 to 72 on the Tyne Cot Memorial in Belgium.

SPENCER, William: Rank: Able Seaman. Regiment or Service: Mercantile Marine. Unit: SS *Toro* (Hull). SS *Toro* was built in 1904, owned by the Wilson Line, as a 3,066 ton steamship, and was torpedoed and sunk off Ushant in 1917. Date of death: 12 April 1917. Age at death: 39.

Supplementary information: Son of Joseph Spencer, of 18 Probys Row, Arklow, Co. Wicklow, and the late Mary Ann Spencer. Born at Gorey. Grave or Memorial Reference: He has no known grave but is listed on the Tower Hill memorial UK.

SPROULE. Alexander Lionel Alolphus: Rank: Private.

Regiment or Service: Royal Irish Fusiliers. Unit: 19th Bn. Date of death: 31 July 1916. Age at death: 23. Service No: 16129. Born in Bray, Co. Wicklow. Enlisted in Monaghan. Died of wounds.
Supplementary information: Son of Elizabeth and W.J. Sproule, of Glaslough Street, Monaghan. Grave or Memorial Reference: IX.B.10A. Cemetery: Etaples Military Cemetery in France.

STAMPER, Hugh Gordon: Rank: Lance Corporal. Regiment or Service: Royal Dublin Fusiliers. Unit: 10th Bn. Date of death: 13 November 1916. Age at death: 32. Killed in action. Service No: 25626. Born in Newtownmountkennedy, Co. Wicklow. Enlisted in Dublin while living in Newtownmountkennedy.
Supplementary information: Son of the Revd J. and C. Stamper, of Monaline, Newtownmountkennedy. Grave or Memorial Reference: II.F.22. Cemetery: Ancre British Cemetery, Beaumont-Hamel in France.

STANNUS, Thomas Robert Alexander: Rank: Major (Acting Lt Colonel). Regiment or Service: Lenster Regiment. Unit: 4th Bn. Date of death: 17 June 1917. Age at death: 47. Died of wounds at Le Toquet in France.

Supplementary information: Born in Battiboys in Blessington. He was the Justice of the Peace for Antrim. Decorated with the Chevalier, Legion d'Honneur and the Distinguished Service Order. Born: 29 September 1870 to James and Rose Stannus, of The Elms, Portarlington, Queen's Co. Husband of E. Stannus, of 23 Earl's Court Square, London. Grave or Memorial Reference: XVII. E.23. Cemetery: Etaples Military Cemetery in France.

STEDMAN, Thomas J.: Rank: Private. Regiment or Service: Royal Irish Regiment. Unit: 7th Bn. He was previously with the 'C' Company South Irish Horse where his number was 1679. Date of death: 22 March 1918. Age at death: 23. Service No: 25800. Born in Rathdrum, Co. Wicklow. Enlisted in Dublin while living in Rathdrum. Died of wounds.
Supplementary information: Son of Daniel and Elizabeth Stedman, of Convent Lodge, Rathdrum. Grave or Memorial Reference: I.A.61. Cemetery: Honnechy British Cemetery in France.

STEDMAN, William: Rank: Private. Regiment or Service: Irish Guards. Unit: 1st Bn. Date of death: 12 April 1915. Age at death: 23. Service No: 3782. Born in Delgany,

Co. Wicklow. Enlisted in Bray, Co. Wicklow.

Supplementary information: Son of Isabella and the late William Stedman, of Kilruddery, Bray. Grave or Memorial Reference: I.E.28. Cemetery: Wimereux Communal Cemetery in France.

STENSON, Samuel: Rank: Stoker 1st Class. Regiment or Service: Royal Navy. Unit: HMS *Partridge*. HMS *Partridge* was sunk by 4 German Distroyers while escorting a convoy. Date of death: 12 December 1917. Age at death: 38. Service No: 290421.

Supplementary information: Son of Samuel and Mary Stenson, of Woodstock, Newtown, Mountkennedy, Co. Wicklow. Grave or Memorial Reference: 24. Memorial: Chatham Naval Memorial, UK.

STEPHENS, Samuel: Rank: Private. Regiment or Service: Royal Dublin Fusiliers. Unit: 10th Bn. He was previously with the Leinster Regiment where his number was 3599. Date of death: 13 November 1916. Age at death: 21. Service No: 26177. Born in Wicklow. Enlisted in Limerick while living in Ashford, Co. Wicklow. Killed in action.

Supplementary information: Son of Henry and Catherine E. Stephens,

of Ballymonéen, Ashford. Born at Bellavista, Blackrock, Co. Dublin. Grave or Memorial Reference: VII.B.41. Cemetery: Ancre British Cemetery, Beaumont-Hamel in France.

STEPHENS, Thomas Willoughby: Rank: Rifleman. Regiment or Service: Royal Irish Rifles. Unit: 13th Bn. Date of death: 21 March 1916. Age at death: 25. Service No: 19215. Born in Ardree, Co. Louth. Enlisted in Newry, Co. Down while living in Ashford, Co. Wicklow. Killed in action.

Supplementary information: Son of Henry and Catherine E. Stephens, of Ballymonéean, Ashford, Co. Wicklow. Native of Ardee, Co. Louth. Grave or Memorial Reference: I. 2. Cemetery: Mesnil Ridge Cemetery, Mesnil-Martinsart in France.

STEVENS, Albert Edward: Rank: Able Seaman. Regiment or Service: Royal Navy. Unit: HMS *Jaguar*. Age at death: 20. Date of death: 26 March 1942. Service No: D-JX 156501.

Supplementary information: Son of Alfred and Emily Elizabeth Stevens, of Bray, Co. Wicklow. Sunk by 2 torpedoes from German Submarine U652. U652 was badly damaged by depth charges from a British Swordfish Aircraft and scuttled by torpedoes from another German Submarine (U81) in the Mediterranean on 2 June 1942. Grave or Memorial Reference: He has no known grave but is listed on Panel 66, Column 3 on the Portsmouth Memorial, UK.

STIVEN, Robert: Rank: Squadron Leader. Regiment or Service: Royal Air Force Volunteer Reserve Age at death: 46. Date of death: 1 December 1944. Service No: 17151.

Supplementary information: Son of Robert and Margaret Stiven. Husband of Dorothy Stiven, of Bray, Co. Wicklow. Grave or Memorial Reference: Plot T. Grave 108. Cemetery: Pembroke Dock (Llanion) Cemetery in Wales.

ST. LEDGER, Peter: Rank: Stoker 1st Class. Regiment or Service: Royal Navy. Unit: HMS *Indefatigable.* During the Battle of Jutland the German Battlecruiser Von Der Tann fired 11-inch shells at the *Indefatigable.* The first two entered 'X' magazine area and blew out the bottom of the ship and she began sinking by the stern. More 11 inch shells from the Van Der Tann destroyed 'A' turret and also blew up the forward magazine and she then sank. There were only two survivors of

her crew of 1,017 men. The Van Der Tann was scuttled in Scapa flow in June 1919. Date of death: 31 May 1916. Age at death: 20. Service No: SS-116654.

Supplementary information: Son of Peter and Annie St. Ledger, Coolkenno, Co. Wicklow. Grave or Memorial Reference: 16. Memorial: Plymouth Naval Memorial.

STRICKLAND, John Foster: Rank: Lance Corporal. Regiment or Service: Irish Guards. Unit: 1st Bn. Date of death: 1 February 1915. Age at death: 30. Service No: 4988. Born in Dublin, Co. Dublin. Enlisted in Dublin while living in Bray, Co. Wicklow. Killed in action.

Supplementary information: From De Ruvigny's Roll of Honour: son of George Foster Strickland, of 2 Prince of Wales Terrace, Bray, retired bank Official, by his wife, Marion, daughter, of John Sopwell, Derryowen, Gort, Co. Galway. Born: Dublin, 10 July 1882. Educated: St Andrews College. He was a Clerk in Congested Districts Board and served in the South African War 1899–1902, with Baden-Powell's Mounted Police. He receiving the Queen's Medal with five clasps; volunteered and joined the Irish Guards on the outbreak of the war in August 1914. Went to France 8 December

1914, and was killed in action at Cuinchy 1 February following, while retaking one of the enemy's trenches. Buried in the cemetery there. Grave or Memorial Reference: I.A.4. Cemetery: Cuinchy Communal Cemetery in France.

STUART, R. C: Rank: Second Lieutenant. Regiment or Service: Royal Air Force. Date of death: 12 December 1918.

Supplementary information: Son of Mr S. Stuart, of Beechgrove, Arklow. Grave or Memorial Reference: North. 2.A.70 West. Cemetery: Arklow Cemetery, Co. Wicklow.

SULLIVAN, Patrick: Rank: Guardsman. Regiment or Service: Scots Guards. Date of death: 7 November 1914. Service No: 6960. Born in Baltinglass, Co. Wicklow. Enlisted in Coatbridge in Lanarkshire while living in Baltinglass. Killed in action. Grave or Memorial Reference: He has no known grave but is listed on Addenda Panel 58 on the Ypres (Menin Gate) Memorial in Belgium.

SULLIVAN, Patrick: Rank: Private. Regiment or Service: Parachute Regiment, A.A.C. Unit: 11th Bn. Age at death: 26. Date of death: 21 September 1944. Service No: 6978471. Enlisted while living in Tyrone.

Supplementary information: Son of Micheal and Jane Sullivan of Wicklow. Grave or Memorial Reference: 5.C.15. Cemetery: Arnhem Oosterbeek War Cemetery in Holland.

SULLIVAN, William: Rank: Lance Sergeant. Regiment or Service: Irish Guards. Unit: 1st Bn. Date of death: 25 September 1916. Age at death: 20. Service No: 4783. Born in Blessington, Co. Wicklow. Enlisted in Dublin. Killed in action.

Supplementary information: Son of Thomas and Elizabeth Sullivan, of The Post Office, Tinode, Co. Wicklow. Grave or Memorial Reference: He has no known grave but is listed on Pier and Face 7.D. on the Thiepval Memorial in France.

SUPPLE, Edward James Collis: Rank: Lieutenant. Regiment or Service: Duke of Wellingtons Regiment. (West Riding) 49th Division. Unit: 1/6th Bn. Date of death: 22 August 1915. Died of wounds. Age at death: 33.

Supplementary information: Son of Mr and Mrs Edward Kerry Supple of Greystones, Wicklow.

From *Claro Times* 27 August 1915.

The death took place at a hospital in France on August 22nd, as a result of wounds received in action on August 20th, of Lieutenant Edward J C Supple, 6th Battalion Duke of Wellington's Regiment, youngest son of Mr Edward K Supple, of Wetherby Lane, Harrogate. Lieutenant Supple was educated at Ripon Grammar School, and later became a master at Skipton Grammar School. Whilst at Skipton he enlisted in the ranks of the 6th Battalion, of which he was later to serve as an officer. Later he obtained a position on the staff of Belvedere School, Brighton, and his military training in Yorkshire was put to good use in the work of the Belvedere Officers' Training Corps. He displayed great enthusiasm in the training of this Corps, which rose to a high state of all-round efficiency, and on several occasions won the challenge cup competed for by the Brighton Preparatory Schools. Lieutenant Supple was a thoroughly good sportsman, and was popular especially in the cricket and football fields. As an officer in the West Riding Regiment, he was a general favourite with officers and men alike, and one of his comrades, writing to the lieutenant's father, says : 'In the greatest danger he was always cheerful, and had a kind word for everyone. He was a good officer, and one of the bravest men I ever knew.'

He is listed on the Skipton Cenotaph, the Craven Roll Of Honour, The Skipton Holy Trinity Church Memorial, the rear plaque on the Harrogate, War Memorial and on a wooden plaque in the Skipton Cricket Club. Grave or Memorial Reference: III.O.3. Cemetery: Wimereux Communal Cemetery in France.

SUTTON, Albert: Rank: Private. Regiment or Service: Black Watch (Royal Highlanders). Unit: 7th Bn. Age at death: 27. Date of death: 16 March 1943. Service No: 3715128. Enlisted while living in Belfast.

Supplementary information: Son of James Albert Sutton, and of Louisa Eleanor Sutton, of Bray, Co. Wicklow. Died in the rout of the Axis troops after the battle of El Alamien when the retreated to Tunisia. Grave or Memorial Reference: III.C.7. Cemetery: Sfax War Cemetery in Tunisia.

SUTTON, Elijah: Rank: Private. Regiment or Service: Irish Guards. Unit: 2nd Bn. Date of death: 30 September 1915. Age at death: 30.

Service No: 2054. Born in Callery, Co. Wicklow. Enlisted in Dublin while living in Kilpedder, Co. Wicklow. Killed in action.

Supplementary information: Son of William Sutton, of The Mountain Tavern, Callery. Grave or Memorial Reference: He has no known grave but is listed on Panel 9 and 10 of the Loos memorial in France.

SUTTON, Joseph: Rank: Private. Regiment or Service: Royal Inniskilling Fusiliers. Unit: 1st Bn. He was previously with the Hussars of the Line where his number was 24265. Date of death: 6 September 1915. Age at death: 23. Service No: 21379. Born in Enniskerry, Co. Wicklow. Enlisted in Bray while living in Enniskerry. Died from dysentery in Malta.

Supplementary information: Son of Joseph and Mary Sutton, of Enniskerry. Grave or Memorial Reference: E.EA.A.668. Cemetery: Addolorata Cemetery in Malta.

SUTTON, Thomas: Rank: Private. Regiment or Service: Connaught Rangers. Unit: 1st Bn. Date of death: 27 April 1916. Age at death: 39, age also listed as 40. Service No: 4998. Born in Enniskerry, Co. Wicklow. Enlisted in Naas, Co. Kildare while living in Enniskerry. Died of wounds in Mesopotamia.

Supplementary information: Son of James and Eliza Sutton, of Killough, Kilmacanogue, Bray, Co. Wicklow. Grave or Memorial Reference: XX.C.5. Cemetery: Amara War Cemetery in Iraq.

SUTTON, William: Rank: Lance Corporal. Regiment or Service: New Zealand Rifle Brigade. Unit: 3rd Bn. 3rd. Age at death: 43. Date of death: 22 November 1917. Service No: 25–682.

Supplementary information: Son of William and Jane Sutton, of Rathdrum. Grave or Memorial Reference: VIII.I.124. Cemetery: Boulogne Eastern Cemetery in France.

SYMES, Thomas Arthur: Rank: Private. Regiment or Service: Royal Dublin Fusiliers. Unit: 7th Bn. Date of death: 18 August 1915. Age at death: 29. Died in Gallipoli. Service No: 14228. Born in Cross Patrick, Tinehely, Co. Wicklow. Enlisted in Boyle Co. Roscommon while living in Tinehely.

Supplementary information: Son of Sandham John and Catherine Chamney Symes, of 'Hill View', Tinahely, Co. Wicklow. From an article in the *People* newspaper; 'Announcement has been received from Alexandria of the death in hospital of Thomas A Symes, of

D Company, 7th Battalion, Royal Dublin Fusiliers. Deceased was the seventh son of Mr Sandman J Symes, Hill View, Co. Wexford.' Grave or Memorial Reference: I.B.37. Cemetery: Portianos Military Cemetery in Greece.

SYNNOTT, Michael: Rank: Private. Regiment or Service: East Yorkshire Regiment. Unit: 1st Bn. Date of death: 12 October 1918. Age at death: 38. Service No: 202660. Born in Arklow, Co. Wicklow. Enlisted in Manchester. Died in Bermuda.

Supplementary information: Son of Michael and Mary Synnott. Husband of Mary Ann Synnott, of 1 Lower Sandwill Street, Great Brunswick Street Dublin. Born at Arklow. Grave or Memorial Reference: 20. Cemetery: St Georges Military Cemetery in Bermuda.

SYNOTT/SYNNOTT, John: Rank: Gunner. Regiment or Service: Royal Garrison Artillery. Unit: 5th Siege Battery. Date of death: 30 May 1917. Service No: 275493. Born in Newtown, Co. Wicklow. Enlisted in Dublin while living in Newtown. Killed in action. Grave or Memorial Reference: I.C.8. Cemetery: Le Targette British Cemetery, Neuville-St, Vaast in France.

SYNOTT, Thomas: Rank: Private. Regiment or Service: Royal Dublin Fusiliers. Unit: 9th Bn. Date of death: 27 April 1916. Service No: 14811. Born in Dublin. Enlisted in Dublin while living in Bray, Co. Wicklow. Killed in action. Grave or Memorial Reference: He has no known grave but is listed on Panel 127 to 129 on the Loos Memorial in France.

T

TALLON, Michael: Rank: Private. Regiment or Service: Royal Dublin Fusiliers. Unit: 1st Bn. Date of death: 2 June 1917. Age at death: 24. Service No: 11245. Born in Arklow, Co. Wicklow. Enlisted in Dublin while living in Wicklow. Died of wounds.

Supplementary information: Son of Paul and Margaret Tallon, of Coates Lane, Wicklow. Grave or Memorial Reference: III. A.2. Cemetery: Niederzwehren Cemetery in Germany.

TAYLOR, George: Rank: Lieutenant. Regiment or Service: Royal Army Medical Corps. Age at death: 42. Date of death: 30 October 1917. Drowned.

Supplementary information: Son of Wentworth and Deborah Taylor, of Tinahely, Co. Wicklow. Grave or Memorial Reference: He has no known grave but is listed on Panel 42. on the Basra Memorial in Iraq.

THOMSON, Herbert Ronald: Rank: Signaller. Regiment or Service: Royal Field Artillery. Unit: 'B' Bty. 174th Bde. Date of death: 25 November 1918. Age at death: 32. Service No: 237526.

Supplementary information: Son of George and Julia Thomson, of Co. Wicklow. Husband of D.M. Thomson, of 112 Muirkirk Road, Catford, London. Grave or Memorial Reference: LI.A.17. Cemetery: Etaples Military Cemetery in France.

THOMPSON, John: Rank: Private. Regiment or Service: Royal Dublin Fusiliers. Unit: 2nd Bn. Date of death: 26 April 1915. Service No: 11450. Born in Rathnew, Co. Wicklow. Enlisted in Dublin while living in Wicklow. Died of wounds. Grave or Memorial Reference: He has no known grave but is listed on Panel 44 and 46 on the Ypres (Menin Gate) Memorial in Belgium.

THOMPSON, Nathaniel George: Rank: Lance Corporal. Regiment or Service: Royal Dublin Fusiliers. Unit: 2nd Bn. Date of death: 21 March 1918. Age at death: 24. Service No: 20199. Born in Laragh, Co. Wicklow. Enlisted in

Bray while living in Tinahely, Co. Wicklow. Killed in action.

Supplementary information: Son of Nathaniel and Frances Thompson, of Tinahely, Co. Wicklow. Grave or Memorial Reference: He has no known grave but is listed on panel 79 and 80 on the Pozieres Memorial in France.

THOMPSON, William: Rank: Rifleman. Regiment or Service: Royal Irish Rifles. Unit: 2nd Bn. Date of death: 17 July 1915. Age at death: 21. Service No: 10191. Born in Kildare. Enlisted in Dublin while living in Bray, Co. Wicklow.

Supplementary information: Son of William George and Emily Thompson, of The Vevay, Bray. Grave or Memorial Reference: V.B.1. Cemetery: Niederzwehren Cemetery in Germany.

TOBIN, John Francis Aviour: Rank: Trimmer. Regiment or Service: Royal Naval Reserve. Unit: HMS *Vivid*. HMS *Vivid* was a Naval Land Base. Date of death: 18 November 1918. Age at death: 18. Service No: 8790/TS.

Supplementary information: Son of Patrick and Mary Anne Tobin, of Hawkstown, Co. Wicklow. Grave or Memorial Reference: General T.4.25. Cemetery: Ford Park Cemetery (Formerly Plymouth Old Cemetery Pennycomequick) UK.

TOOLE, James: Rank: Sergeant. Regiment or Service: Worcestershire Regiment. Unit: 2nd Bn. Date of death: 16 May 1915. Service No: 4320. Born in Bray, Co. Wicklow. Killed in action. Grave or Memorial Reference: He has no known grave but is listed on Panels 17 and 18 on the Le Touret Memorial in France.

TOOLE, Michael: Rank: Lance Corporal. Regiment or Service: Leinster Regiment. Unit: 2nd Bn. Date of death: 16 March 1916. Service No: 7204. Born in Bray, Co. Wicklow. Enlisted in Dublin. Died of wounds. From an article in the Wicklow Newspapers; Lance Corporal Michael O'Toole. Death in France. Loss to the Boy's Brigade. The keenest regret was felt in Bray. Grave or Memorial Reference: VI.D.4. Cemetery; Etaples Military Cemetery in France.

TOOLE, Patrick: Rank: Private. Regiment or Service: Royal Dublin Fusiliers. Unit: 9th Bn. Date of death: 5 April 1916. Age at death: 29. Service No: 19131. Born in Dublin. Enlisted in Bray while living in Wicklow. Killed in action.

Supplementary information: Husband of Bridget Toole, of 39 Woodland Road, Seaforth, Liverpool. Grave or Memorial Reference: C.8. Cemetery: Bois–Carre Military Cemetery, Haisns in France.

TRAYNOR, Thomas: Rank: Private. Regiment or Service: Royal Army Service Corps. Unit, Advanced Horse Transport Depot. Date of death: 11 July 1917. Service No: T2/017739. Born in Bray. Enlisted in Bray while living in Bray. Died in Mesopotamia. Grave or Memorial Reference: XII.B.10. Cemetery: Amara War Cemetery in Iraq.

TREACY, Denis: Rank: Able Seaman. Regiment or Service: Merchant Navy. Unit: SS *Hazelside* (Newcastle-on-Tyne) Age at death: 24. Date of death: 24 September 1939.
Supplementary information: Son of Richard and Julia Treacy, of Arklow, Co. Wicklow. Sunk by Herman Submarine U31 of the coast of Cork. Grave or Memorial Reference: Panel 56. Grave or Memorial Reference: He has no known grave but is listed on Panel 56 on the Tower Hill Memorial, UK.

TREACY, John Joseph: Rank: Private. Regiment or Service: Royal Dublin Fusiliers. Unit: 2nd Bn. Date of death: 25 May 1915. Age at death: 19. Service No: 9100. Age at death: 19. Died of Wounds. Born in Clondalkin, Co. Dublin. Enlisted in Dublin while living in Clondalkin.
Supplementary information: Son of Henry and Bridget Treacy, of Danesrath, Clondalkin, Co. Dublin. Native of Athgraney, Hollywood, Co. Wicklow. Grave or Memorial Reference: VIII.D.47. Cemetery: Boulogne Eastern Cemetery in France.

TREACY, Thomas Joseph: Rank: Able Seaman. Regiment or Service: Merchant Navy. Unit: SS *Fort Pelly* (London) Age at death: 61. Date of death: 20 July 1943.
Supplementary information: Son of Mr and Mrs P. Treacy, of Arklow, Co. Wicklow. Husband of Annie Treacy, of Hull. Grave or Memorial Reference: He has no known grave but is listed on Panel 51 on the Tower Hill Memorial, UK.

TROY, James Joseph: Rank: Private. Regiment or Service: Irish Guards. Unit: No. 3 Coy. 1st Bn. Date of death: 15 December 1917. Age at death: 26. Died of Wounds. Service No: 3889. Born in Kilvaney Co. Wicklow. Enlisted in

Memorial in Rathmichael Church, Shankhill, Dublin. Image courtesy of irishwarmemorials.ie.

Dublin while living in Brentwood in Essex.

Supplementary information: Son of James and Bridget Troy, of Tinahely, Co. Wicklow. Husband of Elizabeth Troy, of 'Methlick', Warley Road, Brentwood, Essex. Grave or Memorial Reference: VIII.A.28. Cemetery: Rocquigny-Equancourt Road British Cemetery, Manancourt in France.

TURNER, John: Rank: Acting Bombardier. Regiment or Service: Royal Horse Artillery and Royal Field Artillery. Unit: 42nd Battery. 2nd Brigade. Date of death: 21 March 1918. Age at death: 30. Service No: 77466. Enlisted in Dublin while living in Bray, Co. Wicklow. Died.

Supplementary information: Son of Samuel J. and Martha S. Turner, of Whitehall, Glassnamullen, Kilpedder, Co. Wicklow. Grave or Memorial Reference: He has no known grave but is listed on Bay 1 the Arras Memorial in France.

TUTTY, Edward: Rank: Corporal. Regiment or Service: Royal Inniskilling Fusiliers. Unit: 9th Bn. Date of death: 1 July 1916, first day of the battle of the Somme. Age at death: 27. Service No: 13579. Born in Baltinglass, Co. Wicklow. Enlisted in Dublin. Killed in action.

Supplementary information: Eldest son of Mathew and Mrs C. Tutty, of 'Glen Brae', Shankill Co. Dublin. Grave or Memorial Reference: He has no known grave but is listed on Pier and Face 4.D. and 5.B. n the Thiepval Memorial in France.

TWAMLEY, Christopher: Rank: Private. Regiment or Service: Royal Dublin Fusiliers. Unit: 3rd Bn. Date of death: 17 March 1916. Age at death: 29. Service No: 24607. Born in Rathnew, Co. Wicklow. Enlisted in Wicklow while living in Rathnew. Died of Pneumonia in Cork.

Supplementary information: Son of Anne Twamley, of Rathnew. Grave or Memorial Reference: R.C. ground 3.B.1222. Cemetery: Rathnew Cemetery.

TYNER, Thomas Goodwin: Rank: Second Lieutenant. Regiment or Service: Royal Dublin Fusiliers. Unit: 9th Bn. Date of death: 9 September 1916. Age at death: 20. Killed in action.

Supplementary information: Son of Thomas and M. Alice Tyner, of Coolalug House, Tinahely, Co. Wicklow. Born in Knockatassonig in 1895. Grave or Memorial Reference: He has no known grave but is listed on Pier and Face 16.C. on the Thiepval Memorial in France.

TYNTE, Mervyn Patrick Arthur: Rank: Major. Regiment

or Service: Royal Munster Fusiliers Date of death: 7 December 1918 Grave or Memorial Reference: Family Plot, West wall of Church. Cemetery: Dunlavin (St Nicholas) Churchyard, Co. Wicklow.

TYRRELL, Alfred: Rank: Master. Regiment or Service: Merchant Navy. Unit: SS *Fowey Rose* (Liverpool) Age at death: 35. Date of death: 5 July 1941.

Supplementary information: Son of Job Tyrrell, and of Susan T. Tyrrell, of Arklow, Co. Wicklow. SS *Fowey Rose* was bombed by the Luftwaffe 20 miles south-west of St Govans head and sunk. Grave or Memorial Reference: He has no known grave but is listed on Panel 51 on the Tower Hill Memorial, UK.

TYRRELL, Charles: Rank: Able Seaman. Regiment or Service: Mercantile Marine. Unit: SS *Astoria* (London). Date of death: 9 October 1916. Age at death: 27.

Supplementary information: Son of Charles and Mary Tyrrell, of 11 Halls Lane, Arklow, Co. Wicklow. Grave or Memorial Reference: He has no known grave but is listed on the Tower Hill memorial UK.

TYRRELL, George: Rank: Boy. Regiment or Service: Mercantile Marine. Unit: SS *Lapwing*

The gravestone of Christopher Twamley.

(Arbroath). The 1,192 gross-tons Steamship *Lapwing* was built in 1911 and was mined and sunk by the German Submarine UC4 in the North Sea 9 miles southeast from Southwold on 11 of November 1917. She was carrying a general cargo from Rotterdam to London. It was reported that all the crew and the Captain were saved. Age at death: 18. Date of death: 10 November 1917.

Supplementary information: Son of Mary Tyrrell (*née* Browne), of 11 Halls Lane, Arklow, Co. Wicklow, and the late Charles Tyrrell. Grave or Memorial Reference: He has no known grave but is listed on the Tower Hill Memorial UK.

TYRRELL, Henry: Rank: Quartermaster. Regiment or Service: Mercantile Marine. Unit: SS *Leinster* (Dublin). Steamship Leinster was hit by a German Torpedo and sank with the loss of over 400 people. It was the greatest maritime disaster in Irish Waters. Age at death: 57. Date of death: 10 October 1918.

Supplementary information: Son of the late Michael and Elizabeth Tyrrell. Husband of Bridget Tyrrell (*née* Blanch), of 2 Jane Villa, Tivoli Road, Kingstown, Dublin. Born at Arklow, Co. Wicklow. Grave or Memorial Reference: N.R 1.92. Cemetery: Deans Grange Cemetery in Dublin.

TYRRELL, Patrick: Rank: Able Seaman. Regiment or Service: Mercantile Marine. Ship; SS *Monmouth Coast* (Liverpool). Date of death: 24 April 1945. Age at death: 60. SS *Monmouth Coast* was a cargo steamer weighing 878 tonnes and built in the Ayrshire Dockyards in 1924. It was owner by Coast Lines in Liverpool. On 24 April 1945 she was *en route* from Sligo to Liverpool carrying her cargo of Pyrites when she was sunk by a torpedo from German submarine U-1305 commander by Helmut Christainson. Only one man of her seventeen crew survived the sinking. U-1305 surrendered in Loch Eriboll in Scotland on 10 May 1945.

Supplementary information: Husband of Julia Tyrrell, of Arklow, Co. Wicklow. Grave or Memorial Reference: He has no known grave but is listed on Panel 71 on the Tower Hill Memorial, UK.

TYRRELL, William John: Rank: Quartermaster. Regiment or Service: Merchant Navy. Unit: SS *Mohamed Ali El Kebir* (London) Age at death: 44. Date of death: 7 August 1940.

Supplementary information: Son of Thomas and Louisa Tyrrell, of Arklow, Co. Wicklow. SS *Mohamed Ali El Kebir* was torpedoed 250 miles west of Malin by German Submarine U38 with the loss of

The gravestone of Mervyn Patrick Arthur Tynte.

approximately 120 lives. One of the survivors William Tough from Aberdeen said he had just come off duty in the galley. He slung his hammock and was making his way to the stern of the ship for a smoke prior to turning in. Fortunately his way was blocked by someone who had made his bed across the doorway. He had to make a detour via the toilet, where Sergeant Bert Rennie was busy with brush and bucket cleaning up the mess of vomit on the floor. The Sergeant asked if he was coming to be sick. 'No', he said, seasickness did not bother him. The Sergeant then asked him to grab a brush and give a hand. Just at that moment there was a terrific bang, and the engines stopped dead. They agreed it must be either a mine or a torpedo. Then came the call to boat stations. Sergeant Rennie had served in the navy prior to joining the army, and seeing that there was going to be a mad rush for the gangway leading to boat stations, he and Mr Tough stood at the foot of the gangway and made them go up two at a time. They started singing 'Roll Out the Barrel', and everybody joined in, preventing any further panic. Mr Tough well remembers William Olley, the Canteen Officer, standing by the canteen shouting 'Come and help yourselves, everything is free, take the money as well, its no use to Davy Jones'. Mr Tough then got on a raft, with a few others, and was rescued six and a half hours later by the destroyer. Grave or Memorial Reference: He has no known grave but is listed on Panel 70 on the Tower Hill Memorial, UK.

U

UNDERWOOD, Henry: Rank: Private. Regiment or Service: Connaught Rangers. Unit: 1ˢᵗ Bn. Date of death: 7 May 1916. Service No: 9751. Born in Dunlavin, Co. Wicklow. Enlisted in Dublin. Died in Mesopotamia. Grave or Memorial Reference: XX.C.6. Cemetery: Amara War Cemetery in Iraq.

V

VANCE, William: Rank: Private. Regiment or Service: Royal Dublin Fusiliers. Unit: D Company, 9th Bn. Date of death: 13 July 1916. Age at death: 30. Service No: 16039. Born in Bray, Co. Wicklow. Enlisted in Bolton while living in Dublin. Died in hospital in Lincoln.

Supplementary information: Son of William and Elizabeth Vance, of 10 Bruce's Terrace, Upper Dargle Road, Bray. Grave or Memorial Reference: D.120. Cemetery: Lincoln (Newport) Cemetery UK.

VENEY, William Joseph: Rank: Private. Regiment or Service: Australian Infantry, AIF. Unit: 'D' Company, 24th Bn. Age at death: 28. Date of death: 5 August 1916. Service No: 967. Born in Gorey, Co. Wexford. Served his apprenticeship with Mr Bates of Gorey. Educated in Christian Schools in Gorey. Age on arrival in Australia, 26. Enlisted in Victoria on 21 March 1916. Address on enlistment; Kongwak, Victoria. Religious denomination: Roman Catholic. Weight: 171lbs. Complexion: browned. Eyes: brown. Hair: brown. Occupation on enlistment: Bodymaker and Mechanic. Address: North Parade, Gorey. Mother, Margaret Veney, Gorey. Marital Status: single. Parents: Frederick and Margaret Veney, North Parade, Gorey. Killed in action.

Supplementary information: Unit embarked from Melbourne, Victoria, on board HMAT A14 *Euripides* on 10 May 1915.

A letter from his Mother dated 12 July 1917 to the Commanding Officer of records

Could you let me have any information concerning Private W Veney No 967, D Coy, 24th Bn, 6th Inf Brigade, AIF Egypt. He joined the Army in Australia and I got word of his being killed in France on the 5th of August 1916. I never got any word on his belongings since I never got any separation allowance from him or money since he joined the army. I am his Mother and I would be thankful if you could let me have any information concerning him.

Yours Faithfully,
Mrs Margaret Varey,

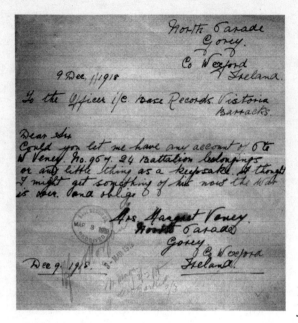

Letter written by William Joseph Veney's mother.

North Parade,
Gorey,

Co. Wexford.

The officer in charge of records replied stating that a search of Private Vereys Kit bag found nothing of his personal belongings. She applied for his pension but she was rejected. A note in the refusal states. 'Rejected, Unable to prove dependance on late son, your husband could earn adequate means of support if he so wished.' Also 'Rejected; Not dependant on the late M. F. for 12 months prior to enlistment.'

From an article in a Wexford newspaper;

Gorey Soldier Killed

The sad intelligence has reached Gorey that Private William Veney, son of My Fred Veney, North Parade, has been killed in action in one of the recent severe engagements. He was attached to the Australian Light Infantry and had been almost twelve months at the front. He was a very popular young man in Gorey, where he was well known. For a long period he was in the employment of Messrs Bates and Sons as a Coach builder, and he also followed up the same trade in Australia. He had been previously wounded in the fighting in France. Much sympathy is felt in Gorey for his father, Mr Fred Veney, in his bereavement. From an article in the Enniscorthy Guardian; News has just been received that Private William Veney, son of Mr and Mrs Veney. North Parade, Gorey, has been killed in action at the front on 5th August last. The deceased left this country for Melbourne over two years ago and shortly after the outbreak of hostilities he joined the Australian Imperial Force, sailing for Egypt a few months later. He subsequently took part in the landing at Gallipoli and Suvla Bay and after the withdrawl of the troops from there he and his regiment were sent straight to France where he went through several engagements. He had been at the front over a year and escaped without a scratch till in one of the big engagements recently in which the British took the offensive where he met his death from shrapnel. Private Veney before leaving this country spent nine years with the firm Messrs Bates and Son, Gorey, as a cartmaker and subsequently motor mechanic and where he was held in the highest respect by his employed and fellow workmen. He sent a postcard home to his people from the front on the 4th August last in which he stated he was in the best of spirits and they had not got any further account from him till the official notification from the War Office that he had

been killed on the following day, the 5th August. He was a fine type of soldier and he died in a noble cause. The deepest sympathy is expended to his relatives in their great sorrow.

Grave or Memorial Reference: He has no known grave but is listed on the Australian National Memorial, Villers-Bretonneux in France.

VIGORS, Arthur Cecil: Rank: Second Lieutenant. Regiment or Service: Royal Munster Fusiliers. Secondary Regiment: Royal Dublin Fusiliers. Unit: 9th Bn. Secondary Unit: Attached to the 3rd Bn Royal Munster Fusiliers. Date of death: 9 September 1916. Age at death: 21. Killed in action at Ginchy.

Supplementary information: Son of Hannah Marion Vigors, of Blessington, Co. Wicklow, and the late Charles Henry Vigors. Brother Capt. C. H. Vigors also died in service. Grave or Memorial Reference: He has no known grave but is listed on Pier and Face Pier and Face 16.C. on the Thiepval Memorial in France. He is also listed on the Great War Memorial in St Canice's Cathedral in Kilkenny.

VIGORS, Charles Henry: Rank: Captain (Acting Major). Regiment or Service: Cheshire

Regiment. Unit: 12th Bn. Date of death: 18 September 1918. Killed in action on Pip ridge in the Balkans. He won the Military Cross and is listed in the *London Gazette*.

Supplementary information: Won Croix de Guerre with palms (France). Son of Charles Henry and Hannah Marion Vigor, of Blessington, Co. Wicklow. Husband of Kate Mary Vigors, of 33 Church Street, Lenton, Nottingham. Brother 2nd Lt. A.C. Vigors also died on service. Age at death: 28. Grave or Memorial Reference: He has no known grave but is listed on Doiran Memorial in Greece.

W

WALKER, John James: Rank: Corporal. Regiment or Service: Royal Horse Artillery and Royal Field Artillery. Unit: 70th Battery. 34th Bridade. Date of death: 25 August 1914. Age at death: 21. Service No: 51512. Born in Wicklow. Enlisted in Wicklow. Died of wounds.

Supplementary information: Son of John I. and Elizabeth Walker, of Kildare Cottage, Bath Street, Wicklow. Grave or Memorial Reference: In north-east corner. Cemetery: La Longueville Communal Cemetery in France.

WALKER, Thomas: Rank: Able Seaman. Regiment or Service: Merchant Navy. Unit: SS *Ocean Crusader.* Age at death: 23. Date of death: 26 November 1942.

Supplementary information: Son of John and Rosanna A. Walker, of Wicklow. Grave or Memorial Reference: He has no known grave but is listed on Panel 75 on the Tower Hill Memorial, UK.

WALKER, William: Rank: Private. Regiment or Service: Royal Dublin Fusiliers. Unit: 1st Bn. Date of death: 4 September 1918. Service No: 21494. Born in Ashford, Wicklow. Enlisted in Wicklow. Killed in action. Grave or Memorial Reference: II.H.19. Cemetery: Bailleul Communal Cemetery Extension (Nord) in France.

WALL, Christopher: Rank: Master. Regiment or Service: Mercantile Marine. Unit: *Laura Ann.* Sailing Vessel *Laura Ann* was captured by a german submarine and sunk by gunfire from Beachy Head. The only casualty that day was the Master Chrisopher Wall. Date of death: 5 June 1917. Age at death: 62.

Supplementary information: Husband of Elizabeth Ellen Wall, of Ardmara, Summer Hill, Wicklow. Grave or Memorial Reference: He has no known grave but is listed on the Tower Hill Memorial, UK.

WALL, Christopher: Rank: Master. Regiment or Service: Mercantile Marine. Unit: *Walter Uric.* Date of death: 29 March 1917. Age at death: 22.

Supplementary information: Son of George and Mary Jane Wall, of 4 Leitlim Place, Wicklow. Grave or Memorial Reference: He has no known grave but is listed on the Tower Hill Memorial, UK.

WALSH, John: Rank: Cook. Regiment or Service: Mercantile Marine. Unit: SS *Walter Ulric* (Carnarvon). Date of death: 29 March 1917. Age at death: 17.

Supplementary information: Son of Hugh Walsh, of Summer Hill, Wicklow. Born in Wicklow. Grave or Memorial Reference: He has no known grave but is listed on the Tower Hill Memorial, UK.

WALTON, James: Rank: Private. Regiment or Service: The Buffs (East Kent Regiment). Unit: 7th Bn. Date of death: 30 September 1917. Age at death: 21. Died of Wounds. Service No: G/13284. Born in Rathmines, Dublin. Enlisted in Dublin while living in Terenure, Dublin.

Supplementary information: Son of A.J. and M. Walton, of Monastery Cottage, Monastery, Enniskerry, Co. Wicklow. Grave or Memorial Reference: VI.C.4. Cemetery: Mendingham Military cemetery in Belgium.

WATCHORN, Abraham: Rank: Private. Regiment or Service:

Royal Dublin Fusiliers. Unit: 5th Bn. Date of death: 26 April 1916. Age at death: 21. Service No: 25026. Born in Wicklow. Enlisted in Naas while living in Rathvilly, Co. Wicklow. Died at home.

Supplementary information: From De Ruvigny's Roll of Honour: elder son of Abraham Watchorn, of Williamstown, Rathvilly, Co. Carlow, farmer, by his wife, Jane, daughter, of George James. Born: Dundrum, Co. Dublin, 20 October 1894. Educated: Lisnavagh. He was a farmer and enlisted 22 November 1915. H was killed in action during the Dublin rebellion, 26 April 1916. Grave or Memorial Reference: CE. 625. Cemetery, Grangegorman Military Cemetery in Dublin.

WEADOCK, Daniel: Rank: Master. Regiment or Service: Mercantile Marine. Unit: SS *Thetis* (Cowes). Age at death: 52. Date of death: 30 April 1918.

Supplementary information: Son of Michael and Bridget Weadock. Husband of Mary Weadock (*née* Dempsey), of 21 The Gardens, Arklow. Born at Arklow. Grave or Memorial Reference: He has no known grave but is listed on the Tower Hill Memorial, UK.

WEADOCK, Michael: Rank: Mate. Regiment or Service: Mercantile Marine. Unit: SS *Thetis*

Steamship *Thetis*.

(Cowes). *Thetis* was a five masted Schooner. Age at death: 17. Date of death: 30 April 1918.

Supplementary information: Son of Daniel and Mary Weadock (*née* Dempsey), of 21 The Gardens, Arklow, Co. Wicklow. Grave or Memorial Reference: He has no known grave but is listed on the Tower Hill Memorial in the UK.

WEIR, William Ritchey: Rank: Gunner. Regiment or Service: Royal Field Artillery. Unit: 4th Reserve. Bde. Age at death: 24 Date of death: 14 May 1917 Service No: 184252. Born in Irvinetown and enlisted in Woolwich in Kent. Died at home.

Supplementary information: Son of William Weir of Ballyross, Enniskerry. Grave or Memorial Reference: W.50. Cemetery: Powerscourt (St Patrick) Church of Ireland Churchyard, Co. Wicklow.

WELDON, Faber Ernest Frederick: Rank: Pilot Officer.

Regiment or Service: Royal Air Force Volunteer Reserve. Unit: 57 Sqdn. Age at death: 31. Date of death: 5 April 1943. Service No: 130519.

Supplementary information: Son of Ernest A. and Maud Weldon. Husband of Bertha Weldon, of Brittas Bridge, Co. Wicklow. Flying Lancaster I W4252 DX-X they took off 2107hrs from Scampton during Operation 'Kiel' and were last heard on Wireless Telegraphy at 0148hrs when its position was fixed at 5420N 0425E. All the crew are commemorated on the Runnymede Memorial and are listed in *'Bomber Command Losses'* Vol.4. W R. Chorley. Gr Shot down during engagement with He11 off Cork 1830hrs. *Fighter Command Losses.* Vol. 1 N L R. Franks. Grave or Memorial Reference: He has no known grave but is listed on Panel 134 on the Runnymede Memorial, UK.

WELLESLEY, Claud Michael Ashmore: Rank: Lieutenant.

The gravestone of William Ritchey Weir.

IN LOVING MEMORY
OF
MAJOR EDWARD
VICTOR COLLEY WILLIAM WELLESLEY, M.C.
ROYAL ENGINEERS,
WHO SERVED HIS COUNTRY WITH DISTINCTION
IN FRANCE, IN THE YEARS 1915 AND 1916
AND WAS ACCIDENTALLY KILLED
ON OCT. 2ND 1916, AGED 27.
"UNTIL THE DAY DAWN!"
ALSO OF
LIEUTENANT CLAUD
MICHAEL ASHMORE WELLESLEY, ROYAL NAVY
WHO DIED ON ACTIVE SERVICE
ON JAN. 31ST 1918, AGED 27 YEARS;
WHEN SUBMARINE K4. WAS LOST WITH ALL
HANDS IN THE NORTH SEA.
"SO HE BRINGETH THEM UNTO THE DESIRED HAVEN"
ALSO
CAPTAIN GERALD
JOHN SHEPHERD WELLESLEY, R.E.
BORN DECEMBER 31ST 1892,
DIED NOVEMBER 12TH 1949.
DEARLY LOVED ELDER SONS OF
EDWARD AND CLAUDINE WELLESLEY

The gravestone of Claud Michael Ashmore Wellesley.

303

Regiment or Service: Royal Navy. Unit: HM Submarine K.4. Age at death: 27. Drowned due to a collision in the North Sea. Date of death: 31 January 1918.

Supplementary information: Son of Maj. E.H.C. and Mrs C.I. Wellesley, of Bromley, Kilpedder, Co. Wicklow. Grave or Memorial Reference: 28 Portsmouth Memorial, UK.

WEST, John Gabriel: Rank: Private. Regiment or Service: Shropshire Light Infantry. Unit: 2nd Bn. He was previously with the Royal Army Medical Corps where his number was 79300. Date of death: 25 September 1918. Age at death: 26. Service No: 31756. Born in Dalgany, Co. Wicklow. Enlisted in Enniscorthy, Co. Wicklow while living in Greystones, Co. Wicklow. Died in Salonika.

Supplementary information: From De Ruvigny's Roll of Honour; Only son of the late Thomas West, by his wife, Rachael (Brooklands Cottage, Greystones), daughter, Thomas Farrell of Windgates, Greystones. Born in Greystones, Co. Wicklow on 29 July 1892. Educated in Greystones. He volunteered for active service, and enlisted in the Royal Army Medical Corps in November 1915. He served in Ireland during the rebellion from May 1916. Proceeded to Malta in the following August and was transferred to the 2nd The Kings (Shropshire Light Infantry); served with the Salonika Army from January 1918 and died 25 September following of pneumonia, contracted while on active service in Macedonia. Buried in Karasouli Military Cemetery. Grave or Memorial Reference: D. 952. Ccmetery: Karasuli Military Cemetery in Greece.

WESTLAKE, George: Rank: Rifleman. Regiment or Service: Royal Irish Rifles. Unit: 1st Bn. Date of death: 27 October 1914. Service No: 10074. Born in Glenealy, Co. Wicklow. Enlisted in Carlow while living in Castledermot. Died of wounds. Grave or Memorial Reference: He has no known grave but is listed on Panels 42 and 43 on the Le Touret Memorial in France.

WHELAN, Peter: Rank: Private. Regiment or Service: Irish Guards. Unit: 2nd Bn. Date of death: 15 September 1916. Age at death: 22. Service No: 6965. Born in Rathdrum, Co. Wicklow. Enlisted in Wexford.

Supplementary information: Son of Mr J. and Mrs M.R. Whelan, of 38 Parnell Street, Wexford. Killed in action. Grave or Memorial Reference: He has no known grave but is listed on Pier and Face 7.D. on the Thiepval Memorial in France.

Herbert Robert White.

WHISTON, James Christopher: Rank: Aircraftman 2nd Class. Regiment or Service: Royal Air Force Volunteer Reserve Age at death: 28. Date of death: 24 February 1943. Service No: 1082520.

Supplementary information: Son of James and Bridget Whiston, of Bray, Co. Wicklow. Grave or Memorial Reference: Grave Y.54. Cemetery: Little Bray (St Peter's) Catholic Cemetery, Dublin.

WHITE/WHYTE, Henry: Rank: Acting Corporal. Regiment or Service: Royal Dublin Fusiliers. Unit: 2nd Bn. He won the Military Medal and is listed in the *London Gazette*. Date of death: 21 March 1918. Service No: 9980. Born in Newcastle, Kilcoole, Co. Wicklow. Enlisted in Dublin while living in Gravs, Essex. Killed in action. Grave or Memorial Reference: He has no known grave but is listed on panel 79 and 80 on the Pozieres Memorial in France.

WHITE, Herbert Robert: Rank: Second Lieutenant. Regiment or Service: Essex Regiment. Unit: 3rd Bn. attd. 2nd Bn. Age at death: 39. Date of death: 1 July 1916. Killed in action on the first day of the Battle of the Somme.

Supplementary information: Son of Henry and Sara White (*née* Brookes). Husband of Marguerite B.E. White (*née* Twiss), of St Margaret's, Kiltegan, Co. Wicklow. Served in the South African Campaign. Born in London, enlisted in the Essex regiment in 1895 at the age of sixteen. Fought all through the Boer was and rose to the rank of Colour Sergeant. He was a Quartermaster Sergeant when the war broke and was recommended for a commission for gallant conduct. He was wounded immediately afterward. Son in law of Mr F.W. Twiss, Kiltegan. Information from De Ruvigny's Roll of Honour: 2nd Battalion (56th Foot). Born: 23 July 1878. Enlisted in the 1st Battalion, The Essex Regt in 1895, served during the South African War (Queens medal and Kings Medal, 7 clasps) was transferred to the 2nd Battalion, The Essex Regiment, after the termination of the hostilities; afterwards served in Malta and England, attaining the rank of Quartermaster-Sergt; served with the Expeditionary Force in France and Flanders from August 1914; Gazetted 2 lt 9 May 1915 for service in the field; was reported missing after the fighting at Mailly-Maillet 1 July 1916 and is now assumed to have been killed in action on that date. One of his men wrote,

Lieut White was my Platoon Officer. He went over in the second wave at 8 to 8.15am 1 July. He got about three quarters of the way between our first lien and the German first line. He turned as if to shout an order, when he was shot an killed instantly. He was a ranker but a gentleman through and through. It broke the mens hearts when they heard he was killed.

and another, 'How I wish Mr White had come through; he was well liked in his platoon, a gentleman and a soldier. Always had a kind word for the men, and one whom any soldier would follow.' He married at St Peters Church, Kiltegan, 23 July 1910, Marguerite Blanche Emmeline (St Margarets, Kiltegan, Co. Wicklow) eldest daughter, of Francis William Twiss, and had three children; Vivien, born 30 December 1915; Valerie, born 13 November 1911 and Irish born 6 March 1914. Grave or Memorial Reference: He has no known grave but is listed on Pier and Face 10.D. on the Thiepval Memorial in France.

WHYTE, Charles: Rank: Private. Regiment or Service: Connaught Rangers. Unit: 1st Bn. Date of death: 23 June 1916. Service No: 6487. Born in Dunlavin, Co. Wicklow. Enlisted in Naas while living in Colbinstown, Co. Kildare. Died in Mesopotamia. Grave or Memorial Reference: V.Q.19. Cemetery: Basra War Cemetery in Iraq.

WHYTE, John De Burgh: Rank: Second Lieutenant. Regiment or Service: Royal Artillery. Unit: 1 Field Regt. Age at death: 27. Date of death: 20 June 1941. Service No: 158279.

Supplementary information: Son of Cecil Hugh de Burgh Whyte and Mary Lloyd Whyte, of Greystones, Co. Wicklow. Grave or Memorial Reference: H. 41. Cemetery: Damascus Commonwealth Cemetery in Syria.

WHYTE, Matthew: Rank: Private. Regiment or Service: Connaught Rangers. Unit: 5th Bn. Date of death: 18 July 1915. Service No: 3879. Born in Baltinglass, Co. Wicklow. Enlisted in Glasgow while living in Glasgow. Died in Gallipoli. Grave or Memorial Reference: He has no known grave but is listed on Panel 181 to 183 on the Helles Memorial in Turkey.

WILCOX, Harold Ray: Rank: Captain. Regiment or Service: Lancashire Fusiliers. Unit: 18th Bn. Date of death: 13 February 1919. Died of sickness contracted on active service in France. Additional information: Husband of Ellen Wilcox, of 'Delgany' Heswell Hills, Cheshire. Grave or Memorial Reference: 26C. Cemetery: Greystones (Redford) Cemetery, Co. Wickow.

WILLIAMS, Gerald Leopold: Rank: Second Lieutenant. Regiment or Service: Royal Inniskilling Fusiliers. Unit: 12th Bn. Age at death: 28. Date of death: 15 October 1918. He won the Military Cross and is listed in the *London Gazette.*

Supplementary information: Son of Thomas and Fannie Williams, of Ashford, Co. Wicklow. Grave or Memorial Reference: II.3. Cemetery: Dadizele Communal Cemetery in Belgium and he is also commemorated on a marble plaque on the walls of the reading room in Trinity College, Dublin.

WILLIAMS, J: Rank: Lance Corporal. Regiment or Service: Cheshire Regiment Unit: 1st Bn. Date of death: 16 April 1921. Service No: 4116554. Grave or Memorial Reference: East of north-east corner of Church. Cemetery: Rathdrum (St Saviour) Church of Ireland Churchyard, Co. Wicklow.

WILLOUGHBY, Charles: Rank: Private. Regiment or Service: Irish Guards. Unit: 1st Bn. Date of death: 17 June 1916. Service No: 9266. Born in Wicklow, Co. Wicklow. Enlisted in Liverpool while living in Killavaney, Co. Wicklow. Killed in action. Son of the late Mr George Willoughby of Togher. From a Wicklow newspaper article of the time,

> Sincere and widespread regret was occasioned in the Tinahely district, when it was learned that Pte Charles Willoughby, of the Irish Guards, had been killed in action in France on June 17th. He was the eldest son of the late Mr George Willoughby, of Togher, and he was most popular with all classes and creeds, while

The gravestone of J. Williams.

to his more intimate friends his kind and unassuming disposition endeared him in a binding affection. Pte Willoughby was a giant in stature, though he had the disposition of a child, so very kind and gentle to all was he. A sad feature about his untimely end was that he was shot on the very day he entered the trenches.

Grave or Memorial Reference: I.P.21. Cemetery: Essex Farm Cemetery in Belgium.

WILLOUGHBY, William: Rank: Private. Regiment or Service: South African Infantry. Unit: 2nd Regt. Date of death: 8 July 1916. Age at death: 33. Service No: 6230.

Supplementary information: Son of the late John and Martha Willoughby, of The Fields, Tinahely, Co. Wicklow. Grave or Memorial Reference: III.K18. Cemetery: Warlencourt British Cemetery in France.

WILSON, Alexander: Rank: Lieutenant Colonel. Regiment or Service: Royal Army Medical Corps. Age at death: 55. Date of death: 18 September 1919.

Supplementary information: Son of Alexander Wilson. Husband of A.M. Wilson, of 18 Liverpool Street, Dover. Born at Wicklow.

Grave or Memorial Reference: OO.153. Cemetery: Sheerness (Isle of Sheppey) Cemetery, UK.

WINDER/WINDERS, James: Rank: Private. Regiment or Service: Royal Dublin Fusiliers. Unit: 1st Bn. Date of death: 2 May 1915. Age at death: 33. Service No: 10960. Born in Wicklow. Enlisted in Naas while living in Tallaght, Co. Dublin. Killed in action in Gallipoli.

Supplementary information: Son of Patrick Winders, of 511 Main Street, Tallaght. Grave or Memorial Reference: He has no known grave but is listed on Panel 190 to 196 on the Helles Memorial in Turkey.

WINGFIELD, Richard James Trench: Rank: Second Lieutenant. Regiment or Service: Royal Field Artillery. Unit: 9th Bde. Age at death: 19. Date of death: 27 April 1916. Awards: Mentioned in Despatches.

Supplementary information: Son of the Revd Lt. Col. W.E. Wingfield, DSO. (late RFA), and Mrs E.M. Wingfield, of Broome Rectory, Bungay, Suffolk. Also served at Gallipoli. Born at Greystones, Co. Wicklow. Grave or Memorial Reference: XXI.D.4. Cemetery: Amara War Cemetery in Iraq.

WINTLE, Armar Lowry-Corry: Rank: Captain and also down as a lieutenant. Regiment or Service: Royal Inniskilling Fusiliers. Unit: 9th Bn. Date of death: 22 August 1917. Age at death: 20. Died of wounds.

Supplementary information: Son of Florence and Col. Fitzhardinge Wintle, (87th Punjabis) of Bamba House, Bray, Co. Wicklow. He won the Military Cross and is listed in the *London Gazette* and there is also a photograph of him in the *Sphere* dated 17 November 1917. Grave or Memorial Reference: II.O.1. Cemetery: Wimereux Communal Cemetery in France. He is also listed in the Haylebury Roll of Honour, the Worcester Kings School Memorial, the Worcester Cathedral, Kings School Cloister window War Memorial and the Bray Memorial, Church of Ireland, Bray.

WISDOM, Wlliam: Rank: Private. Regiment or Service: Royal Dublin Fusiliers. Unit: 1st Bn. Date of death: 16 April 1917. Age at death: 24. Service No: 8532. Born in Newcastle, Co. Wicklow. Enlisted in Dublin while living in Newcastle. Killed in action.

Supplementary information: Son of Laurence and Elizabeth Wisdom. Grave or Memorial Reference: He has no known grave but is listed in Bay 9 of the Arras Memorial in Turkey.

WRIGHT, Stanley: Rank: Sergeant (W. Op.). Regiment or Service: Royal Air Force Volunteer Reserve. He was one of the four crewmen from 50 Squadron based in Waddington that lost their way returning from a cancelled raid (Convoy AD730) on Berlin. They flew a Hampden Bomber. Age at death: 23. Date of death: 17 April 1941 Service No: 751744.

Supplementary information: Son of William Henry and Alice Wright, of Old Trafford, Manchester. Grave or Memorial Reference: north-east Corner. Cemetery: Blessington (St Mary) Church of Ireland Churchyard, Co. Wicklow.

WYNNE, Charles Wyndham: Rank: Captain. Regiment or Service: Royal Garrison Artillery. Unit: 182nd Siege Battery. Age at death: 22. Date of death: 24 June 1917. Died of Wounds. Born: 25 May 1895.

Supplementary information: From De Ruvigny's Roll of Honour: Youngest son of Albert Augustus Wynne of Tigroney, Avoca and Glendalough Cottage, Co. Wicklow, Civil Engineer, by his wife Alice K., daughter of the Revd John Wynne of Corrie, Bagenalstown. Born: 29 May 1895. Educated: Lancing College (Methematical Exhibition), and Balliol College, Oxford, where he was a member of the

Stanley Wright is the headstone on the left.

O.T.C. Gazetted 2nd Lt RGA. 28 February 1918. He was promoted to Lieut and Captain, September 1916, served for a time in Ireland. Subsequently volunteered for foreign service, and served with the Expeditionaly Force in France and Flanders from September, 1916. Second in Command of the Battery, took part in the battle of Arras, 9 April 1917, and of Messines, 7 June and died at the General Hospital, St Omer, 24 June 1917 of wounds received in action at Armentieres 10 June. Buried in St Omer. A brother officer wrote; 'He was one of the best. Beloved by his men, and excellent officer, with a tremendous interest and whole-heartedness in our work' and a Private; 'You will understand what a high opinion we all had of him, and now that he is no longer with us, we realise of what irreplaceable value he was, and would give all we know to have him with us again.' Grave or Memorial Reference: IV.C.38. Cemetery: Longuenesse (St Omer) Souvenir Cemetery in France. He is also listed on the Balliol College WW1 Memorial.

The gravestone of William Wyse.

WYSE, William: Rank: Driver. Regiment or Service: Royal Field Artillery. Secondary Regiment: Royal Engineers Secondary Unit: attd. 4th Field Survey Coy. Age at death: 17 Date of death: 22 February 1919. Service No: 119824. Grave or Memorial Reference: Near north-east corner. Cemetery: Kilcommon Cemetery, Co. Wicklow.

Y

YEATES, Harry: Rank: Private. Regiment or Service: Cameron Highlanders. Unit: 5th Bn. Date of death: 3 May 1917. Age at death: 24. Service No: S/15881. Born in Woolston, Hants. Enlisted in Glasgow while living in Southampton.

Supplementary information: Husband of Sarah Yeates, of Castle Street, Wicklow. Grave or Memorial Reference: He has no known grave but is listed in Bay 9 of the Arras Memorial in France.

Lest we forget.....